ACTIONS SPEAK LOUDER THAN WORDS

How do educators engage students in community action projects without telling them what to think, how to think, or what to do? Is it possible to integrate social justice organizing into the curriculum without imposing one's political views on students? In *Actions Speak Louder than Words*, longtime activist and teacher educator Celia Oyler delves into such questions through firsthand accounts of social action projects. By moving beyond charity work or volunteerism, she shows how community activism projects offer fertile ground for practicing democratic engagement as part of classroom work.

Actions Speak Louder than Words is a systematic, qualitative study offering in-depth and detailed portraits of teachers who design social action projects as part of the regular classroom curriculum. Each case forms a chapter organized as a narrative that includes excerpts from classroom dialogues, and interviews with students, teachers, and parents describing their social action projects with sufficient detail to give educators guidance for designing such projects for their own classrooms. The final chapter examines power, pedagogy, and learning outcomes across the cases, providing specific guidance to educators wishing to take up such projects and offering instructional and procedural advice as well as cautions. A fresh new example of taking up the challenge to teach toward equity and social justice, *Actions Speak Louder than Words* is an invaluable resource for educators who are passionate about the possibility of integrating activism and advocacy into curriculum as a means to engage in strong democracy.

Celia Oyler is an Associate Professor in the Department of Curriculum and Teaching at Teachers College, Columbia University.

THE TEACHING/LEARNING SOCIAL JUSTICE SERIES
Edited by Lee Anne Bell, Barnard College, Columbia University

ACTIONS SPEAK LOUDER THAN WORDS

Community Activism as Curriculum

Celia Oyler

Routledge
Taylor & Francis Group

NEW YORK AND LONDON

First published 2012
by Routledge
711 Third Avenue, New York, NY 10017

Simultaneously published in the UK
by Routledge
2 Park Square, Milton Park, Abingdon, Oxon OX14 4RN

Routledge is an imprint of the Taylor & Francis Group, an informa business

Library of Congress Cataloging in Publication Data
Oyler, Celia.
    Actions speak louder than words : community activism as curriculum / Celia Oyler.
    p. cm. — (The teaching/learning social justice series)
    Includes bibliographical references and index.
    1. Community and school—United States. 2. Schools—Public relations—United States.
    3. Communication in education—United States. I. Title.
    LC221.O95 2011
    371.19—dc22
    2011010060

ISBN: 978-0-415-88161-6 (hbk)
ISBN: 978-0-415-88162-3 (pbk)
ISBN: 978-0-203-80508-4 (ebk)

Typeset in Bembo and Stone Sans
by EvS Communication Networx, Inc.

Printed and bound in the United States of America on acid-free paper
by Walsworth Publishing Company, Marceline, MO.

Dedication

This book is dedicated to my parents: To my Mother, who taught me not to be afraid to take a stand for justice, and my Father, who always insisted, "Honey, actions speak louder than words."

CONTENTS

SERIES EDITOR INTRODUCTION

The Teaching/Learning Social Justice Series explores issues of social justice—diversity, equality, democracy, and fairness—in classrooms and communities. "Teaching/learning" connotes the essential connections between theory and practice that books in this series seek to illuminate. Central are the stories and lived experiences of people who strive both to critically analyze and challenge oppressive relationships and institutions, and to imagine and create more just and inclusive alternatives. My hope is that the series will balance critical analysis with images of hope and possibility in ways that are accessible and inspiring to a broad range of educators and activists who believe in the potential for social change through education and who seek stories and examples of practice, as well as honest discussion of the ever-present obstacles to dismantling oppressive ideas and institutions.

Actions Speak Louder than Words responds to this call in every particular. In this vivid and engaging book, Celia Oyler argues that the skills and habits of civic participation, so crucial to a democratic society, can and should be explicitly taught. She makes the case that schools ought to be places where young people learn how to work with diverse others to analyze and solve social problems and act collectively to make a difference in the world. Not only does she want students to learn about representative democracy, she wants them to learn the skills and dispositions of "strong democracy"—concern for the common good, the ability to constructively engage with diverse opinions and thoughtfully explore how particular decisions affect the greater good for all. In fact, given the enormity of social problems that we face as a nation, and the rancor that characterizes too much of public debate these days, teaching the social literacy skills of deliberative democracy may be as important as any of the other kinds of literacy that are the typical focus of curriculum.

Clearly, this task is not without challenges. As Oyler points out, teachers ought not impose their political viewpoints on students or ask them to take particular positions. This concern is a central focus of the book: "How can teachers thoughtfully engage students with real world social problems without telling them how to think or what actions to take?" Too often, teachers address this challenge by avoiding engagement altogether in an attempt to stay "neutral" and avoid controversy. Yet that decision is itself a political one that implicitly supports a status quo more typified by student passivity and narrow self-interest, sidestepping altogether the thornier questions so thoughtfully taken up in this book.

This richly detailed and engaging book shows us the many forms that "community activism as curriculum" can take, and extracts the academic, social, and emotional lessons that students take away from such engagements. As readers, we vicariously enter seven public school classrooms where we watch students collectively examine issues of local importance in their communities. We witness classroom interactions, listen to the voices of students and their teachers discussing, questioning, challenging each other, and taking collective committed action on their decisions. We hear teachers grapple with the challenges of encouraging thoughtful and informed civic engagement without dictating its form. We also see the ways that such teaching instantiates constructivist teaching and learning, inclusive classrooms, active student engagement and other attributes of skilled teaching in general.

The author meticulously teases out the tensions and lessons in each case, probing potential pitfalls as well as possibilities for enriching curriculum through democratic civic engagement. Students not only learn social action skills of problem solving, coalition-building, public testimony, and collaborative action, they also learn to deal with criticism and controversy constructively, work cooperatively in groups, wrestle with complex topics, think critically, conduct in-depth research, engage multiple perspectives, ask higher order questions, write and speak persuasively, and claim ownership of their own learning. Taken together, these cases illustrate an education that is hopeful, visionary, loving and respectful of students' capacities and agency. I can't think of anything more inspiring for an educational agenda truly worthy of a democratic society.

Lee Anne Bell, Series Editor

ACKNOWLEDGMENTS

The genesis for this book was provided by Earl Hatley and Kathleen Kesson, to whom I remain deeply grateful. It was Earl who told me about my first case, Rebecca Jim and her work on Tar Creek. In addition to being an activist, Earl is also a scientist, and I thank him for patiently explaining some of the science needed to understand the lead poisoning of the water and land. It was Kathleen who introduced me to that northwest corner of Oklahoma and encouraged this project at the start.

The other cases collected here would have never come to my attention without the existence of alternative print and radio media. Specifically, I acknowledge the leads provided by Amy Goodman of *Democracy Now!* (visit www.democracynow.org for more information), *The San Francisco Bay Guardian*, and Ira Glass of the radio show *This American Life*. Public and non-commercial, non-corporate media are essential elements for a well-educated and politically engaged citizenry. (As are small presses which need independent bookstores to survive.)

Most of all, I owe boundless thanks to the teachers who welcomed me into their classrooms. Although I met two of them at professional conferences, the others were total strangers, whom I "cold called" via telephone or email. Amazingly, each one of them upon hearing of my project, said, "Sure, come spend a week in my classroom. No problem." I still marvel at such trust. Obviously, this book would not exist without them. I am grateful that they all agreed to use their real names and I also thank them for the time they took to make corrections on the chapters about them, and for their important contributions to the Afterword.

The students interviewed at each site were astoundingly articulate, wonderfully confident, and truly welcoming. I often concluded group and individual interviews marveling at their ways with words, wishing this book could just be verbatim transcriptions of their insights. I am indebted to these students and do not have the space here to acknowledge them individually. Because of research guidelines, I cannot thank them by their real names as I use pseudonyms throughout the book for all minors. However, the adult students are named, if they requested this on their permission form at the time of the interview.

I thank Jean Clandinin for providing years of mentorship on this project, including inviting me to share early stages of the work with her students and colleagues at the University of Alberta's Centre for Research for Teacher Education and Development. I have come to rely on her for both wise counsel as well as critical questioning. I am grateful for both.

To Jonathan Arias, Bill Lamme, Robin Semer, and Alexandra Lola Semer-Lamme I offer thanks for providing car, room, and board during Chicago data collection as well as years of listening and encouragement for the project. I continue to draw much political inspiration and grounding from the Arias-Semer-Lamme family.

So, too, I thank Ann and Harold Berlak for putting me up (and putting up with me) while I was doing fieldwork in the San Francisco Bay area. The Berlaks are an important intellectual and political "north star" for me as I navigate my life as an academic. I continue to rely on their example of academic integrity and politically engaged scholarship as a model for what is possible.

In the course of this decade-long project, I received help in conversation from many students, colleagues, friends, and family. Apologizing to those I have mistakenly forgotten as I age, let me thank: Doug Biklen, Sari Biklen, Michele Genor, A. Lin Goodwin, Katherine Gregorio, Britt Hamre, Markie Hancock, Saigyo Terrance Keenan, Nancy Lesko, Leah Mayer, Carole Oyler, Claire Ryder, Carole Saltz, Mara Sapon-Shevin, Ruth Vinz, and Megan Williams. And I offer a huge thank you hug to Robert Carter who carried the ball on our Experiencing Diversity project while I worked on the final manuscript. I am indeed blessed to have such generous colleagues.

This project was partially supported by three internal grants from Teachers College—including the tenured faculty research grant that provided a semester free from teaching. I thank my colleagues Marjorie Siegel and Bill Baldwin for pushing me to apply for that funding; and to colleague Doug Grier for offering support across paradigms.

The administrative brilliance of Felicia Smart and Michelle Hill from the Department of Curriculum and Teaching at Teachers College ensured that my fieldwork proceeded smoothly. I thank them for continually extending themselves.

I owe a very hearty thank-you to Michele Mondo, transcriber extraordinaire who typed most of the interviews. More than her flawless transcription, though, it was her enthusiasm for my research participants' words that continually buoyed my spirit.

Catherine Bernard at Routledge Press was so very welcoming of my book and made the entire process enjoyable; her warmth came through in every email and always cheered my spirits.

Shira Epstein's close, careful, critical, and constructive feedback was instrumental in improving this work. I am so honored to be in a scholarly community where a former student can be my teacher. I thank her for her multiple readings of the manuscript and the stimulating conversation over the years as we worked through our ideas on social actions projects in the classroom.

I am so pleased that Susan Liddicoat agreed to serve as editor on another book of mine. Her keen eye greatly improved this volume, and her deep grounding in educational scholarship proved invaluable. She is not, of course, responsible for the errors and gaps that remain.

Lee Bell—the Routledge series editor—offered much encouragement for this book, for which I am very appreciative. However, I am even more appreciative of her unwavering dedication to justice, multiculturalism, and anti-racism, which helps sustain me when I get discouraged by the comodification of public education and the assault by big business on public school teachers.

I want to thank my wife—Florence Sullivan—for not only being the videographer for my case in Chicago, but for providing significant support (meals, encouragement, endless cups of tea, feedback on chapters) during the last years of this project. Writing is hard for me, and her warmth and commitment provided the wind beneath my sails. She kept telling me I could finish this book, and I finally believed her.

Finally, deep thanks to Ella Baker and Bernice Johnson Reagon, for the song (Sweet Honey and the Rock's "Ella's Song") that I hummed as I wrote this book: "We who believe in freedom cannot rest until it comes." Goodness knows, we have our justice-oriented work cut out for us on this planet.

Visions of a better world are created and sustained in no small part through the debates and dialogues nurtured in life-long communities of learning. Why not make schools such places?

Cover Image

Together We Are Strong, 2011 Peace Calendar cover artwork, Karen Kerney, digital collage, SCW©2010.

Syracuse Cultural Workers catalog is 32 color pages of feminist, progressive, multicultural resources to help change the world and sustain activism. The Peace Calendar, Women Artists Datebook, over 100 posters on social, cultural and political themes, holiday cards for Solstice, Christmas, Chanukah, plus buttons, stickers, T-shirts, notecards, postcards, and books. Great fundraising products. Box 6367, Syracuse, NY 13217; 800-949-5139; Fax 800-396-1449. 24-hour ordering—Visa/MC/Discover. www.SyracuseCulturalWorkers.com.

Permission for Use of Lyrics on p. 141

What's Going On

Words and Music by Renaldo Benson, Alfred Cleveland and Marvin Gaye.
©1970 (Renewed 1998) JOBETE MUSIC CO., INC., MGIII MUSIC, NMG
MUSIC and FGC MUSIC

All Rights Controlled and Administered by EMI APRIL MUSIC INC. on
    behalf of JOBETE MUSIC CO., INC., MGIII MUSIC, NMG MUSIC
    and FGC MUSIC and EMI BLACKWOOD MUSIC INC. on behalf of
    STONE AGATE MUSIC (A Division of JOBETE MUSIC CO., INC.)

All Rights Reserved   International Copyright Secured   Used by Permission

Reprinted by permission of Hal Leonard Corporation

INTRODUCTION

Teaching with Social Action, Activism, and Advocacy Projects

Ask most teachers why they went into education and you will invariably hear: I want to make a difference in the world. Many teachers express this commitment by staying late after school listening to the trials and tribulations of young people as they struggle to find meaning and negotiate identities. For some teachers this commitment takes the form of working in schools with poor children and youth under conditions of overcrowding and under-financing that would shock the general populace. Teachers also live out this commitment to make a difference in the world by spending long hours on weekends, nights, and summers creating unique and challenging curriculum materials designed to fully engage their students.

Among these teachers, many are moved to include social justice curriculum and materials that relate to real-world struggles for freedom, justice, and equality. They believe that curriculum must be more than a dry list of standards drawn up by some anonymous committee. Instead they view curriculum as where students can encounter the world—its histories and peoples—analyze its current conditions, and prepare to act with and on the world in moral and responsible ways. Teachers can also take these social justice commitments and build on them even further, by designing curriculum around social action projects that involve community education, outreach, or organizing. In short, such teachers realize that as curriculum designers, they have the opportunity to help their students make a difference while on this planet.

Many more typical versions of school curriculum focus on the preservation of a society's knowledge, skills, and values. Indeed, some people argue that schools should be conserving institutions: preserving the society and maintaining the status quo. Other people, however, want schools to be sites of social change, democratic renewal, public investment, and transformation.

The rationale for this version of curriculum is simple: the students of today will live in a world different from the one they were born into. This world of their future will require new solutions to new problems, and potentially, new solutions to old problems as well. Therefore, school curricula should not only transmit the knowledge and skills that have been accumulated throughout human history and prepare students to analyze those histories and traditions, but should also prepare students to participate fully in shaping the future life of the community. For those of us committed to creating a more just world for as many as people as possible, we are drawn to versions of school curricula that help prepare graduates to care deeply about the welfare of others.

I began research for this book after hearing about the projects of a guidance counselor working in Miami, Oklahoma, who helped organize high school curriculum around the problem of lead contamination in the local water and soil from improperly closed-down mines. The work of this educator—Rebecca Jim, see Chapter 1—inspired me to systematically study teachers who involve students in social action projects. I wanted to understand what got them started with these activist projects, how the teachers themselves viewed their work, and how they thought about issues of power and imposition.

After visiting Ms. Jim in Miami, Oklahoma, I studied six other teachers who move their social justice curriculum beyond the walls of their classrooms into the realm of social action, advocacy, and activism. The teachers, projects, and students profiled in this book were selected because their classroom curricula were designed around small or large community or global action projects. These projects began with the premise that all is not right with the world and that school can prepare students to engage in authentic problem solving. This, then, is what social action curriculum is all about:

- Observing that the world has problems
- Understanding that these problems have root causes
- Analyzing the current problems and its causes
- Joining together with others to create solutions

Throughout data collection for this project, countless leads were offered to me of teachers who get students involved in worthwhile and meaningful curriculum projects. So many people—educators and non-educators alike—offered me suggestions of teachers they know that are making a difference. For instance, one class in Long Island, New York, conducted oral history projects with seniors in a nursing home; and a teacher in Boston designed a unit on volunteering in the community that he launched with a series of class trips to work in a local food pantry. My research, however, was a little more specific; I searched for teachers in public schools who designed regular classroom curriculum around community or global action projects that were predicated on more than "helping" others. As Kirschner (2008) explains: "People enter the democratic fray in order to solve a problem that affects their lives or the lives of community members. In contrast, when social action is framed as charity or service, it is often apolitical and can reinforce a deficit view of the community" (p. 93).

Building on this idea, my framework for this project is heavily influenced by Rahima Wade's (2000) typology of service learning, as directed either toward (1) developing solidarity with people in need, such as working at a soup kitchen; (2) engaging in indirect service to benefit others whom you never meet, such as raising money for a food program; or (3) advocacy projects that are focused on community improvement. It is the third type of project that I sought to find; and indeed, I was given scores of leads of classroom teachers whose curriculum included activist and advocacy projects designed to improve some aspect of the local or global community.

What Is Social Action?

To probe the distinction between studying *about* social justice versus engaging in social action, we can turn to the work of Hannah Arendt. In her book, *The Human Condition* (1958/1988) she distinguishes among three modalities of life: labor, work, and action. Labor is what the body needs and does to keep alive; work involves production and relates to what humans do to change their natural environment through construction of materials. But action means to bring something new into the world, to take initiative: "With word and deed we insert ourselves into the human world and this insertion is like a second birth.... This insertion is not forced upon us by necessity, like labor, and it is not prompted by utility, like work" (pp. 176–177).

Social action projects, then, involve some sort of creation that involves connecting to other people. This may take the form of street theater or leafleting; it may involve writing letters to elected officials or petitioning bureaucrats who are in decision-making offices. The important idea for classroom projects is that social action is never possible in isolation and by its very definition, involves the recipients of entreaties and advocacy. As Arendt explains, "Plurality is the condition of human action" (p. 188). As can be seen from the projects profiled in this book, much of the teachers' pedagogical efforts went into helping students understand this plurality. And this plurality can be understood as having two dimensions: (1) the plurality of actors and factors involved in the social issue the project is taking up; and (2) the plurality of knowledge and viewpoints among class members themselves. So each classroom that took up a social action project was learning to work more skillfully within the plurality inherent in all human communities. What, one might ask, could be more essential for the life of children and youth as we prepare them to move courageously into active adulthood than to have experience taking up matters of the common good and to take them up collaboratively and cooperatively with others?

At its root, school-based social action curriculum is designed to foster engaged civic agency rather than passivity or self-interest. I draw upon Walter Parker (2003) here, in his explanation of the ancient Greeks and the distinction they made between "idios" and "polites":

> ... the root *idios* ... means private, separate, self-centered—selfish. This conception of idiocy achieves its force when contrasted with *polites* (political) or public. Here we have a powerful opposition: the private individual and the public citizen.... An idiot is one whose self-centeredness undermines his or her citizen identity, causing it to wither, or worse, never to take root in the first place. An idiot does not know that self-sufficiency is entirely dependent on the community. (pp. 2–3)

Unfortunately, much of the U.S. school system relies upon individual and competitive patterns of engagement with learning. Yet outside of school—whether playing or working—the vast majority of human time is spent in collaborative, rather than competitive, activities. Most home life relies upon working together, many workplaces depend on people functioning in teams, and almost all civic and political life is undertaken in collaboration. Clearly, citizens are required to cooperate.

It is essential to note that throughout this book, I use the term *citizen* not in regard to national identity papers, but rather, to describe people who live and work in a place, and engage in a public manner as advocates and activists. Hence, one need not be a U.S. citizen to engage in citizenship activities. However, the struggles over who can be counted as a citizen of this country have been with us since the founding of this country and are of critical importance today. In acknowledgement of this I also use the term *civic agent* to draw attention to the reality that many actively engaged community members may not have written documents that align with their community membership.

The Politics of Action

The teachers I profile in this book differ in their classroom pedagogies and also in their autobiographies. However, they share an important viewpoint: that is, they view their curriculum as being necessarily linked to important social problems. And rather than merely study *about* these issues, these teachers invite their students to engage in direct problem solving. These teachers want their students to actively participate in community decision-making and action. Indeed, it is this community-based participatory action that is politics itself. I agree with Benjamin Barber (2003) when he explains, "Politics is the art of planning, coordinating, and executing the collective futures of human communities" (p. 53). Yet often when people think about classrooms, they think politics should be kept out. But as Walter Parker (2003) points out, "Democratic education is not a neutral project, but one that tries to predispose citizens to principled reasoning and just ways of being with each other" (pp. xvii–xviii).

To my mind, all decisions about what to include in any curriculum—and how to include it—are by very definition political. Some teachers are understandably afraid to include controversial topics in their daily lesson plans, so try to neutralize their curricula as much as possible. They fear complaints from parents or from administrators; most of all, they fear the negative consequences that could occur if they bring attention to the political nature of such curriculum work.

Certainly, we do not want teachers imposing their political viewpoints on students by asking them to take a specific side or another in an election, or even telling students what positions they should take on controversial issues. How, then, can teachers organize classroom work around active community engagement with real-world social problems and not be in the business of telling students *how* to think and what to do? This was a principal question that motivated my decade-long study, as neutrality in the face of social, racial, economic, or environmental injustice does not seem an option to me. I found Bill Bigelow (1997), a founder of *Rethinking Schools,* helpful here. In writing about his own elementary-classroom teaching in which he incorporated a lesson about corporations and labor practices around the world, he discusses this critical question about what to do with his own point of view:

> On the one hand, I had no desire to feign neutrality—to hide my conviction that people here need to care about and act in solidarity with workers around the world in their struggles for better lives. To pretend that I was a mere dispenser of information would be dishonest, but worse, it would imply that being a spectator is an ethical response to injustice. It would model a stance of moral apathy. I wanted students to know these issues were important to me, that I cared enough to do something about them. On the other hand, I never want my social concerns to suffocate student inquiry or to prevent students from thoughtfully considering opposing views. (p. 14)

This is the tension that propelled me into this project. Given the enormity of social issues, we as teachers cannot adopt a stance of neutrality. Yet to prepare students to engage in truly deliberative democracy, we cannot afford to impose our viewpoints on them. I was eager to investigate this challenge with teachers and students engaged in advocacy and action projects.

The projects I profile do not all have fairy-tale endings where the students and teachers successfully triumph over corporate greed and uncaring bureaucracies. Indeed, I did not consider the "success" of the project as a criterion for inclusion in my research because I was most interested in visiting the classrooms and speaking with the students and teachers while the projects were still taking place. The question of how effective the students and teachers were in bringing about change is more complex and is—in most cases—beyond the scope of this book. However, it is important to address this issue of "success" because if teachers limit their selection of social action projects to only struggles that have a good chance of being "successful," they may select "non-controversial charitable activities which tend to send the message that kindness and charity will transform society, rather than offer redress for complex social problems" (Kahne & Westheimer, 2006, p. 290).

The students in this book—elementary school through graduate school— were immersed in projects that demonstrated the complexity of such matters as sustainable land use, school financing, environmental racism, and globalization. The idea that individual citizens can make a difference through collective action is integral to increasing civic participation. This book rests on the premise that learning to do this can take place in classrooms.

Democracy, Civic Agency, and Social Action

In focusing on education for civic agency, it is essential to first explore the conceptions of democracy and citizenship that underlie social action. The school-based social action projects described here hinge upon an understanding of civic agency as requiring active involvement in local decision-making. This is in contrast to the more common form of citizenship education that mainly emphasizes voting for representatives during election years and then lobbying these elected officials in regard to particular issues.

I want to argue that in addition to teaching young citizens to navigate representative democracy, we also must educate for "strong democracy" (Barber, 2003). This version of democracy requires direct community involvement. According to Barber, "Only direct political participation—activity that is explicitly public—is a completely successful form of civic education for democracy" (p. 235). This form of democracy relies upon citizens who understand that their own individual well-being is tied up in the commonwealth of the community. Rather than the individualist orientation of liberal democracy concerned with individual rights, property contracts, and privacy, this more communalist orientation toward democracy is concerned with pluralism, the common good, and understanding human difference. Rather than approaching decision making as "majority rules," it is essential to engage in dialoguing across difference. The goal with such dialogue is not to reach a (potentially weak) consensus, but instead to struggle toward a solution that most advances equality and social justice.

But, of course, what is "the common good" is contested. How then are educators to make curricular decisions and help their students learn how to make decisions that advance the common good? What *is* the common good in any given situation, and how does a citizen learn to work toward this aim? Walter Parker (2003) urges us to teach for what he calls "democratic enlightenment," which is a stance and position that is fundamental to acting from a place of mutual interest, rather than individual self-interest. As Parker explains—using the example of fascist or white supremacist groups—civic engagement without justice-oriented knowledge, values, and principles can be regressive and oppressive. Thus, simply advocating for students to be involved in the public realm is not sufficient for justice-oriented educators: we must simultaneously be creating opportunities to discuss and debate how particular decisions affect all community members.

These are complicated matters, complex enough in the community arena, but made even more complicated when taken into the classroom. After all, students arrive in classrooms with particular cultural models (Gee, 1999) for understanding the purpose of schooling, with widely divergent interests and skill levels, as well as sometimes advanced home training on the appropriate behavior for a student or a citizen.

The Research Project

I spent five years collecting these classroom cases, and in that time span, had leads on many more teachers than I had the money or time to pursue. Even in the current context of high-stakes testing, scripted curriculum, and a focus on "teaching to the standards," there are teachers from elementary school through graduate school who systematically carve out the space to also teach for active civic agency through social action. This book is meant to be a careful study of seven such teachers. Specifically, I was interested in

1. Finding out directly from the teachers how and why they used social action projects in their classrooms
2. Finding out from students what and how they were learning
3. Exploring with teachers and students the issues of power, authority, and decision making that circulated throughout the projects

My methods were simple (see the Appendix for more detail). After negotiating schedules and formal permissions, I spent a week (or its rough equivalent) at each site. At my initial meeting with each teacher, I

- Explained in person the purposes of my study
- Heard the story of the social action project
- Established a schedule for the week of classroom observations and important people to interview
- Learned more about the teacher and his or her autobiography

At each site I interviewed and held focus groups with as many students, parents, administrators, and school staff as volunteered to meet with me. I conducted the interviews and focus groups in classrooms, restaurants, coffee shops, offices, hallways, people's homes, on campus/school lawns; and one time, over beers in a bar.

At the end of each day of data collection, I typed the field notes I had collected. This exercise triggered comments and questions that I recorded and drew upon in subsequent interviews and observations. I concluded each site visit with a final interview with the teacher. This was a time when the teacher was able to explain to me aspects of his or her pedagogy that I may not have understood at our initial meeting. It was my time to ask questions that related to power, authority, and decision-making. Thus, both the teacher and I had quite a bit to say. Sometimes, the teacher was concerned that I understand the nuance of particular instructional events that she or he carefully explained. Most exit interviews lasted approximately an hour and a half. Also near the end of each week in the field, I organized some sort of small thank you to the teacher and students. Most often this took the form of food: with elementary children, it was a pizza party in a park; with a college professor it was dinner at a beautiful spot on the California coast. Upon returning home, I began the process of transcribing all classroom observation audio recordings and focus groups recordings, and I sent the interview tapes to be transcribed.

Much has been written about social action projects, and I have been drawing upon this rich literature base over the course of this study. Having compiled an extensive literature review, I finally arrived at three questions that I used to frame my data analysis. Pouring over the data, through multiple readings, I asked:

1. What advocacy and activism activities did the students engage in and how were they structured for learning? (Wade, 2000)
2. What role does the "public good" play in classroom instruction and in the teachers' motivations? (Barber, 2003; Parker, 2003)
3. What opportunities existed for students to engage with multiple viewpoints? What opportunities existed for discussion where difference and pluralism were visible? (Arendt, 1958/1988)

Using the above questions to guide my data analysis, I then sought an organizational structure for the book. I found many similarities and differences among the teachers' pedagogies and the social action projects themselves that I could have presented as a research monograph. However, persuaded that many teachers are looking for inspiration and also a little guidance in beginning projects such as these, I have chosen to write this book as a narrative: telling the story of each classroom as I encountered it. However, to provide a focus for each chapter, I concentrate on a few key themes prominent in each classroom story. Also, it should be noted that the week (or its equivalent) I spent at each site offered different types of interactions. Thus, some chapters include detailed classroom dialogues, and other chapters rely more heavily on retrospective reflections by students and teachers.

The Cases

As I explained earlier, I began with the case of Rebecca Jim—a Cherokee guidance counselor in Miami, Oklahoma. Much of her life work has been spent combating lead contamination left from mining companies that are no longer in business in the local area. Ms. Jim has helped integrate social action into the high school curriculum. The student organizing that stemmed from this curriculum was a part of a successful grassroots campaign to stimulate the Environmental Protection Agency—having formerly abandoned their own Superfund site—to reopen the case and begin lead clean up. I used this case (Chapter 1) as a pilot for the subsequent studies and refined my methods after that visit.

I next traveled to Seattle, Washington, where I studied a high school globalization class during the year of the World Trade Organization meeting there. (This December 1999 meeting sparked massive global justice protests and marked the beginning of many global justice coalitions.) Joe Szwaja, the white teacher from this case (Chapter 2), invited me to come to Nova High School in early January and witness the globalization course in action. When I arrived at the school, I found out that Nova is an alternative public school where the entire curriculum is designed in close collaboration with students. Many students and teachers from the school generously shared their knowledge and expertise regarding planning public school curriculum around advocacy and activism in general, and around public protest in particular.

The third case was in San Francisco, in the predominantly African American neighborhood of Hunters Point, where the community-based organization *Literacy for Environmental Justice* put me in touch with Lance Powell, a white science teacher in his fifth year of public school teaching. I was scheduled to study his Advanced Placement Environmental Science class, but happened to arrive in the midst of an additional controversy (related to the school's academic high school status) that sparked a quick social action curriculum in his ninth grade integrated core class. It was in this classroom where I first saw "teaching the commons" in action (see Chapter 3).

On that same trip to San Francisco, I moved next to the Mission District where I was hosted by Derrlyn Tom, an Asian-Pacific Islander teacher active in many community-based organizations, including *Teachers for Social Justice*. Ms. Tom's pedagogy shows a teacher designing instruction to support low-income students to meet high academic standards while simultaneously addressing the issue of emissions from the local power plant and its effects on the San Francisco Bay. This case (Chapter 4), then, offers a clear model for culturally relevant pedagogy (Ladson-Billings, 1995) merged with social action.

Quite a few years after having launched this research project, and almost ready to give up on finding an elementary school case, I perked up when I heard some Chicago fifth graders speak on a *National Public Radio* show about their campaign to get a new school built in their Cabrini Green neighborhood. I tracked down their teacher—Brian Schultz—who, in his second year of elementary teaching, learned alongside his students how to be an activist. The classroom project mushroomed, gaining substantive national and international media attention, which the students took gracefully in stride. Spending a week in the dilapidated school building, surrounded by administrators, parents, and children who rallied around this common cause, I was able to study how an entire science, social studies, math, and language arts curriculum can be integrated through a community-organizing project of major importance (see Chapter 5).

I met the teacher of my college case (Chapter 6) at the American Educational Research Association Conference when I found myself constantly seeing the same tall, bearded white man at session after session. Finally, Eric Rofes and I introduced ourselves, and I quickly found myself telling him about my project documenting teaching for social action. Within minutes he had agreed for me to spend a week shadowing him at Humboldt State University in Arcata, California. Eric taught a class—"Education for Action"—designed to teach the organizing skills he had honed, mostly in the gay rights movement, to young activists. After my week with Eric, he greatly assisted me in further thinking about this book as I sorted through methodological, political, and pedagogical dilemmas I encountered.

Wanting to have as many cases at different age levels as possible, I was excited to find a case taking place in a graduate school of education. Barbara Regenspan, then a professor at the State University of New York-Binghamton, taught a class aptly titled, "Social Action as Curriculum" and generously opened her course to me. In turn, the teachers in her class invited me to accompany them as they embarked on their individual social action projects. It turned out that Professor Regenspan and I shared many of the same worries about social action curriculum, often pondering issues of power, authority, and imposition. In her case (Chapter 7), I had the opportunity to explore some of the emotional/spiritual aspects of asking students to take a step toward action grounded in critical consciousness.

All of these projects—and the students and teachers who created them—concretely answered my burning questions about what curriculum, teaching, and learning look like when organized around social action projects. The curriculum in these classrooms took up weighty matters of environmental, educational, and racial justice. These teachers—through their choices of reading materials, field trips, guest speakers, and films—helped their students ask questions about what is right, what is fair, what is just. They organized their classroom instruction around the essential questions that animate so many people: What kind of world do we want to live in? And how, then, do we build a more just and peaceful future? Students' responses to these curricula of social action reinforced my view that most people have deep interest in making the world a better place. This phrase—so oft repeated—was brought to life in these seven communities, and found specificity in the large and small actions these classes undertook to rebuild the world one piece at a time.

These teachers, who welcomed me into their classrooms and trusted me with their pedagogy, help all of us understand ways to build education around social issues that matter. Learning the skills of activism, advocacy, and organizing for justice and equality, while developing the knowledge, values, and principles that lead to democratic enlightenment (Parker, 2003), can and should be at the center of public education. Knowing that the project of strong democracy requires deliberation across difference, I have no intention of presenting these cases as examples of "best practice." Indeed, I eschew such dogmatism—or mythology—knowing that teachers' work involves local decision-making, grounded in moral and political frames that cannot be grasped in the short time I spent in each site. The teachers themselves add their own words about their classroom pedagogies in an Afterword, generously offering details about their projects and their most recent thinking on activist-oriented classroom curriculum.

I hope that readers will approach these classroom stories with a spirit of collective collegiality, knowing that justice-oriented pedagogy for social action takes many forms and that dilemmas of practice always surround our work as classroom teachers. This pedagogical project, is, after all, not substantively different from the project of democracy itself: it is strengthened and kept alive by vibrant and respectful debates and is nurtured by new generations of citizens who push the Unites States of America to live up to its dream of "liberty and justice for all." In the final analysis, teaching for social action is not that much different from organizing for social action, and we must remember that "We don't have to engage in grand, heroic actions to participate in the process of change. Small acts, when multiplied by millions of people, can transform the world" (Zinn, 2002, p. 208).

1

CURRICULUM FOR CIVIC AGENCY

Rebecca Jim and Tar Creek

> The students are the key to getting Tar Creek cleaned up. They're the ones
> that are going to do something about it. I think they're going to keep it going
> after they graduate from high school. I think they're going to stay involved.
> Because these kids, I guess you probably noticed, they can tell you everything
> about Tar Creek.
>   —Nancy Scott, Cherokee Nation Learn and Serve Director

No matter where in the world a school is located, a focus for a social action
project can be found. As humans we always have the opportunity to improve
conditions for ourselves and for others. Indeed, classrooms can be laboratories
for active engagement in the most pressing issues facing us on planet Earth, and
curriculum can be organized around creating a more humane, a more just, and
a more sustainable planet. In the hands of a creative and committed teacher
purposeful links can be made in almost any school subject area. The decision
about what sorts of projects and issues to take up may come from either the
teacher or the students, and are most often a negotiation and point of discussion
that is part of the classroom curriculum.

I use this case of Tar Creek to underscore the central assumption of social
action projects: that school curricula can be a site for leadership development as
well as learning the skills and dispositions of public activism and advocacy. In
Miami, Oklahoma, the students I met were all acting as powerful citizens advocating on behalf of their land and their community. They learned and practiced
a wide range of skills central to engaged citizenship. They courageously and
publicly tackled a local issue, which many adults in the town were studiously
ignoring. Their creativity and commitment serve as inspiration for teachers to
take up real-world problems as part of the regular school curriculum.

Indigenous peoples, including the Quapaw, Seneca-Cayuga, Miami, Modoc, Wyandotte, Ottawa, Peoria, Cherokee, and Eastern Shawnee, still heavily populate this area of Oklahoma. Indeed, according to Nancy Scott—the Cherokee Nation coordinator of the service-learning grant that supported some of the Miami High School projects—approximately 63% of students at Miami High School have some Native American Indian ancestry. The Cherokee Nation is investing in promising school-based projects because the Native American high school graduation rate is the lowest for any ethnic/racial group in the United States. In an interview at her office, Ms. Scott explained why the Nation was supporting this particular service-learning project:

> The reason why our kids are in so much trouble nowadays is because they don't know who they are. They're lacking their identity. They don't fit into the Native American world because they don't really know anything about their culture, or they're not being taught, or they don't have that person that can tell them who they are. And then, on the other hand, in the non-Indian world they don't fit there either. So, to me, it's like an identity crisis that they're going through. So, through this program, I thought maybe getting the students involved in the community … would help them feel like they were part of something.

Ms. Jim—in her capacity as a high school guidance counselor and with the support of the Cherokee Nation *Learn and Serve Project*—began to spark that involvement.

The Tar Creek Superfund Site

I returned from my trip to Miami, Oklahoma, wearing a cream colored t-shirt with a large orange design on the back: *Tar Creek Fishing Tournament and 10K Toxic Tour*. Orange, you see, is one of the colors of Tar Creek—a body of water that runs through the town. Residents remember when their parents and grandparents used to fish in Tar Creek—now there are few living fish in the waters. A few years earlier, the city leaders responded to the visually disturbing site of the discolored water by building walls on the sides of the bridges so the water is not visible. Signs saying "Tar Creek" were removed. The t-shirt, however, was one of the fundraisers that Miami High School students made for their campaign to address the lead poisoning in their community.

Ottawa County, Oklahoma, is now part of what the U.S. Environmental Protection Agency (EPA) calls the *Tri-State Mining District*. However, back in the 1830s when white settlers were angling for prime Arkansas farmland, the area was simply called "Indian Territory" and was considered worthless and highly undesirable land. Hence, the federal government gave a portion of the area to the Arkansas-based Quapaw People, and as part of the Indian Removal, program forced the tribe to move there.

Many years later, however, at the turn of the 20th century (before Oklahoma became a state), lead and zinc were discovered. Suddenly, this worthless Indian land was deemed valuable, and the Bureau of Indian Affairs facilitated a way for mining companies to lease the land from the Quapaw. Eventually over 300 mines were opened, and ended up supplying lead for the vast majority of bullets manufactured for World War I and II. Hundreds of thousands of tons of lead and zinc were extracted from a forty square mile tract, a site that includes the towns of Picher, Cardin, North Miami, Quapaw, and Commerce. In the early days, these were mining boomtowns, and the local economy flourished. By the early 1960s, mining activity slowed, and finally came to a halt in 1974. Since that time, the area has been economically depressed.

When the mines were shut down, most of the hundreds of mineshafts were abandoned by the companies and were not properly sealed. Surface and ground water filled the underground caves and shafts, and the sulfuric acid reacted with metals left in the caves, creating acid water filled with lead, zinc, cadmium, sulfates, iron, and other heavy metals. After a few years, this acid water surfaced and began to run into local creeks.

However, polluted water is only one of three environmental disasters. The second comes from the abandoned mines that honeycomb the entire forty-square mile site. When the companies dug for lead and zinc, they were required to leave pillars of earth for support. When the mining companies pulled out, the former workers used the heavy equipment left behind to mine the pillars, leaving no support for the ground above. So over the last forty years when the mines filled up with water, some of these areas collapsed leaving huge sinkholes. Different field surveys indicate that hundreds of shafts have already collapsed. While there are few reported instances of destruction of buildings and roads, eighteen homes were affected by one collapse just north of Picher High School in 1967. In this collapse, the ground dropped approximately twenty-five feet, and five minor injuries resulted. One local woman remembers that when she was five years old her family's house "fell in." Police and fire department officials had to come to get the family out.

Aside from the toxicity of the ground waters and the destructive nature of the sinkholes, acres and acres of mine tailings (chat) left over from years of mining operations dot the landscape. These are places that look like a moonscape—dusty grey mountains stretch as far as the eye can see. Local knowledge regarding the health effects of the chat was slim. For a long time, the chat was a cheap or free source of fill for many projects. Much of it has been utilized in the construction of driveways, roadbeds, playgrounds, and baseball fields. The chat piles, some of them 200 feet high, are mostly unfenced, and provide a tempting place for recreation. As a mother of one of the high school students explained, "I let my kids play on the chat piles when we moved to town a few years ago. I let my kids climb on it, we thought it was fun.... We didn't realize that dust we had on us could potentially make us sick. We had no idea." Adults and youth rode motorized bikes up and down the slopes of the chat piles, not knowing that they were ingesting lead through the dust they created.

Residents' lead levels are extremely high in the area and are suspected to bé an explanation of many children's learning and behavior problems. It is well documented that lead poisoning can cause cognitive disabilities, decreased growth, hyperactivity, impaired hearing and even obesity. At the time of my visit, researchers from Harvard University were measuring area children's lead levels by analyzing their baby teeth as they fell out. They judged the lead levels unusually high and extremely dangerous. Tests by the EPA triangulate this finding. For example, between 1994 and 1995, the EPA (U.S. Environmental Protection Agency, 1997) tested 2,055 families' yards and found that 65% had concentrations of lead in at least one part of the yard at or above 500 parts per million. In this same report, the EPA extrapolated that 21% of children could have blood levels at, or exceeding, 10 micrograms per deciliter (ug/dL), the level at which the Centers for Disease Control say that children experience adverse health effects. The effects of lead poisoning are lifelong: "Exposure to lead is particularly dangerous to the unborn and to young children less than 72 months of age. Lead can effect [sic] virtually every system in the body. Lead is particularly harmful to the developing brain and nervous system of fetuses and young children" (EPA, 1997).

Due to the constellation of environmental disasters in the area, in 1981, the EPA ranked Tar Creek the nation's *worst* hazardous waste site, and by 1983, declared the area a Superfund site. Residents believed cleanup was imminent. Yet, by the late 1980s, the EPA had quietly left town, much as the mining companies had done in years past. By the time of my visit, however, the EPA had begun to dig up contaminated yards and driveways, and quarantine the debris in a storage area. And according to many local citizens, the EPA had returned to Tar Creek due—at least in part—to the campaign waged by the high school students.

Meeting Rebecca Jim

Like most of the teachers I met as part of this project, Rebecca Jim is both dynamic and understated; dynamic in her passion for the subject of ameliorating environmental degradation, and understated regarding her own individual role as a catalyst for student activism. Throughout the visit, she continually moved the conversation away from herself and focused on her strategy of following students' initiations:

> I've followed what they've wanted to throughout my career and this is where they are now. And they're having the time of their life. And so I'm going to follow it, if that's where they want to go.... We find a way to incorporate their ideas in a way that is a learning thing. For example,

the Fish Dance. They wanted to have a school dance. And in twenty-one years I've never sponsored a dance. Didn't see that you could make it a learning thing. Couldn't see a way to do that ... And then we found ways to make it be one of the best learning situations we ever could have thought of.

Ms. Jim traces her style of blending community organizing and education to her early training in the Teacher Corps. This was a federal program—with roots in the anti-poverty money of the Johnson administration—which based preservice educators in low-income communities. Teaching interns spent a third of their time in classrooms, a third of their time studying, and a third of their time doing community work. As Ms. Jim describes it: "We had to organize people to do things. The Teacher Corps will always be remembered in that little town of three hundred people because it was amazing. Everybody had to come up with their own plans to spend that amount of time. And it was just full blast. And so, ever since then I've just run it full blast."

Rebecca explained that her training as an educator grounded in a community-organizing model was complemented by the courses and workshops she took in group process. Indeed, the students spoke repeatedly about how she is able to bring out the shy or "depressed" student and encourage them to talk. Cheryl—a senior—went on at some length about how Ms. Jim's pedagogy encouraged participation from all students:

> She just brings everybody together, and it's like you're learning how to associate with people, you're learning how to talk to people, you're learning how to stand up in front of groups, and you're learning how to voice your opinion.... You wouldn't think it was that hard to think of how you feel about something. But then, once you actually have to get up there and say something about it, because I mean she'll always give everybody an opportunity to speak their mind ... I really respect her for that because it's got to be hard with some of the kids that we have to just sit there and listen to them half the time because some of them can ramble on and on, like me, and then some of them can just sit there and say, "Ah, uhm, ah, ah...I don't know what I think, pass." And then she'll say, "Well, what are you thinking right now?" It's amazing. I mean, it just floors me to think how one person can bring such a huge controversy, such a huge group together, such a community.

This pedagogy of helping students find their opinions and then find a way to voice these points of view to others was central to all the teachers I studied. In fact, it was in this pilot case at Tar Creek that I also realized how essential it was for me to observe in classrooms as the teaching was taking place. (In the Tar Creek case, school was already finished for the summer when I visited so I didn't actually observe any of the classroom instruction.)

Overall, it was quite fortuitous that Tar Creek was my pilot study, and Ms. Jim my first educator. Upon arriving at Miami High School, she gave me a list of all the interviews she had already pre-arranged. Not only had she planned an interview with local reporters, but she had also arranged many hours of interviews with students, school personnel, and parents.

Integrating Social Advocacy and Action into the Curriculum

When people think about the role that guidance counselors play in the school, many people think first about their work with students on social, emotional, and academic issues of adjustment. However, some guidance counselors conceptualize their roles more broadly and seek to work with classroom teachers on designing instruction to better meet the needs of learners. Rebecca Jim took this latter approach and explained that she volunteered to come into classrooms to help discover ways to engage students in learning. She said, "I beg teachers to let me come into their classrooms. I want to allow for all the ways that people can learn." And in the year of my visit, Nancy Scott (from the *Learn and Serve Project*) said that Ms. Jim had integrated the Tar Creek Project into ten classrooms. Ms. Jim explained that the school administration was very supportive of service-learning and had also required that the sports teams do some service projects.

Teachers from a range of subject areas collaborated with Ms. Jim on curricular integration, including English, science, and government. One English class studied Arthur Miller's adaptation of Henrik Ibsen's *An Enemy of the People*. In this play, the theme centers on the conflict in a community between an environmental problem and economic development. In a government class, students studied the organization of government bureaucracies and also learned about citizens' movements, including boycotts, petitions, lobbying; in science classes, students learned a variety of water testing techniques. To support this scientific inquiry, Ms. Jim wrote and was awarded a $25,000 EPA grant to get meters with long probes so the students would not have to touch the water to test it. She obtained enough equipment to have three area schools link up via laptop computers that were also part of the grant. And using an integrated curriculum approach, seniors in an English class wrote individual poetry, essays, and scientific reports about Tar Creek, which were ultimately collected and published in a book, *Tar Creek Anthology: The Legacy* (Scott, 1999). A few years later, high school students wrote another book, *The Tar Creek Anthology 2: Our Toxic Place* (Scott & Jim, 2002).

Educational Outreach

A major focus of the high school students' activism was education and outreach in the elementary school and high school. The year I visited they had organized two large high school events: The Fish Dance and the Tar Creek Conference. Regarding the conference, one student explained, "The last week of school, we took over the fifth and sixth hours of the day and had four different sessions that people could go to. It was mandatory so everybody got some education whether they wanted to or not." High school students led some of the sessions, and scientists and environmental activists led some. In a focus group, students reflected on their organizing skills and how the first year of the conference it was not well attended so in the second year they decided to make it part of the school day. They outlined for me all that they had learned about organizing an effective conference.

Because the students spoke in such detail about what they had learned about organizing, the power of student-led decision-making in activist projects became very obvious. If Rebecca had stepped into the early details of their first conference planning, they may not have made the mistakes they did. But, the students were clear that they had learned from their mistakes and had changed their plans the following year. I know as a teacher it is often very difficult to step aside and allow students to lead, but from this example (and other examples in other case studies), it is obvious that learning by doing requires that teachers not overly intervene to guarantee "success." Indeed, learning community and educational organizing skills is better served by letting students make plans, enact them, and then reflect on the successes and failures, rather than having a "perfect" teacher-led event. The ownership that all the students in this case (and in all the others) felt about their work was overwhelmingly evident.

At the elementary school, the high school students designed instructional materials and collaborated with elementary teachers (whom they knew from their own time at the elementary school) to teach the lessons. They taught children to wash their hands after coming in from playing outdoors and that taking recreational vehicles up the mountainous chat piles was extremely dangerous. Ryan—one of the young men interviewed—said the teachers in the elementary school were very supportive of their efforts: "They're one hundred percent willing to let us teach them, because by teaching them, they'll teach their parents and their parents will teach other people."

A Sense of Efficacy

To decorate the gym for the high school Fish Dance, students invited elementary school children to submit 3-D fish for The Tar Creek Fish Contest. Carrie narrates the story:

> We were going to have a fish dance. Decorating for the fish dance would be all these elementary classes that had entered their fish ... and each class got their own fish to do ... Each class got to decorate one side that was Tar Creek fish, the other side was future Tar Creek fish after we get it

cleaned up. And that made the little kids realize, "Oh, well, this is bad; this is what we have, this is good, this is what we want," and realize that this is how it could harm us. And this is how we can stay away from it and get it cleaned up and realize that it's contaminated and that the water's orange. Not because there's orange fish in it, but because there's very bad, harmful minerals and acids and lead in it that causes it to change color. It all comes from the mines. You [could tell] what actually sunk in with them, because they're not just drawing this ugly colored fish, they're drawing fish with three eyes and four tails and a couple of fins that go the wrong way and just really getting extravagant with it and then turning it over and having this beautiful fish that should be in there, you know. And I know that that had to have a lot of impact because I was getting questions asked to me even days after they had already handed all the fish in.

It is important to note Carrie's reflection on the effectiveness of the educational outreach work they conducted with the elementary school children. After all, having a positive impact is exactly the desired outcome of advocacy and activism. And as Kahne and Westheimer (2006) explain: "Researchers have identified a strong connection between an individual's sense that they can make a difference—their sense of efficacy—and their level of civic participation" (p. 289). Therefore, for Carrie (and perhaps the other students as well) to have completed her educational outreach work with a sense of effectiveness is a strong indication that she may continue future involvement in civic life. This, of course, is one of the most important reasons to design school curricula around social action and advocacy projects: to foster life-long civic agency and community involvement.

Learning Outcomes

Some of what is learned in these projects are specific skills—or organizing tools—and some of what is learned are ways of thinking and understanding such work. A later case—of Professor Eric Rofes at Humboldt State University—offers an in-depth examination of activist and advocacy skills instruction (see Chapter 6). Indeed, he designed an entire graduate level education class around teaching these. In each case in this book teachers integrated:

a. content regarding the social problem;
b. analysis regarding the root causes of the problem;
c. content regarding activism and advocacy that people have tried in the past; and
d. direct skill development for organizing, educating, and advocating.

Along the way, however, students also often learned lessons beyond the teachers' control that could not have been shaped by even the most carefully sequenced lesson plans. These lessons regarding ways of thinking about and understanding civic agency and social change are of critical importance. Without a large-scale longitudinal study, it is impossible, of course, to say what the life-long learning outcomes were for students in each case study. However, after only a few days with the students at Tar Creek, evidence of what students had learned did emerge.

In addition to all the media, education, and organizing skills students learned, they also learned important skills in group work. They spoke often about how their group strength is derived from diverse individuals working together. One student noted quite explicitly: "We all contribute something different to the group. Everybody specializes in one area, and when we pull it all together, we make things happen." Students listed the group skills they learned in the Tar Creek Project: holding meetings; working out interpersonal conflicts; stating their opinions; and (most frequently noted of all) listening to each other. They had a very strong sense of group identity as they talked about their work, speaking repeatedly about finding collective solutions to problems: "we" have to pass legislation; "we" have to educate people; "we" have to solve these problems. This collectivity was expressed at a micro-interactional level as well: throughout the visit the most talkative students worked continuously to prompt the quieter ones to answer particular questions. As Ned put it: "The one thing we did learn that we don't usually learn in school is how to work together—group efforts. We learned a lot of manners."

Students also learned that social change takes time. In the interviews the students explained on a number of occasions, "It's just going to take time." This is reminiscent of the title of the book about Myles Horton—the wonderful activist who founded the Highlander Research and Education Center in Tennessee. Horton devoted his entire lifetime to organizing for social change, first in the labor movement, and then later in the Civil Rights Movement. When he wrote his autobiography, he titled it, *The Long Haul* (1997). We know that social change is a long-haul process. If young people recognize this in high school and develop realistic expectations, they may be more likely to stay politically involved as adults. This is a lesson that cannot be learned by a teacher telling them, and may not be understood by reading about prior and contemporary social change movements. However, by being involved in a long-term, sustained project such as Tar Creek, these Miami High School students spoke confidently about the long-term nature of their project as well as their commitment to it. This finding parallels Kirshner's (2008) recommendation based on his study of multiracial youth activist projects; he recommends educators should plan on spending *more* than one or two semesters on civic engagement projects. The Tar Creek work offered this type of long-range involvement.

Controversy and Criticism

Educators who design curriculum around social action projects should be prepared for public controversy. In every case I studied for this book, the teachers had worked hard to establish open lines of communication with their school or university colleagues and administrators. Although this did not always make them immune to criticism, it certainly helped keep controversies at the manageable level. Of all the cases, Rebecca Jim ran into the most public criticism due to a series of letters to the editor in the local newspaper. But even this potentially challenging situation turned into a learning opportunity for some of her students.

During the spring, right before my visit, concerns started to be raised about water pollution from a local poultry plant that had been built in the area. Many of the students who were very involved in the Tar Creek lead-pollution project became active around this newer concern. As part of a school club, with Ms. Jim as the faculty sponsor—The Cherokee Volunteer Society—students planned an educational outreach program. As the campaign unfolded, they ended up also doing leafleting at the local supermarket. When the student group announced their plans for a boycott of the poultry product, someone wrote a letter to the editor decrying the high school's involvement in commercial and political affairs. The letter criticized Rebecca Jim by name. A student explained: "They were saying that she was supposed to be a school counselor, and she wasn't supposed to be doing all this stuff." The principal then wrote a letter to the editor disavowing any relationship between the school and the boycott. When Ms. Jim was called in to speak with the school administration, the superintendent told her that the project was "harming commerce."

This pressure, however, did not deter the students who jumped right into deeper civic engagement by writing letters of their own. Cheryl explained that it was the first time she'd ever written a letter to the editor. Her letter defended the high schoolers' protest. More controversy followed when Cheryl was called into the principal's office. He suggested that she was just parroting Ms. Jim and didn't know what she was talking about. She was extremely angry that he did not credit her with being able to form her own opinion on important topics and proceeded to explain facts and figures about the case to him. Cheryl said she spent a better part of the class period in his office, and at the end he apologized to her. When asked what other teachers said about her letter, she relayed that a couple said,

> "What's going on? What's this about?" But mostly it was kind of like the teachers don't want to be controversial, they don't want to really have anything to do with it because it's like they're worried about how some of the parents might think of them. They're not worried about their own opinion or about how they actually feel about things, they're just worried, "Oh, well such and such might not like this." That's how most of the town is, always worried about what everybody else thinks.

I was moved by Cheryl's acknowledgement of how often people are afraid of sticking their necks out on controversial topics, and I was encouraged that even though she was not yet old enough to vote, she was taking a public stand about a local issue of environmental and economic importance.

I used the poultry plant controversy to explore with parents if they shared the principal's criticism that students were being indoctrinated, rather than educated. One mother was quite loquacious in her response to my questioning:

> I think people underestimate teenagers' intelligence. I mean, these are young adults that are on the verge of being our next political leader or the next religious leader or whatever. I think that's underestimating their intelligence if you say, "Well they're just spouting her rhetoric.".... So you're saying my child's not intelligent enough to speak up for herself? They see the water, they see the consequences of what happens. They see the kids needing to go in and get a blood test because they might be high in lead.... I think sometimes it's easier to stick your head in the sand and say, "You know, there's no problem," or, "That's just one of those radical hippie teachers who's trying to get everybody in this, her own agenda." I don't see that with Ms. Jim. When this all came down, I kind of questioned at first, you know, the [poultry] thing, and I thought, okay, let's look at both sides. But then I thought, there's nobody else out there speaking about this. There's nobody else out there that has the guts to say, you know, "Maybe there's a problem." And basically that's what Ms. Jim is saying, "Let's look at this, let's see what we can do. Look at this creek, look at what we've done to our environment." And she's not saying ... she's never said once to Carrie ... "You do this. This is the way I want you to do it." She says, "What do you think, Carrie? What do you think?"

This, of course, hits upon one of the central fears concerning taking up activist and advocacy projects in the classroom: can teachers and students engage in critical inquiry and advocacy about real-world problems without being dominated by the educator's agenda? Every educator who integrates social issues and social problems into the curriculum has opinions and points-of-view about the issues. Ms. Jim, for example, was a Clanmother for the Quapaw Tribal Efforts Against Lead and thus was an activist in and for the community.

This research project was propelled by my own questions about how I as a social activist and teacher should negotiate my power and influence while integrating social action curriculum into the classroom. Throughout this book, I take up a consideration of issues of power that swirl around such work, and indeed in all classrooms as, of course, no curriculum is ever neutral. This interview with Carrie's mother offers two very important lessons: The first is that we must not infantilize students—in this case teenagers—and portray them as empty vessels who are not capable of forming their own opinions and commitments. When Cheryl read the letter in the newspaper about Ms. Jim that accused her of misusing school funds to indoctrinate students, she immediately reached for a pen and paper to offer an alternative viewpoint. This is the action of an engaged citizen or civic agent, who acts on her own initiatives, and acts on behalf of her community.

The second lesson that must be noted in Carrie's mother's explanation of the Tar Creek environmental curriculum is that the teacher's pedagogy was centered not on action, but on thought. Thus, the focus for Ms. Jim's curriculum can be seen as inquiry-oriented. It is by beginning with inquiries that invite students to look out into the world, see its problems, and imagine alternatives that social action and advocacy curriculum springs. The actions students then take emerge not from following the lead of the teacher, but from deliberating with the teacher and other young citizens about the nature of the problem and possible steps that can be taken to tackle the problem. Clearly, teachers who use social action projects as part of the regular school curriculum do initiate by bringing content knowledge and often process knowledge into the classroom. They also bring their commitment to engaged citizenship with them. This should not be confused, however, with indoctrination, which is what the school principal and the letter-writer feared. The students with whom I spoke did not want to be viewed as passive vessels or pawns. Rather, they spoke as knowledgeable members of a community in distress. The difference, however, between them and many of the adults in the community, is that they were committed to investigating and solving this decades-long environmental disaster.

Finding Receptive Public Spaces

Long after leaving Oklahoma, after I had finished all the data collection for this project, I examined the cases to find unique aspects of each teacher's. For Rebecca Jim, a recommendation from Randy and Katherine Bomer (2001) articulates in a nutshell a central aspect of her approach: "To educate for public participation must mean, in addition to supporting students' acquisition of strategies and dispositions, also to contribute to the construction of public spaces receptive to their voices…. Otherwise we are just teaching kids to talk to walls" (p. 157).

Rebecca Jim helped create these public spaces. Students had been interviewed by print and television reporters, and thus gained experience with speaking to the media. Such interviews did not always go as well as everyone would have liked, but that too is an essential aspect of the learning process. Rebecca helped arrange the interviews by teaching students media outreach skills such as writing and faxing press releases. She helped prepare them for what to expect in a media interview, but she insisted that the students develop their own talking points. Thus, she can be seen creating the public space for their voices, but not putting words in their mouths.

Rebecca also helped create spaces receptive to students' voices when she networked with the elementary school teachers on the lead poisoning education program. Although the high school students planned and taught the lessons, it was Ms. Jim who often handled the bureaucratic side of the educational outreach project. She was also involved in helping coordinate the high school conference, negotiating with the principal for time built into the last two periods of the school day.

The students also created The Tar Creek Toxic Tour as a feature of their fundraising campaign. Traveling around the area by bicycle, car, or van, participants arrive at sites that illustrate the range of environmental problems facing Tar Creek. Students serve as tour guides and also created installations at various sites. The tour is a prime example of Ms. Jim's creation of public spaces for students' voices. Taking the tour, one sunny, hot May day, we went from site to site, each marked with signs put up by students. "They're graffiti artists," Rebecca explained, "And the paint was donated by the Lion's Club." Students demonstrated great ownership and agency as they narrated the tour; they spoke about their plans for next steps in the project and of the various scientific solutions with which they were experimenting. Given toxic land, Ms. Jim had helped the students find a genre to bring together students, the public, and the toxic land, thus finding productive engagement as artists, scientists, speakers, and activists.

Perhaps, more than any other aspect of teaching with social action projects, students most need role models for civic agency and creative political engagement. Rather than turn her head as many adults in the community had done for years, Ms. Jim helped harness the high school students' creativity and commitment so they could play a central role in addressing a dire need in their community. Along the way, these Miami High School students learned important lessons about leadership, engagement, and social change. As Carrie explained:

> If we can touch one person by doing the things that we do then, I mean, eventually it's going to spread. One person can make a difference; it's been shown in the past. There's a quote [from Martin Luther King, Jr.]. It's: "History will have to record that the greatest tragedy of this period of social transition was not the startling clamor of the bad people but the appalling silence of the good." If we can all … you know, we all sit back and we complain about the things that happen in our community, but not too many people get out and actually do something to change what's happening. And if one person can do that, if one person can start a group and get people interested, then eventually people are going to see there's a problem and start to help.

2

A CURRICULUM OF PROTEST

Joe Szwaja at Nova High School

It's good to learn about activist skills by doing it.

—Sante, 15 years old

... we can see that the tiniest acts of protest in which we engage may become the invisible roots of social change.

(Zinn, 2002, p. 24)

The second case I studied came to me via the daily radio news and commentary show *Democracy Now!* In the days following the massive demonstrations against the World Trade Organization (WTO) in Seattle, a public high school teacher and two of his students were guests of Amy Goodman and Juan Gonzalez, the hosts of the show. The students explained that they organized street theater, including a *Sweat, No Sweat Fashion Show*, as a project for their class on globalization at Nova High School. (For the entire segment, see http://www.democracynow.org/1999/12/8/high_school_students_at_anti_wto.) I immediately contacted the teacher of the class, Joe Szwaja, explained my project to him, and wrangled an invitation for a week of observing and interviewing in early January, 1999. Because of the informal instructional climate at Nova, students had ample time for interviews throughout the day. I was able to immerse myself in the school community, sometimes interviewing students on the couch in the lounge, sometimes meeting them in a local coffee shop, and sometimes lingering in classrooms after the rest of the students had left.

Various students told me that the globalization class and the WTO protest were not their first experience with activism. Previously, they had leafleted about genetically modified food and had also done fund-raising to save an old-growth forest. One of the classes they had taken the year before was called, "Activism." The students in that class had learned about fair trade and had protested at Starbucks. They had studied and had joined campaigns about the Hanford (Washington State) nuclear power plant waste-disposal problem. In another class, called "Bureaucracies," they focused on schools and went to school board meetings, including making a presentation about the school-funding formula.

The globalization class, which I had come to study, had been examining the WTO in the build-up to the big meeting in Seattle. Then they planned the *Sweat, No Sweat Fashion Show* and a street theater piece with large Bread and Puppet style puppets. (The Bread and Puppet Circus makes massive papier-mâché puppet heads, which are carried on tall sticks and stand out very boldly in a large demonstration.) According to a student named Amber, they had about 500 people watching the street theater at one point in time. Then, after the protests were over, the class created a quiz for the media to take related to facts about globalization because they were dismayed that the coverage was about the small incidents of violence rather than about the major issues. They sent out the quiz as a press release and invited journalists to come to their class.

A School for Activism

Nova's curriculum is designed around in-depth studies on a wide range of topics, and most classes provide connections to the outside world. Here, then, was a perfect place for me to investigate teachers (and students) planning curriculum that took place beyond the four walls of the classroom. Part of Nova High School's mission statement underscores the necessity for learning to be rooted in community, and insists that education include more than mere knowledge acquisition: We seek "to promote in our students an awareness of responsibility to self and community." Being responsible to one's community is, of course, a laudable goal and one that proponents of democracy insist is central to forging active citizens. Yet how this sense of responsibility to the community is actualized and expressed is, by its very nature, subject to debate, disagreement, and contestation.

The students and teachers at Nova who organized their learning around the meeting of the WTO and subsequently undertook various action campaigns can be seen as moving well beyond any traditional service-learning notion of volunteerism. Researchers have found that volunteering among young people is on the rise, but political involvement is not (Sax, 2004). As Kahne and Middaught (2006) noted in their studies of high school seniors' civic, political, and patriotic commitments:

> For democracy to work, citizens must be willing to act. Less than half of
> the students we surveyed, however, shared this belief.... Participation in
> many forms of civic and political engagement has declined markedly over

the course of the past several decades. To a significant degree, we seem to be a nation of spectators. The risk this tendency poses to democracy is substantial. (p. 604)

The teachers and students at Nova were certainly not spectators, but instead planned and enacted curriculum around major problems such as globalization.

These teachers and students did not evidence a passive conception of citizenship. Indeed they were learning about and practicing many of the freedoms that many citizens think are against the law. In a large survey Gibson (1993) uncovered a sizeable percentage of citizens who thought the law prevents them from publishing a leaflet, making speeches against the government, or organizing protest marches. In contrast, he found that the small percentage of people from his study who were knowledgeable about their freedoms had prior political experience. Therefore, it is my assumption that the students at Nova—if surveyed later in life—would be in that minority due to their experience with direct protest as part of the regular school curriculum.

As I went from case to case for my research and studied teachers whose curriculum involved activism and advocacy, I wanted to understand how teachers negotiated their authority and dealt with the overtly political nature of their curricula. At each site I consistently asked about and sought evidence for how teacher power was used in making decisions about how advocacy and activism actions were planned. Although only the Nova case involved direct protest (and thus was potentially the most extreme), it is evident that the very structure of the school's student-teacher relationship helped mitigate strongly against the teacher imposing his will on the students. Nova High School was certainly alternative: students received course credit not through attendance in classes, completion of homework, and scores on assignments and tests, but through contracts that were individually developed and negotiated between students and teachers. For Joe's globalization course, quite a few of the students I interviewed did not end up receiving credit because they didn't complete their contracts. At Nova, if the students did not want to do the projects or studies the teachers proposed, then they would just opt out. In this way, the very structure of Nova protected the students from teachers' imposition and protected the teachers from having to worry so much about such imposition. Of course, persuasion can take many forms, and power can be deployed in subtle but strong ways.

Because students did not have to complete assignments that were given to them by teachers (which, of course, is not the way it works in traditional schooling), any political action students took was based in large part on their own initiatives. I found quite a few examples of this when speaking with students, and indeed, this acting on individual and collective initiatives is what a school like Nova is all about. Throughout my interviews at Nova, most students explained to me the actions they had taken toward activism or advocacy or else mentioned the fact that they had ideas for actions that they actually never carried out. Stefan, for instance, said, "I was interested in doing something about Hanford [nuclear power plant with waste-disposal issue], but never did." Thus, it can be seen that Nova's approach depended on students' initiative to actually take action. This works as a bit of a safeguard against teacher authority. Even though Joe was very outspoken in his political viewpoints (some of the students reported knowing other students who didn't like how "political" he was), because the pedagogical structure of Nova did not allow teachers to impose assignments on students, Joe was protected from needing to significantly worry about teacher imposition.

Although I had arrived at Nova to interview and observe Joe and his globalization class, the school principal—Elaine—made it clear to very clear to me that I needed to interview other teachers and other students in addition to Joe. She explained to me, "We are seen, I think, as a school of activism by a certain segment of the population." Students echoed this sentiment; Clara Lathrop explained that Nova is

> an alternative school so [the students] are interested in alternatives to the mainstream.... Independent thought is very much supported and promoted here. But, I mean, that doesn't translate to, you know, "Go out and protest everybody." So there are a lot of kids that do, and others that don't involve themselves. There are really cool kids who do all kinds of things on their own, too. That's what I think is really cool.

Nova High School is the only case in my study where activism was accepted as part of the school culture. This is, of course, a rarity in public schooling. Nova is a unique setting, and its activist classes and curricula must be viewed within this unusual context. This does not mean, however, that Nova has nothing to teach those of us who work in more typical (non-activist) settings. Specifically, Nova offers an opportunity to examine how power and knowledge circulate through teacher and student decisions and pedagogy. I close the chapter by pointing out particular safeguards and practices that helped students develop nuanced perspectives on political engagement.

Permission to Protest

A typical worry for teachers involved in projects that involve activism and advocacy is related to complaints from parents or administrators. All of the K–12 teachers in my study maintained excellent lines of communication with the building principal. In all cases, I was able to interview the principal and discuss the specifics of the cases. The principals were knowledgeable about the activities of the students and did not express any worry about "fall out" from parents or school superintendents. In fact, the only principal who discussed any special steps taken in relation to teachers' projects was Elaine at Nova. Although Nova was known as the activist school and much of the entire school curriculum revolves around out-of-school projects, Elaine knew that the massive anti-WTO protests planned for Seattle required some special steps on her part. She explained to me at the start of the interview that "the kids went out on their own for the WTO. I have to make that very clear." But she also contacted the Seattle School District general counsel a week before the protests and told him:

> I want you to know that we have a class on globalization. We've taught both points of view. Our kids are going to do street theater [on the first day]; but [the next day] if they go out for the protest they're going out on their own and so are the teachers. So if anybody asks any questions that's what we've done. And I'm telling you at least a week in advance if you have any questions about it.

The principal went on to explain that, in fact, some phone calls were received:

> So we got a call from parents. A parent had called the superintendent's office and complained that our teachers were taking the kids out. And they called me and I said, "That's not true." I called the parent back and I said, "That's absolutely not true. We have a class, they went out for a scheduled venue, and the play was the first day on the street. It was street theater, apparently it was very good street theater, and it was part of the class, and they were very supervised by the staff." And the next day when everybody did the big walk people were out on their own, they had to have parent permission. And then I had a parent call to say, "My daughter went out and she wasn't supposed to go out, but she said the school told her to go out." I said, "That is not true. I was personally here, and when they went out I said, 'Do you all understand that you have to be out with parent permission? You're taking a day off of school.'" Then I had a parent whose kids, three of them who go here, were very involved in the protest, and she was very upset because she's worried about her kids, and she said, "I believe in activism, Elaine, but this is just going too far."

Joe Szwaja, the globalization teacher, was very careful to explain:

> On Tuesday when we knew it was going to be a lot more sticky, I was there as a private individual, and I wasn't there as a Nova teacher, but some of our students were there, and I was with them and was there trying to keep it as peaceful as possible. I was proud of how our students knew a lot about the issues and judging from some of the coverage, our students knew a lot more than some of the reporters covering it. I was proud of how peaceful they were.

This is the only case in the book in which the students were involved in an international and large-scale demonstration; from the teacher's and principal's comments, it is easy to see that even in this school dedicated to activism, the educators made sure to distinguish between school-sponsored activities (the street theater) versus attendance at the very large anti-WTO protest. This carefulness was demonstrated in the principal's proactive phone call to the Seattle school district counsel and to the advance distribution of permission slips.

Meeting Joe Szwaja

As could be expected, many of the teachers from my research have active political lives outside of school. Joe is no exception and may be the most politically visible teacher I studied. Before moving to Seattle, Joe lived in Madison, Wisconsin, where he was an elected member of the City Council for six years. Subsequent to my visit in 1999, Joe ran for two more elected offices: in 2000 he ran for U.S. Congress (as a member of the Green Party) and garnered almost 20% of the vote; then in 2007, he ran for Seattle City Council. He lost to the incumbent both times. Joe is also involved in non-electoral politics: he is a long-time member of the *East Timor Action Network* of Seattle and a founder of the *Seattle International Human Rights Coalition*. Over the years while a teacher at Nova, he has taken many student groups on overseas trips, either related to his work as a Spanish teacher and/or trips tied to human rights activism.

Making links between school and issues in the wider world is not a new enterprise for Joe, so when the WTO announced plans to come to Seattle and anti-globalization groups planned protest, he thought it would make a terrific focus for a fall semester study. He found students to be very interested since it was going to be a "huge thing," and he collaborated with the theater arts teacher—Bobbi—to create street theater. They "invited people from both sides" to the school for a teach-in (a genre he and Bobbi had used many times before). The principal also spoke to me about the teach-ins and stated that Joe and Bobbi made certain that various positions on issues were represented. Joe explained to me that if he couldn't get outside speakers to represent different viewpoints, then he himself would speak from that position. Indeed, I heard him do that very thing while I observed him in class, and have included the classroom excerpt later in this chapter.

The Globalization Curriculum Project

Class assignments tied to the globalization curriculum included an essay on a topic of the student's choice and a test Joe created about the General Agreement on Tariffs and Trade (GATT) and the history of the WTO. A student explained that they also had to log outside hours showing that they were working on issues of globalization in some way. "You know," she reported, "we could even be working on it from the other side—helping the World Trade Organization to organize."

In reality, no students worked for the WTO, but they all contributed toward the street theater, which was clearly a high point of the class. Students designed the *Sweat, No Sweat Fashion Show* and also created a play about sweatshop practices around the world and alternatives to such practices. In her interview, Bobbi explained that every year she does a theater piece with Nova students and then described the genesis of the street theater for the WTO protests:

> I decided to do a street theater piece this year because I went to *Arts Edge* and I saw this most wonderful piece that was completely done in silence with these big huge puppets—head puppets. And I just went and I said, you know, "Gosh, this is so beautiful. I would love for students at Nova to have the experience of creating something that would be like this and that wouldn't use a lot of words. And that would … be a very different thing that we've done, than we've ever done at Nova." We've never done puppets and big puppets. And I also was very concerned about what was going on with the WTO, so I thought this would be an interesting thing to do … to have the students create a piece that they felt in response to the WTO. And Joe said he wanted to do a piece on globalization economy, so I said, "Well it's really important people become informed before we make this piece." So I saw the first part of it being like a way to become informed about the issues; and then people create a response. It was definitely created by the students, their ideas as they learned about the issues. So, again, it's the idea of drama or it becomes an expression in a sense of what people find out about the world and then put in a form to share it in a way that's aesthetically beautiful and touching. And that's what makes me excited: to light other people up in terms of their involvement and commitment to a project. Because you know what's really unique is that really things don't happen unless students want them to happen. Because there's nothing that makes a student have to stay in a class at Nova, it's just by their … I mean, there's no grades so you don't have that hanging over people. ·

One of the students in the globalization class—Amber—told me that making the puppets and doing the street theater was a highlight of the globalization course. When I asked her to explain what she learned by doing the street theater, she said, "We made huge puppets. We used cardboard and newspaper and rags. We made masks too. I could probably make a big puppet with someone."

But at the same time that Amber felt confident about making large papier-mâché puppets, she was much less positive about her knowledge of issues surrounding globalization. She was ultimately disappointed in the class and explained that a lot of the other students knew a lot about the issues of globalization before the class even began and that the class "went too fast" for her. She elaborated on this: "About half the class probably already did know that stuff and half the class didn't know anything. Or just knew a little tiny bit. I think

Joe went over it briefly. But even the basic stuff is confusing. It's not an easy subject to understand. There were all of us who were like, 'What's going on? What are we talking about?' And then there were the people who were into it.... There were long discussions I didn't even follow and didn't understand it at all."

In stark contrast with Amber is Nicole Bade who was interviewed on the radio show *Democracy Now!* Her account of the content of the globalization course differs quite significantly from that of Amber:

> In the globalization class the first couple of weeks were just researching the WTO, finding the history, reading about GATT and all of the different legislation from the US that had been changed, some in Europe, how the World Trade Organization differed from the GATT, how their view of the free market differed from Adam Smith's view of the free market, stuff like that.... We read excerpts from various sources, we heard a lot of lectures from my teacher, Joe, who's read all of the Marxist theories, all of the capitalist theories. And we had little study sheets and stuff like that. We also read a lot of information that was being printed by the WTO on their web site and by the anti-WTO. And we had a few people for fair trade who were at this point going into schools and teaching in classes, and people that come in and tell what it's like to work in a free trade zone, basically what this version of free trade is doing to people all over the world and how it's demeaning, in many cases, women's rights and a lot of labor standards in different countries, and environmental standards.

Nicole—one of the lead organizers for the street theater—explained how it worked:

> We decided on a street theater of the devil versus the people playing a board game, the devil being any personification of the WTO: the GAP, the capitalists, whatever, and just kind of leaving it up to the imagination. Basically what we did is we had a gigantic dice and someone would roll a three and we had drums and stuff like that, and shakers, and everyone would shout, "One, two, three," and they would take three symbolic steps on the board game in different directions. And then they would get a chance card of some sort that would become something. Like, for instance, one person got a shopping spree and went to the GAP, but then it showed the other side of what happens. The basic story line for this is you have these people and they're working in the fields, and they're sewing, and they're going to school, and they're fairly happy; they're sustaining their way of life. But, you know, it's hard, hard labor. And so these little devils are down in hell ... well, actually, these two big devils with legions of little devils ... and they make a bet. One says that he can completely dissuade the humans from this style of life and make them unhappy and turn against themselves. And the other devil's like, "Eh, I

think humans are smarter than that." So they make this bet and they go up on it, and they're like, "So, do you guys want to play this game?" And all of the little devils, you know, scurry around and say, "Yes, play the game. Play the game. There's lots of money." And we had a whole bunch of big dollar bills and stuff like that. And the people are like, "Oh, okay, it doesn't cost anything, I can only win." And so the first one wins the shopping spree. And we, the little devils, bring over this little bag that has GAP clothing in it, and she takes it out and the clothing has blood all over it. And she gets really, really horrified and runs away. Then the father gets a better paying job and the job is shut down because it went overseas. And the concluding thing was that the mother got a whole bunch of genetically engineered pesticide-filled strawberries in winter and gave birth to a mutant child. And then they're all like, "We're not playing this game anymore." The little devils all run off.

When I asked about the other street theater piece—the *Sweat, No Sweat Fashion Show*—Nicole explained that it was "Joe who actually organized it." She described how it worked: "Models would come out and model things that have been made in sweat shops and they would have blood on them and stuff like that. And then a representative from one of the sweatshops that made it: "representative" because we couldn't find anyone who would come out and explain the labor conditions that they were made under and the grotesque human rights abuses that occurred in the employment places." Although Joe was excited about the fashion show and he referenced it in his discussions with me, Nicole's explanation that it was the teacher's project and not the students' helped clarify why no students referenced it, or explained what they had learned by doing it.

Genres for Social Action Pedagogy

As I traveled around the country collecting these cases of teachers whose regular classroom curriculum centered around social action projects, I began to generate a list of the products or genres that were used. As is true for all classroom curricula, students are invited to participate in a number of learning experiences throughout the school day. In its most traditional form and perhaps what comes most readily to many people's minds when they think of teaching and learning, curriculum and instruction involves a teacher with a textbook and teacher's guide of some sort. The teacher's job is to impart knowledge and the student's job is to listen, copy information into a notebook or onto the page of the workbook. Then the teacher tests the students to see how well they have memorized the information the teacher has imparted.

Using social action projects as part of the regular school curriculum involves an inherently different form of demonstrating knowledge. Taking part in an action that moves outside the four walls of the classroom involves some sort of audience for the students' knowledge products. So rather than a report or a test, students in social action projects generate products for the public. This "public" may be the students and employees within a school building, if the social action project is focused within the school building; for example, if the project is to decrease the amount of waste sent to the landfill every day from the school cafeteria. But whatever the social issue that is the focus of the project, students are involved in producing a product of some sort for a live audience.

In the case of the Nova globalization class, the main product that most students spoke about—and that first drew the attention of Juan Gonzalez, the reporter for *Democracy Now!*—was the street theater that Nicole described above in great detail. This theater piece offers an opportunity to analyze both power and knowledge as it circulates through this unusual pedagogical genre. Notice, for example, how it was Bobbi's experience at the community group, *Art's Edge,* that led her suggest street theater with puppets as an exciting genre. Understanding that the genre of street puppet theater required substantive knowledge to undergird and stimulate it, she collaborated with Joe to infuse the theater piece into his globalization class. Yet all of this background work is, of course, invisible to one of the lead student organizers—Nicole—who described how inspired she and her classmates were by the artists and their puppets that they decided to make their own big puppets and write a street theater piece. And then we have Amber, representative of a different sector of students who, although she enjoyed making the puppets and felt she would know how to make them again should she need them in the future, was much less confident about her knowledge of the main issues of globalization.

Because I am an advocate for integrating social action projects into the curriculum, as a researcher it is important to offer a critical but friendly analysis of how power/knowledge circulates within the genre of pedagogical activities such as this street theater piece. Although decisions about what actions to take may appear on first glance to be the students'—and indeed at Nova if the students didn't buy in, no external mandates existed to pressure them to do so—teacher power and influence runs deeply beneath the surface. It was Bobbi's and Joe's prior knowledge and commitments that stimulated them to bring street theater and globalization into the curriculum. It is important, I think, for teachers to claim—as did both Joe and Bobbi—their influence on the curriculum. It is a mistake for teachers involved in social action curriculum to deny their influence as they seek to assuage public criticism that they are possibly indoctrinating students. The more that teachers can claim their authority for both classroom process and knowledge construction (Oyler, 1996), the more capable they will be of analyzing and then interrogating their (possible) influence on student knowledge construction and student advocacy and activism.

The street theater piece also offers another cautionary tale and that one derives from Amber's disappointment with the course. Although quite pleased to participate in the street theater production, she finished the class not feeling very confident about her content knowledge related to the main issues of globalization. This may be partially explained by the mixed age groupings of most Nova classes. Amber was a first year student, and Nicole was a few years older. However, in all classrooms—whether mixed age or not—students arrive and depart with a great range of knowledge and skill differentials. No matter if the classroom curriculum involves social action projects or not, teachers face the challenge of creating instructional opportunities that are multilevel (Oyler, 2001). In the case of social action projects, which sometimes require much time spent on product production, it is important for teachers to work closely with students and assess their content knowledge. The teacher is most often the expert in the classroom regarding content, concepts, and skills pertaining to the topic or issue of study. He or she should decide—perhaps as negotiated with students—what knowledge students will be expected to learn. Although participating in a community action project can be a powerful induction experience with regard to strategies of activism, if students miss important knowledge about the issue at hand, they are certainly less prepared to engage in *enlightened* political action.

Teachers' Political Commitments and Classroom Pedagogy

In my interviews with students, some students spoke less about the curriculum of the class and the social action projects and more about the influence Joe had on them as a teacher and as an activist. In one interview Thomas explained to me, "What Joe does is teach from the heart and that's what makes all the difference. He cares, and it is that caring that makes me care too." Such "teaching from the heart" is a subject of great interest to me as I seek to understand the power that circulates within such potentially provocative pedagogies.

The role of the individual teacher who is very inspiring oftentimes cannot easily be separated from the content he or she teaches. And yet a teacher can be inspiring about a great range of things. When asked to recall an inspiring teacher—and I have asked hundreds of preservice and inservice teachers to do just this over the years—a great range of experiences come to mind. For some people, they recall a teacher who made a subject come to life simply because the teacher had so much enthusiasm. For other people, they recall a teacher who scaffolded some social or emotional learning. (I recall, for instance, how my second grade teacher—Mrs. Benbow—helped me learn how to join group play at recess, rather than stay inside and read a book which is what my first grade teacher allowed me to do.)

It was at Miami High School and then continuing on to this case at Nova that I started hearing from students about the influence of the teacher's political commitments and passions. In setting out to conduct this research study, I was concerned about the issue of teacher imposition and very interested in documenting the ways that students understood the teachers' political commitments. It seemed to me that teachers motivated to design curriculum around real world issues of equity and justice might need to be extra careful about their own pedagogical practices. Specifically, I was concerned that teachers convinced of their moral and political certitude not impose a dedication to human liberation and social betterment upon students. The dangers of requiring, for instance, students to advocate for the teachers' causes loomed large for me. Believing—along with Hannah Arendt (1958/1988)—that "plurality is the condition of human action" (p. 188), I sought to uncover the ways that the teachers' pedagogy created spaces for students to understand and explore multiple viewpoints, and not just swallow the viewpoints of the teacher.

A number of students at Nova described how Joe taught them so much about the world and about being an activist. As James put it, "Joe opened up my eyes" to various issues of social and economic injustice. "Joe is great," he says, "the stuff he brings to Nova. He's always doing this activism stuff." Likewise, Clara described how seeing Joe at meetings outside of school time motivated her to be more active herself. She explained that when Joe invited special guest speakers to speak at Nova lots of the students show up and "it's just because of Joe that they come."

Nicole also described in great detail the influence Joe had had on her; and she was able to elaborate on specific details of his pedagogy, particularly as it related to matters of influence and imposition. "Joe really tries to make you think. No matter what your point of view is, he'll always state the other point of view—which I find to be very, very helpful because that's how I think. I very rarely have one point of view on any subject." A student such as Nicole, who had honed many of her political positions within community organizations such as the Direct Action Network and the Catholic Worker community, was able to appreciate the pedagogical moves Joe made. Specifically, Joe asked students to consider multiple viewpoints on the issues under examination. Indeed, while observing his globalization class during my January visit, a classroom excerpt demonstrates this commitment.

Joe was engaging the students in a review session on the main concepts from the semester's globalization class and was using an interactive, Socratic-type lecture. When asked to define colonialism, one student offered an answer. Joe then replied, "Okay, so that's the Marxist perspective, what's the other side of this? What's another perspective?" It is overt and intentional pedagogical moves like this one that are so important in helping students understand that many school content and concepts—particularly in the social studies—are not purely factual and objective, but rather are shaped by different paradigms and perspectives. Instead of attempting to only present "facts," Joe's commitment was to help his students understand that even the very definitions of words and concepts come from particular positions. Committed to presenting the point of view *not* in the room, this version of progressive pedagogy opens up the possibilities for pluralism and democratic debate.

But not everyone in the class had the developmental maturity to understand Joe's pedagogical moves. Nicole described some of her classmates' responses:

> But that [stating the other point of view] at some points caused a little bit of tension in the class just because: "Well, he said this the other day and now he's saying this." The main thing that Joe was trying to do is trying to get us to back up our sources and stuff like that. So even if we had something that he thought was right on track and could be backed up very, very well, he wanted us to justify it with those things.

Nicole had a deep understanding of what this pedagogical approach offers to a strong democracy (Barber, 2003): "Everyone was coming from all these different angles.... It was very healthy controversy. At Nova, we're really used to disagreeing."

Clara too, had a sophisticated political analysis and could understand Joe's pedagogical techniques:

> You know, everybody has a bias ... and Joe probably has a biased account when he talks to people about his biases. All teenagers are doing is ... taking somebody's opinion and somebody else's and saying, "Yeah, that's my opinion" and then seeing how it sits, and then saying, "Oh, no, I hate that opinion."

The classroom structure at Nova did not require that students take up teachers' suggestions, thereby providing a strong measure of protection against teachers imposing their political decisions on students. This sort of teaching requires a fair amount of content knowledge so that the teacher can offer the opinion or point of view that is not present in the room. This was a skill that Joe had carefully honed, sometimes through inviting guest speakers in, and other times by taking on the alternative viewpoint himself. Additionally, it helps to have authentic and complex issues as the focus of study. As Nicole explained, "Another thing that was emphasized is that nothing in this issue is black and white." Most social justice issues are inherently complex and thus always can be examined for nuance. Students' "black and white" thinking can be challenged as they seek greater and greater sophistication of their political viewpoints. Thus, we can learn from Joe Szwaja how the influence of a teacher whom students admire and seek to emulate can be balanced by overt attention to ensuring that multiple viewpoints are carefully considered. Indeed, it is the insistence of teachers such as Joe on critical thinking over dogmatism that nurtures the very habits so necessary for pluralism and deliberative democracy to flourish.

It is helpful to conclude with advice from Walter Parker (2003) here in underscoring how important it is that civic action be guided by enlightened political engagement. He uses the examples of the Ku Klux Klan and the Nazi regime to explain that without democratic enlightenment to guide the activism, apathy and no action are actually preferable. An essential element of this enlightenment comes from the inclusion of multiple viewpoints and people with different social identities. It is through this inclusion that students can become more nuanced and critical in their thinking. It is the insistence of the teacher to move beyond "black and white thinking" that helps students progress toward deliberative democracy. As Parker explains, "the presence of multiple perspectives increases the likelihood that dominant norms and beliefs are subjected to observation and critique" (p. 99).

By taking advantage of an international, local event and organizing a semester-long class on the issues of globalization, Joe Szwaja gave his students the opportunity to engage in a curriculum of public protest. But he did this with full attention to cultivating a stance toward political engagement that is deliberative and educated, rather than dogmatic and simplistic. By continually insisting that multiple perspectives be brought to the table, he offered a version of public engagement built on deliberation and pluralism. That this pedagogical act increases students' ability to observe and critique dominant norms and beliefs is a theme that runs across the cases of this book and is an essential component to understand these teachers' classroom practices. How can schools and classrooms become sites for unpacking the status quo and create more just and equitable communities?

3

ADVOCATING FOR THE COMMONS

Lance Powell and Hunters Point

> We're learning about environmental science injustices ... And we actually
> get to participate in ways that we could help fix it.... So we actually get
> to feel part of the community more.
>
> —Sandia, 12th grader

For quite a number of years I spread the word among friends and colleagues
that I was looking for teachers who used social action projects as part of the
regular school curriculum. At various points, people would send me leads, and
I worked to sort out which sorts of cases "counted" for inclusion in this book.
I knew the case had to involve some sort of real world social, environmental,
or economic justice issue. I knew the project had to involve students doing
classroom work that reached out beyond the four walls of the classroom. And I
knew that I was looking for cases that could offer some degree of controversy.
That is, I wanted to find some politically charged issues about which adults in
the community held differing opinions.

One day Ann Berlak, a friend from Oakland, California, sent me an article
from the *San Francisco Bay Guardian* about high school students tackling issues
of environmental racism. Mentioned in the article was a local community-
based organization by the name of Literacy for Environmental Justice (LEJ).
Just as I had done with Nova High School, I cold-called the agency, explained
my project, and asked for leads on teachers with whom they were working.

The organizers were very welcoming and gave me the names of three teachers to contact. One of the three was leaving the classroom the next semester for
a school leadership position, but the other two, Lance Powell and Derrlyn Tom,
agreed to hear about the details of my project, and both ultimately agreed to
have me come and study with them. I spent a week with Lance Powell in his

science classes at Thurgood Marshall Academic High School (TMAHS) and then another week with Derrlyn Tom, who taught in a different school also in San Francisco (see Chapter 4).

This chapter begins with a portrait of Lance Powell and the context of his school and then presents two very different forms of teaching with social action projects. I happened to arrive at the school in the midst of a surprising activism project that had not been planned ahead of time and involved a complicated situation with the local school board. This project unfolded with Lance's ninth grade team-taught class "Urban and Wilderness Survival Challenge."

The second focus of this chapter takes place inside Lance's Advanced Placement Environmental Science class. In selecting the cases for this book, I was eager to have as much diversity of course levels as possible, so I was pleased to have the opportunity to study an AP class. During my time in this class, Lance was organizing his instruction around "The Tragedy of the Commons." I use his short "teaching the commons" unit—which was tied to a small social action project—to explore the importance of this critical aspect of strong democracy: helping citizens consider their individual liberties and rights within the context of what is best for the community and the planet. At no point in world history has this perspective been more important. As the gap between the rich and the poor—the haves and have-nots—expands, it is essential for engaged citizens to move beyond an individual gain perspective. Although mainstream success these days in U.S. society is closely tied to individual profit and material success, our very survival as a planet is dependent on citizens who are able to solve public social problems and act for the common good. This chapter offers a chance to listen carefully to many micro-interactions in a classroom as a teacher engages in lessons designed to teach students to actively participate in shaping the common good.

Meeting Lance Powell

After arriving in San Francisco, I made my way to Thurgood Marshall Academic High School—an *academic* high school located in the working-class neighborhood of Hunters Point. As the school principal explained in an interview, the school was opened ten years previously as an outcome of a lawsuit initiated by the National Association for the Advancement of Colored People. The NAACP demanded equal access for poor, students of color to a rigorous college-prep curriculum. Greeting all who enter the high school is a large permanent display board listing all the colleges TMAHS graduates attended. Indeed, according to the principal, 95–99% of graduates go on to college. However, unlike the other San Francisco academic high school (Lowell), students are not selected by test scores for TMAHS; rather, they "choose" in, by indicating the school as their first choice. In this way, the school provides open access to an elite education. Students here take science, math, English, and foreign language for four years; they also have ethnic studies and pre-engineering and robotics and access to a large number of Advanced Placements courses. Half the students qualify for free lunch, and many of the students attending the school from this zip code live in government housing. The principal tells me that the Latino and African American students from the previous year's ninth grade did better than their peers at any other school in the city on the California School Exit Exam: Latino students from Marshall scored 30% better than the city average, and African Americans scored 20% better.

For my first day, Lance asked me to meet him in his office next to the science lab before school. In his fifth year of teaching, Lance is a tall, slim, white man who keeps his bicycle—which is how he commutes to school—leaned up against his desk in his office. His classroom is a science lab with tall tables and stools, and there are five computers at stations around the room. The entire room is filled with carefully hung student work related to environmental issues, including solid waste, Styrofoam, recycling, and paper production. The room is sunny and offers a spectacular view of the surrounding hills. On the front wall are poster-size assorted colorful pictures of Earth, along with numerous bumper stickers presenting succinct advice: "Question Assumptions"; "Justice, Not Vengeance"; "Imagination is more important than knowledge" (with a picture of Albert Einstein); and "Success is not a matter of chance, but a matter of choice."

Lance is very proud of the science lab, telling ninth graders during one class period that the district spent $250,000 to renovate it. He is dedicated to inquiry-based, project-oriented teaching and spends most of his planning time creating and organizing scientific investigations. In fact, it is through such "hands-on" science that Lance actually made his first foray into science teaching. Having graduated with a degree in conservation biology, he thought he would go into environmental law or environmental consulting. However, moving to the San Francisco Bay area after his post-college world travels, he fell into working for a for-profit company called Science Adventures in which he went to different schools conducting science demonstrations for large assemblies and teaching in after-school science programs. Lance found he really enjoyed being in front of children making science accessible, but wanted to do more; "The problem with Science Adventures," he said, "was that after-school only comes once a day." Being networked into the teaching world for the first time, he found out that because of San Francisco's desperate need for science and math teachers, there was a special program that paid for his teaching credential from San Francisco State and put him immediately into a high school classroom.

Currently in his fifth year of teaching, Lance shows no signs of slowing down. Indeed, while teaching, he bounds from the front of the room to the back, making his way through the thirty-five seniors packed into his Advanced Placement Environmental Science class, or running from table to table as he works to keep his ninth graders focused and engaged. His expressive tone and energetic pacing convey a real seriousness of purpose; he uses every single minute of class as teaching time. Mr. Powell also works to build strong, positive relationships with students; as they enter the classroom, he stands at the door, greeting each one. Throughout the course of instruction he constantly extends compliments and encouragement, from numerous comments to individual students such as "Very convincing speech, Maurice," to comments to the entire class such as "Mr. F. was proud and impressed by your speaking."

Lance is also a hawk-eye teacher who pays total attention to the work of individual students, circulating all over the room, focusing on quiet kids too— even though the loud joker teenagers could easily dominate. His "with-it-ness" (Kounin, 1970) seems to earn the respect of students; at one point in a ninth grade class, he called a student's name at the end of a sentence because he noticed him playing with some sort of game. David was clearly amazed that Lance had noticed and turned with a little smile and shook his head as if to say, "Mr. Powell catches everything." He uses humor to confront non-complying students and takes time to connect with students individually: showing great interest, for instance, in a girl's photo album she brought for him to see.

The positive student relationships Lance Powell seeks to build are interwoven with an overt commitment to foster student decision-making and a valuation of student voice. For example, a ninth grade class was working on crafting their statements for a San Francisco School Board public hearing and a couple of students asked Lance, "Why are we doing this?" There was a brief pause and instead of the teacher providing the rationale for the classroom activity, another student explained, "You're going to have to speak out in life." As this was the special unit on Wilderness and Urban Survival, Mr. Powell echoed the student's explanation and added, "Finding your voice is part of survival." Helping students find their voice emerged as a key feature of Lance's pedagogy. In the thirty single-spaced pages of classroom discourse I transcribed (see the Appendix for methods related to transcribing classroom talk), there were eighty instances in which Lance used the words *speak, speaker,* or *speaking.*

Defending the Academic High School

Across each of the cases in this book, teachers consistently taught and or scaffolded many basic skills of active citizenry. Among the most essential of these skills is what Lance Powell called, "finding your voice." I happened to arrive at TMAHS while the school was in the midst of a major controversy related to the "academic" status of the high school and would get to observe a special unit designed to teach students how to offer testimony in a public hearing. Right before my visit, the superintendent of schools had brought forward a proposal for the academic schools to *reduce* the number of required graduation credits to be consistent with most other high schools; thinking that the requirements may partially explain the high attrition rate at the school. Meanwhile, the ninth grade "family team"—of which Lance Powell was the coordinator—was at the beginning stages of their two week "Urban and Wilderness Challenge," a special team-taught unit that involved field trips and a culminating camping trip to a redwood forest campground across the Golden Gate Bridge in Marin County. The students have four core teachers who co-plan and integrate content for ethnic studies, academic literacy (reading across the content areas), science, and language arts.

So quite serendipitously, I had stumbled into a special, quickly designed unit created to take advantage of this authentic "urban challenge." The ninth grade teaching team was excited to integrate this real world controversy regarding the number of credits needed for graduation into their project-based curriculum. The schedule the teaching team created was elaborate, and it involved all the ninth graders preparing a statement for public testimony. It would culminate with a mock board meeting at the high school, which would be a practice run for the official school board meeting.

Writing a Statement for Public Testimony

I began my observations in second period ninth grade science. After collecting field trip permission slips for the scavenger hunt coming up on Friday, Mr. Powell asks for a show of hands for how many students had attended the community meeting on Saturday related to the school board proposal to lower graduation requirements. Quite a few say that they went, along with their mothers and grandmothers. He invites one student to give a report, and her explanation makes clear that the people attending the meeting are quite concerned about the proposal that the academic standards of TMAHS be reduced. She concludes her report, and Mr. Powell says, "Well spoken, Aliza." She beams while the class claps. All eyes are on the teacher, and he starts talking:

> The topic today is not geology. We are shifting gears, as promised, from normal science, because we are in the midst of, yes, the 9Y Urban and Wilderness Survival Challenge. And a big part of our urban survival is finding our voices, not that you can't find yours because you're very well spoken, finding our voices and speaking out about things that affect us and the timing couldn't be more impeccable with the proposal from the superintendent coming down. A big part of urban survival is you guys realizing how you can become a part of that [public] process.

He asks the class to take out the charts that they worked on with Ms. Finkelstein in a previous class. They were supposed to outline five points on both sides of the argument—for or against the change in school graduation requirements. Only seven of twenty-one students can actually produce the charts. Seemingly undeterred by this lack of organization or completion, Lance begins an explanation of what to expect at the board meeting.

Here's the idea, the superintendent has come up with this proposal and has a big influence over the Board of Education and how the members vote, but what happens at this meeting is that it is open to public testimony. Anyone that wants to speak in favor or against the proposal is able to. That means people like me and you. So you have all these people looking this way, and there's the board sitting this way. And there's a line of people. And they have two minutes to speak their mind. You have two minutes to say what you want to say in favor or against. So depending on what's happening, regardless of what's happening, you want to be real focused and clear about what you're talking about. So basically your goal is to be real concise, say what you have to say and be convincing. You're trying to convince the board members that this is either the best thing that's ever happened to this school or it's going to be the worst thing, one way or the other. So you want to think about what you would do if your parents told you something you didn't like. For example, your birthday party's cancelled; there will be no birthday party. You'd be like, why, why? You know how to argue. All right? Some of us are better arguers than others. And I imagine, I know for a fact, we have some pretty talented speakers in this room. So this is basically something that's real, that's on your plate, and definitely related to urban survival. Hopefully you can see that education is part of urban survival.

It struck me right away that this is a good example of providing students access to the culture of power (Delpit, 2006). These are all students of color, and almost 100% from families where they will be the first to attend college. By painting a strong visual image and outline of what to expect, Lance can be seen directly transmitting his cultural capital (Bourdieu, 1986) and his knowledge of the codes of power (Delpit, 2006) to them. (I found out in a subsequent interview that Lance had never actually attended a San Francisco Board of Education meeting himself!) Students interrupt Lance's explanation quite frequently, peppering him with questions. One student queries: "Will they really be listening?"

"Yes," Lance explains, "What you say really matters, you need to convince them. But you have to really hang in there, because often the public testimony doesn't come 'til really late: like 11:00 at night." Moving quickly to the task at hand, Lance tells the students,

We're not going to tell you *what* to think, hopefully you have an opinion based on the research you've done. You're going to write that statement. When I say statement, I mean what you're arguing. It's like you're going up and your life depends on it. You want to be convincing, you want to be passionate, you want to be loud. We've got 15 minutes.

Students take out papers and start to work, but do not work in silence. Questions continue to be asked by individuals as the writing proceeds. For me, this short class period was filled with an important observation: Lance is careful to explain that students must develop their own opinions, but these opinions should be informed ones arrived at through systematic research and defended in their statements.

Wanting to find out how controversial topics were pursued inside this classroom, I perked up my ears when a student asked Mr. Powell: "Is tomorrow the walkout?" Lance had mentioned to me that if they didn't get a delay on the school board vote, that there was talk circulating among students about a school walkout. Supporting such an action could clearly present danger to the activist teacher: at what point would teachers cease to have the support of their principal for this sanctioned school-community activist project? Lance quickly replied: "Walkout? You're talking to the wrong guy." Questions from students continue:

Question: How do we get to the board meeting?
Lance: I don't know, maybe we could organize something.
Question: What if you don't want to write a statement?
Lance: If you really don't care, pretend you do.

Mr. Powell begins to pass out the rubric that will be used to evaluate "How you speak your statement," and one boy states quite loudly that he'd "rather be doing science." Explaining that the students "won't have as much science if this goes through," Lance also adds: "I imagine Martin Luther King would have rather been with his family; sometimes it's not about what you want to do to be comfortable."

Implicit in these remarks is clear indication of Lance's own stance on both the school board issue and some strong pressure to (as the song lyrics say) "be like Doctor King." This is the aspect of teaching with social action projects that I am most eager to tease out; clearly, Lance has his point of view about the value of science and that a reduction in academic requirements would not be a good path for the school. Also, implicit in his remarks is the strong admonition to rise beyond your own desires and work for some collective, common good.

Lance can be seen doing a careful dance here: he doesn't hide his viewpoint on the particular issue; he uses class time to pursue a controversial topic; and he invokes one of the most common icons of the U.S. struggle for racial equality in his attempt to motivate students to care. At the same time, he wants the process to be non-impositional, "We're not going to tell you *what* to think." One piece of evidence that at least some students felt free to disagree with their teacher was the fact that a number of students did end up writing statements supporting the proposal to lower the number of required credits.

The other important point during this classroom exchange occurred in the conversation about the student walkout. Student walkouts have a bit of a history in California, and sometimes during campus walkouts teachers do choose to accompany them. For Lance Powell, however, this was not one of those times.

The teaching team was under a fair amount of pressure from the principal who had sent out a memo halfway through that very school day asking teachers to work with him and not to "storm the meeting."

Lance tells the class, "Your goal is to convince the board members, and some of these people are really educated, with Ph.D. level educations. I know you've convinced your parents of things and they are smart people."

A student interjects: "I want to use big words."

Lance replies, "Big words sometimes make you sound smart. Or sometimes it can backfire. Anyway, can we go to our stations? I'm coming around with stopwatches. Okay, everybody go to their lab station." The students move very quickly into groups of about five and many of them start working on their statements right away. Mr. Powell moves from group to group passing out a stopwatch to each group. He gives further directions:

> While the person is speaking their statement, someone else in the group is the timekeeper. We gotta keep it under two minutes. Before you start talking, the idea is you're not going to be reading your statement, you're going to be saying your statement…. You want to be speaking with as much eye contact as possible. At the board meeting, some people have little note cards so they can remember what they want to say. You want to be looking at these people [the board members] in the eye. Remember, they're all adults, they're all educated adults. You want to be talking to them convincingly.

I place the microphone at one small group table, and later transcribe two of the students rough draft statements they spoke to the members of their small groups (for transcription notations, see p. 181 in Appendix):

> I feel that it is necessary to keep the 280 credits at Thurgood Marshall. We are after all an academic school and by lowering the credits we will no longer have such status. In fact it was the school district who recommended that the 280 credits be applied at Thurgood Marshall, in order to boost academic achievement. Our school is already set up to work co-existingly with 280 credits. If we were to change that we would have to adopt another system. Based on statistics about 99% of the students that graduate from this school go to college. Students with 280 credits get recognized for their achievement and have more chances for getting into a university. Reaching the standards, students become more responsible, learn more, get prepared for college, and this gives the school a better reputation.

> I've been waiting to go to Thurgood Marshall. From my friends, I heard great things about this school. I came to this school wanting a great opportunity to go to college. The reason I picked this school is because of the credits and it being an academic and a college prep school because

I wanted to go to college with a scholarship and become what I want to be. So taking away credits is a big step I don't want to have to take. Me being African American and wanting to go to college is a great thing to do. In my neighborhood, not a lot of people go to college. I'm going to - - (laughs). Okay. Going to an academic school makes me work harder and prepares me for college. I need something to challenge me and that is my testimony.

After both students finish, the small group members spontaneous clap for them, and I am struck by how seriously these 15 year-olds have risen to the challenge presented.

I realize how powerful this pedagogy is as I notice one boy sitting at the back of the room with an electronic Chinese-English dictionary. I wonder if he is a new arrival in this country when he doesn't seem able to answer a peer's question, "How old are you?" (The oldest person in the group has to present first). Yet, he manages to write a statement and delivers it in his small group, with the help of another Chinese-speaking student. It is lovely to watch the peer support that enables this boy to be fully included and successful. It is evident to me that this social action-oriented group work can be conducted because the students have become accustomed to working in small groups; collaborative small group work is clearly a norm in this classroom.

There is a tone in the room of utter diligence and no one seems to be wasting even a second of time. Earlier, when only a third of the class had managed to produce the charts, which were supposed to have helped scaffold the assignment, I thought this might be a serious impediment to getting the statements written. I was quite surprised (and delighted) when at the end of the fifty-minute class period, all students had practiced their statements in their small groups. The class ended with Mr. Powell explaining that in the next class in their schedule that each person would give their statement again, and this time give it to the whole class. The teacher would use the same rubric they had used in their small groups (see Figure 3.1), but this time it would count as their grade for the day.

By fifth period, it is the third time I have heard the explanation of what the students are to do, but I am still a little in awe of Mr. Powell's fair, firm, and friendly style.

What we are doing here matters a great deal because you need to find your voice to speak up when things affect you. The goal of today is *not* to have me up here talking the whole time. Nicole, can we put the make-up away? Inappropriate. The bigger goal is to have you come out of school feeling confident that you can get involved and testify at public hearings.

This particular class is being held after the teaching-team's collaborative prep period, and Lance tells the students that there has been some controversy

PRESENTATION RUBRIC					
Name:					
Assignment:					
Presentation Skills	FIX-UP ZONE				
1) Did you face the audience?	0	1	2	3	4
2) Did you maintain eye contact with the audience?	0	1	2	3	4
3) Was your voice loud and clear enough for the audience?	0	1	2	3	4
4) Did you speak with expression and energy (like you mean it)?	0	1	2	3	4
Argument					
5) Did you strongly state your opinion?	0	1	2	3	4
6) Did you back up your opinion with examples or other points?	0	1	2	3	4
Language					
7) Was your statement grammatically correct? (especially perfect verb forms/tenses and perfect sentences?	0	1	2	3	4
8) Did you use persuasive language?	0	1	2	3	4

FIGURE 3.1 9th grade team statement presentation rubric

among the teachers and staff about when to go to the media. I am struck by how this demonstrates to students that this work is contested ground, and that adults have differences of opinions. It reinforces that this problem is real and is complex. I realize this is a major part of what I seek to find in my cases: When does curriculum get to deal with real problems that are happening in the world? I write in the margins of my field notes: "What are the markers of pedagogy designed around the real? One is that it is complex and people disagree." This is so different from so much of academic knowledge presented in schools: the knowledge is fixed, there are right answers and wrong answers. This kind of banking approach (Freire, 1980) to education means that the learner is not able to bring something new to the table. Thus, the learner is positioned in a passive role; and the good student is one who is quiet and compliant. This is, of course, the image of citizenship that some wish to inculcate in public schools: teach children to follow directions, color within the lines, and comply with authority. However, in this classroom, and among this teaching team, students are asked to take an active role in shaping the world around them. They are actively teaching civic agency, not passive compliance.

Presenting the Statements

By sixth period it is apparent to me just how carefully scaffolded this activity is. In a succession of classes, each of the four ninth grade groups had a chance to decode and decipher the arcane language of the board proposal; outline five points on both sides of the argument; write an individual statement; practice the speech in small groups; and then practice delivering the statement in front of the whole class. Because the teachers had planned the sequence together, as the four classes of ninth graders moved through their day, each teacher actually conducted different lessons, depending when in the sequence of instruction each group was at by the time they arrived at the teacher's room.

Now in Lance's sixth period the students are to practice the speeches in front of the whole class. Lance whispers to me as the students are switching classes that his next group has a large number of more newly arrived immigrant youth and he knows some of them will be very nervous about getting up to speak in front of the whole class.

The class period begins with a very detailed report by an African American girl who attended the community meeting on Saturday. Lance thanks her, "I couldn't have summed it up better myself. Not a chance. I can't believe your recall." And then he adds, "One thing I'd like to stress that you said is that there are a lot of different opinions going around out there. One thing that I think everyone in that room was in agreement on—everyone in that room had the best intentions—people want the best for their children, for the students at Thurgood Marshall in general, but there's some controversy over the methods. How do we get to point B? There's some controversy over it. There's some pros and cons on either side of the proposal. You guys have taken a position. You don't have to be locked into your position. But for the purposes of today you've got your statements. Can everyone pull out their statements please?" All students manage to find their papers. "The meeting will come to order, please."

A student jumps in: "I have a question. How are they going to decide who's on the board?"

Lance replies: "Who's on the board is already determined. They're elected."

Student: "No, no I mean, for our mock board meeting."

Lance: Oh, we're going to get some intimidating teachers to play the roles. We're working on that. Okay, so the first thing I'd like to ask is, basically, today is not going to be geology, sorry about that Erica, we're putting rocks on hold so we can get down to something that is very important which is public speaking, public presentations, about an issue that affects you guys. So out of fairness, the way to go about the order is, what do you think, reverse alphabetical order or alphabetical order?

A student quickly pipes in: "Alphabetical order."

Lance: "That's the first one I heard, so it will be alphabetical order. The order of speakers. So people are set up for it in their minds, Okay, take a deep breath." Lots and lots of lots of student voices are raised in protest or concern and some time passes, "So did you guys all bring your rubrics?" A loud chorus of yeses follows.

"We've never really done this before in this class, public speaking, and because you all are decent human beings, I don't think this is going to be a stretch for you but okay, when we're not speaking, can we be…"

A student: "Quiet"

Lance: "Totally quiet. We're not shifting around, we're not doing anything that might distract the speaker because there's an expression I learned, a saying out there that the number one fear of most people is public speaking, the number two fear of most people is death. Meaning that lots of people would rather die than public speak. For some of us maybe it looks easy when we're up here jabbering all the time. But for some people it takes some nerve to get up here. I hope people feel safe in here. I've seen people be very courageous in this room before. So no matter what happens, I want people in the audience to be super, super respectful. If you're not speaking, you're going to be like the wind beneath the speaker's wings."

Lance then says that he will stand at the back of the room and let the speaker know if they need to speak louder. "You're trying to convince folks to vote one way or another. You want to put some passion in your voice. You want to say it like you mean it. And it does directly affect you. It's real. And last but not least, even though you don't have to memorize it, you want to be looking up. If you're not making eye contact, it's not a good thing. Okay. So, our first speaker today." Mauricio is the first student and when he finishes the kids clap profusely for him (and continue to do so for each student in turn).

Lance: "You thought you weren't going to do a good job, but you did a great job. What did we like about what Mauricio did?" Classmates offer a long list of compliments.

The second student is now up and is taking real pleasure in speaking—he's got quite a smile. When he finishes, a student suggests he should be louder. Lance adds: "I agree with that; if you could increase your volume a little bit, that would help you out a lot, and another thing I'd like to point out is at the very end, you kind of looked up and smiled and said, 'And furthermore …' That was good. Furthermore's a power word."

To another student, Lance gives a tip about how to "Look up while you're reading. Keep your finger on your spot. When you look up, it changes everything. You can have your paper up there. I don't want you to memorize it, but every once in a while, maybe when you're comfortable with where you are, just kind of look up. You don't even have to look at anyone really, it just seems like you're looking at somebody."

The next day when the first class of ninth graders come in, Lance explains the next stage of the project: "What we're going to end up doing is that each group will select two people to speak at the mock board meeting. The next step will be to develop what those speakers will say. And to let the cat out of the bag, just to make it interesting, we don't want everyone to say the same thing, so each group will have two speakers, and we're going to set it up like a debate. And one speaker will be in favor of the proposal, and one speaker will be against. No matter what you're arguing, it's kind of nice to know the other argument. You can argue more effectively."

Each small group meets, and they select the two people from their group who will present at the mock meeting that will be happening the next period. They have just enough time for everyone to rehearse. An African American girl named Shantel goes first. She is poised and confident, but stumbles on some words near the end of her talk. The students all clap for her and Shantel's quickly comments, "I messed up."

Mr. Powell reassures her: "That's okay. If that happens when you're speaking, it's no big deal, you hear me tripping on words *all* the time. No big deal, don't let it rattle your cage." The students all laugh. "So one thing for all the speakers, and this is the last one, if you're up there speaking, and all of a sudden you have like a moment of clarity and something comes to you, you can add it. You don't have to stick to your script."

Near the end of the class period, all the students who will be delivering their statements have practiced, and Mr. Powell explains what will happen next period in the auditorium:

> What we're going to be doing is modeling the meeting that's going to happen with the Board of Education. But one quick announcement. Initially we were going to want everyone to go to the board meeting tonight. We were going to actually show up and have you publicly testify. So Darlington, Ashley, Greg, Shantel would have all been publicly testifying before the superintendent. But we've actually made some gains in what our school's stance is on this. And [the principal] has now asked us not to go. He feels that if we all show up we'd jeopardize this.... That was the original goal to get a thousand people to show and say we mean business. Because one of the criticisms was that a lot of their decisions were made behind closed doors and guess what? We're the people that are involved. You and your parents that chose to come to this school for whatever reason. His feeling is that would jeopardize the progress that we already made and we're going to respect the superintendent and that in good faith she's going to do what she told us she's going to do. So we're not going tonight, you guys, some of your parents might be planning on going. So please ask your parents NOT to go to this meeting, and we'll do it next time. When the vote does come up, we'll be going.

The Mock Meeting

At 11:30, the entire ninth grade "family" of eighty-five students files into a freezing cold auditorium and sits in rows, filling in from front to back. On the podium are teachers and parents playing the role of school board commissioners. The names of the real commissioners are on placards in front of each mock commissioner. The audience of students is quiet. A teacher calls the school board roll. An African American mother acts as the superintendent (the real superintendent is also an African American woman) and reads the eleven philosophical tenets from the consent degree of 1985, which is, apparently, how all board meetings begin. Among them:

1. All individuals should learn to live and work in a world that is characterized by interdependence and cultural diversity.
5. All individuals learn in many different ways and at varying rates.
8. If individuals do not learn, then those assigned to be their teachers should accept responsibility for this failure and should take appropriate remedial action.
11. Parents want their children to attain their fullest potential as learners and to succeed academically.

The "clerk" then reads the proposal to reduce the number of credits required at "academic" high schools to 230. The audience starts booing, and teachers don't seem to mind. Student speakers are then called up in groups of four. The first speaker receives wild clapping, and the second speaker has a crisis of confidence, drops her head on the microhpone and says, "I can't do it." A nearby teacher calmly helps her by putting her finger on the lines she is to read. The girl reads haltingly. The audience is patient and quiet. I keep track of gender and ethnic distribution of speakers, and there are more African American girls and Asian and Asian American girls than any other subgroup.

The speeches are well delivered, and the audience is patient and quiet for quite some time. As it drifts closer to 12:30, the audience grows restless, and I must admit I've heard most of the arguments and am getting a bit bored myself. A spitball fight erupts, and Mr. Powell exiles one girl to the back of the auditorium. But then the chair of the board calls for a vote, and the audience visibly sits up. They clap and hoot and holler loudly when the outcome is what most of them want: no reduction in credits. Watching the teachers try to calm the students down enough to dismiss them to their next period, I write in my field notes that I am relieved not to be in charge.

Assessing Student Learning

The next morning in class I had a chance to listen in on what students had learned about fighting for social justice. Mr. Powell started the class by writing on the board, "Write about the 5 most unfair things that you or your friends face in life." Out loud, he adds: "You can think about school rules, the police, parents, anything you want." As the students begin developing their individual lists, he circulates among them, reading and speaking quietly with individuals. When most students have a few items on their pages, he explains, "What we want to do here is link issues of fairness to justice, which is related to urban survival." He segues into a short debrief of yesterday's mock board meeting and asks for their comments and reflections. He begins by saying, "You've got some proud teachers." Then he adds that things got really out of hand at the end of the meeting: "We teachers can take responsibility for not having an activity, but there was a frightening energy in there." He then gives some short advice about the importance of being calm in large group situations.

He doesn't belabor the lecture and students get to work developing their lists, which include: we face racism and stereotypes, classism, pay taxes, can't vote, college isn't free, weekends are too short, there's too much violence. One boy states, "Kids and teens don't have power over anything." When Mr. Powell says, "You feel like you're powerless," the boy and others add on, "Yeah, that's true about a lot of things." Lance then writes on the board: "You have to pick your battles," and says, "What would make me happiest is if you can step into the community debates. Let's look at these lists, like all the kinds of racisms that exist and the inequality of school districts. But I hope you'll get in and pick a battle. Some of us teachers have chosen to pick the battle of keeping Thurgood Marshall at 280 credits." He talks about the next board meeting coming up in a few weeks and having them go and how important it is that they are preparing for it.

The next and final activity of the class that day is to get into groups and do some strategic planning around fighting an "amendment" (which he passes out to the students) setting an 8 p.m. curfew for teenagers during the week, and 10 p.m. on weekends. (The amendment turns out to be a simulation that he has made up, but most of the class doesn't figure this out until near the end of the period.) "When I saw it, I thought, no way. Here's what I'd like you to do: One reaction to the amendment, why do you think it's unfair? What could you do (if you chose to pick this as your battle) to stop this? List three or four things."

Students offer a range of answers, and then Lance gives them the next direction: "Go to your groups. I'm getting magic speaking objects. Each person will share three ways to get involved. One person has to be the note-taker. It can't be the person who spoke on the microphone yesterday." Lance passes out objects—which are used to signal that the person holding it should be the only person talking—and I'm reminded that ninth graders are still children in some ways as they seem to care which object they get. The moose seems to be all the group's first choice. The other objects are: a crystal, an elk vertebrae, a magnetic perpetual motion sculpture, a stick of wrapped sage (no one picks this in either class).

In the small group I sat in on, students discussed methods of fighting against this injustice. A small part of the conversation follows:

Student 1: We could call the press.
Student 2: What will that do?
(Many students discuss this strategy for a few minutes.)
Student 1: We could have a protest, have a sit-in
Student 2: Have a petition
Student 3: How do you spell petition?
Student 4: What's a sit-in?
Student 1: Didn't you learn anything in Ms. Goldstein's class?
Student 4: I'd tell my family not to vote for it cuz it's not right.
Student 2: How will we go out on Halloween?

What ensues next is a quite a long exchange when the student worried about Halloween says that is a darker night than all the others; the other students try to correct her misconception with scientific explanations. She isn't convinced and they finally drop the subject.

Lance then addresses the entire class and asks: "Was the walkout an effective way to organize?" Students engage in a fairly lengthy discussion about advantages and disadvantages of the walk out, including saying that it demonstrated togetherness and pride. He then asks more questions to them about what message they want to send and to whom they want to send the messages. He comments, "You need to think about consequences of actions ahead of time. Is it worth it for the higher cause? So go over your lists and pick the best two things. Then make a presentation." He writes the guidelines on the board.

Issue:
1. Reasons this is *unjust*
   • list of things
2. What your group wants to do and why
   • why would it work?
   • what would be the consequences of your actions, positive and negative?

Students start working fairly energetically on this task, and I roam contentedly around the room listening in while these young people carefully consider injustices and how to organize to change them.

I have one more day at this school, and there still is seventh period Advanced Placement Environmental Science, but I am satisfied that I have witnessed a carefully sequenced small spontaneous unit on taking a public stand. I feel I am that much closer to some of the answers I seek through this research project.

Advanced Placement Environmental Science: Trail-Blazing, Project-Based Curriculum

At the same time Mr. Powell's ninth graders were working on the school board proposal, his AP Environmental Science class was working on a unit he called, "The Tragedy of the Commons." This was the first year the AP Environmental Science class was being offered at TMAHS, and as with the ninth grade curriculum, Lance was busy developing materials and creating a cohesive, project-based curriculum. "I feel like I'm a project manager," Lance explained to me as he described the course. Quite proudly, he added that when he came to the school, "We didn't have any textbooks, we didn't have any curriculum. I have been working with other teachers, and we created and trail-blazed the curriculum."

Lance explains how great it is to teach in the Bay Area as there are so many opportunities to engage students in environmental projects. The class has been working with LEJ on the restoration of Heron's Head Park right in Hunters Point and also on the public debate about the expansion of a power plant by the Mirant Corporation. He elaborates on the particular environmental issues facing the neighborhood: "This is where we are—there are 325 toxic sites in the neighborhood of our school with two Superfund sites. One of them is one of the largest Superfund sites in the United States. There was a nuclear toxic fire there last year that burned for three months."

Lance invests a great deal of time and energy in designing labs; in interviews, students mentioned ones on bioremediation and garbage as highlights from the year. Some of the labs are conducted at City College where he takes the class so they can work with a professor. He explains to me that the lab facilities at the high school are actually better than at the college, but he wants students to have the experience of being on a college campus and being taught by a professor. He has also partnered with the director of environmental education at the University of California, Berkeley, and two of the doctoral students are scheduled to come to lead a lab for the AP students.

The class also takes a lot of other field trips, including trips to do water sample collection and testing in the bay; throwing nets out and collecting samples; using microscopes at the edge of a pond; going to a golf course and testing for nitrates; and going to the Water Waste Treatment Center. He specifically requested that the AP course be scheduled for the last period of the day so the class can—as one student put it—"go all over and not have to worry about getting back to school." Some students I interviewed explained that they find the field trips to be inconvenient for them in regard to after-school jobs and/or needing to be home to care for younger siblings.

In addition to some complaints from students about field trips, some explained to me in a group interview that the community service hours that Mr. Powell required were a burden. The only two criteria are that it has to be outside of school and it has to be environmental. Lance explains about this requirement:

> My goal is … to make people aware, number one, and then…best case scenario is to … take it a step further. Some of them already are so psyched about doing this stuff. After school today some people from the San Francisco Department of Environment came to have a meeting … because two of the girls … [are] going to … speak at a retreat with all these other students that are going to be environmental educators.

One student described the importance of the field trips and community service in fostering a sense of responsibility to the community:

> And also it's like we get to see like all the stuff that we're doing. Like we're learning about environmental science injustices; and then we also get to see about [things like] the plant expanding the cooling system. And we actually get to participate in ways that we could help fix it. Like I remember signing these post cards for a petition to close down the power plant. So we actually get to feel part of the community more.

Protecting the Commons

Central to all consideration of teaching with social action projects is the concept of the common good. Dr. Martin Luther King, Jr., in his famous letter from the Birmingham jail explained that as humans: "We are caught in an inescapable network of mutuality, tied in a single garment of destiny. Whatever affects one directly, affects all indirectly" (King, 2011, Chapter 5, para. 4). Although King was writing this letter to white clergy who had criticized the direct action tactics being used in the civil rights movement, his explanation of the "common good" is as crystal clear as any I have found. All the teachers spotlighted in this book can be seen organizing classroom instruction focused around skills needed for people to pull together and work for the common good.

What Lance Powell did in his environmental science class is build a series of lessons around the idea of "the commons," leading up to a letter writing campaign about a proposed expansion of a power plant. He started the unit with a history lesson going back to "the olden days" and the "King of England." He offered an engaging mini-lesson leading into a challenge for students to consider how the commons can be protected. Near the end of class, Lance frames the issue as urgent:

> Put a star on this in your notebooks because it underlies a lot of the global problems in the environment, and it's called the "Tragedy of the Commons" … We've got a big problem. It's as real as it can be. The fisheries are getting wiped out. You guys have read about global warming, the

greenhouse effect, the ozone layer, rivers, lakes, all that stuff is commons. You guys have to think about the environmental damage to air and water, which are commons.... Okay, we'll pick that up later. Reminder, please come in with what's happening with the Potrero Plant fresh in your head. That's a perfect example of the commons, because what they want to do with their expansion is to take all this additional water into their power plant and use it for a cooling system and to make their power plant more profitable, but the reality is it's killing a half million fish and is a huge source of pollution for the bay. It's part of the commons. It ties right in. What could be some ideas to protect the commons? So come in fresh tomorrow. Be prepared.

The next day, when the students walk into class, Mr. Powell has written on the board:

Tragedy of the Commons
—Bay water is a commons.
—Bay landscape is a commons.

He offers a detailed explanation of what is happening with the proposed power plant and why a large coalition—including the U.S. Fish and Game Administration—has come together to fight the proposed expansion. Lance tells me from the front of the room that he is "adlibbing" because the guest speaker— Patrick—from LEJ was supposed to be here by now. Lance continues,

But the question of the day is, and I know what Patrick was going to talk about, is how do we handle any of these problems? From the PG&E power plant, to the Navy shipyard, to any type of company that is allowed to basically trash the commons where they don't actually pick up the expense of it. How do we confront that?

Patrick arrives and begins talking as soon as he enters the room:

So you all are talking about the Tragedy of the Commons. I have a little more information. I went to the hearing yesterday about the expansion of the Potrero Power plant by the Mirant Corporation. It was one of the most interesting hearings I've ever been to. It was very emotional, very packed. There were lots of different people there from different elements of the environmental field, people really concerned about the Bay, people really concerned about environmental justice for the southeast community. People who are really concerned about air emissions.

He explains that public comment is due today and that if the students decide to write letters they have to do it now.

Passion and Point of View

Lance tells the class, "I pride myself in not jamming my opinion down your throat, but I want you to write a letter for or against the expansion or to request more information." Continuing this advocacy with a back door escape hatch so he is not using class time to tell students that they must write letters advocating for the point of view of the adults in the room, Patrick elaborates:

> I'm trying to be objective, but you're hearing my opinion about this. I care a lot about San Francisco Bay. I could just go through a few ways to argue this and discuss this, and I could show you some sample letters you could write. If you're against doing anything at all, and expansion is the way to go, then you could write a letter arguing that. If you feel like you haven't been given enough information, then you don't have to do anything. I don't want you to feel like your grade depends on doing anything at all.

Students ask, "Can we write letters together?" Lance replies, "You could try to reach consensus and write one together," and about half the class gathers in their groups.

There's not much time left in the class period, and Patrick says the vote is going to be held tomorrow; there is a seriousness of purpose in the room, and I can't quite believe it is the spring of these seniors' last year in high school, they are packed in like sardines, some without even access to a writing surface, and every single one of them is involved in writing a letter, or appears to be engaged in helping draft one.

After class, Lance faxes the letters to the commission and gives me copies for my files. The letters are all different, no one uses the sample that Patrick brought. Here are three examples, one from an individual (Figure 3.2), one from a group of five (Figure 3.3), and one from a group of three (Figure 3.4).

Watching this episode unfold—and reading the letters, none of which argued for expansion of the power plant—I knew I had a juicy episode to chew on. Concerned, as I am about teacher imposition in social action projects, this advocacy project gave me a perfect vignette to analyze. Teachers who organize curriculum around real world problems and then ask or permit or support students to go public with their products face the issue of how their own points of view intersect with the assignments they require from students. At every single interview throughout this entire project—with teachers, with parents, with school secretaries, principals, and students—I asked over and over again my questions about power and imposition.

The unavoidable dilemma is this: any authentic real-life problem has complexity and at least two—if not many more—positions, with different stakeholders taking differing positions. And any teacher who designs curriculum around authentic problems probably has a well-developed point of view on

Dear Commissioners,

I am writing to you about a concern I have as a student from Thurgood Marshall Academic High School. I've been participating in an Environmental Science class and have learned about issues that affect me personally. I have visited Herrings Head Park and it is already in a state of recovery.

I've studied data and statistics of different information about the Hunters Point Area, and even seen the atrocities that have endured due to the race for profits.

Alternative solutions must be explored before going forth with such a big step in building the power plant. Please consider hearing about what affects the communities and the organisms before the decision is final.

Thank you for taking the time to hear me out.

FIGURE 3.2 Advanced placement student's letter

what is to be done. Add to this mix that teachers make decisions regarding what assignments are required and then how those assignments are graded. Students are aware of this relationship, and even if the teacher has provided a way out (as Patrick and Lance did), they still exert an incredible amount of influence, due to their relationships with students. Perhaps a student really respects a teacher

Dear Commissioners,

As high school seniors at Thurgood Marshall Academic High School, we feel strongly against the usage of San Francisco Bay water by the new power plant. We are deeply outraged that nearly 1/3 of the bay water will be used just for cooling purposes at the power plant.

By initiating this expansion, we are posing several dangers to our precious ecosystems. We are endangering our fish species, our wetland environments, and the clarity of the water. Water is a resource that is shared by all, not just one species. It is both greedy and arrogant to not even consider the effects this power plant will cause.

San Francisco Bay is already damaged. Can we damage it any more? We understand the need for power, but there are definitely other options to consider instead of using our limited resource, water.

FIGURE 3.3 Advanced placement students' letter

Dear Commissioners,

As the seniors of Thurgood Marshall Academic High School, we are seriously outraged on the issue of expanding the Potrero Hill Power Plant. We feel that this expansion is unnecessary. It is not only harmful to the species in the bay, but also indirectly harmful to our environment.

As AP Environmental students, we are volunteering our own time to improve the water quality in our bay. And now you're telling us our work is about to go to waste? But we understand that energy is a very important resource to our survival, but please put our comments under consideration. Thank you!

FIGURE 3.4 Advanced placement students' letter

but has not truly developed his or her own point of view on a matter. Is the teacher, then, by sharing his or her own point of view and advocating a certain action (writing a letter) exerting undue influence?

But, I argue with myself, it is equally dangerous to design curriculum around the authentic problems of the world and not demonstrate that you have a position: to teach, for instance, about any form of injustice or discrimination and not make it clear that you find it wrong. By their very nature, social action projects involve matters of justice. To be silent in the face of injustice is not a stance we can afford to model in the classroom. How then to deal with this pedagogical dilemma? Over pizza, five of Mr. Powell's seniors shared their thoughts on this matter.

—He's a … yeah, he's a pretty extreme environmentalist.

—You can see where his passions lie. It's not like he's like, "You have to believe in this," but you can see how the way he talks about it and the way he's…trying to give us all the information; you can see that he really cares about what he's talking about.

—He kind of has ways to open up your eyes. Because I'm the person who would like to see different points of view about something, and sometimes when we did have those discussion groups, like I'm sitting there in that group with my opinion. Then later on, once I hear everyone's opinion, kind of, "Oh yeah." It kind of makes you think of another point of view and kind of consider that later on.

—Yeah, Mr. Powell tells us his opinion, but he's not like, "Oh, you have to do what we say."

By the end of the group interview, they had concluded that making sure students had lots of opportunities to dialogue and debate with each other helps mediate the powerful influence of the teacher. Their Environmental Science class included many such debates, and one girl explained how helpful these discussions were in sorting through her own ideas:

> It would get really rowdy because people feel really strongly about one way and the other people disagree, and that's why we had to hold on to objects to talk because people would argue. But then it really shows you what other people are thinking about, you know. And I thought it helped you understand more too because if you talk about it then you understand it and you get other people's ideas, so you better understand it as you talk about it.

It is exactly this sort of dialogue and debate that is so necessary to sustain democracy and is what seems central to non-impositional social action projects.

Indeed, it is within issues that involve "ambiguity, contradiction, instability, and fluidity" that students learn to "engender dialogue and action" (Varlotta, 1997, p. 475). By engaging in such projects in schools, teachers can scaffold the development of political and civic participation among young people (Wade & Saxe, 1996). By not shying away from controversial, opinion-laden, complex environmental issues, Mr. Powell was preparing the seniors to enter the fray of democratic deliberation. What an important set of skills and dispositions to learn in school—that environmental issues are complicated, that the public has to learn the issues, that responsible people do not always agree, and that it is important to develop a point of view. The teacher modeled all this by both asserting his own point of view and creating a space for debate and dialogue in the classroom.

A Big Win

A couple of months after returning to New York City, I received a letter in the mail from Lance:

> Our AP Environmental Science class just had a big win that I wanted to share with you. The day we had that guest speaker from Literacy for Environmental Justice speak about the potential expansion of a local power plant in the Bay, which was followed by our letter writing campaign which we faxed to the BCDC—well, it looks like it had some effect. Actually, we were told specifically by the BCDC that the letters made a difference. So we're all feeling pretty good right now.

Lance enclosed a letter from the executive director for LEJ, which reads:

Dear Mr. Powell and Students,

I am writing to congratulate your students on their success in helping to oppose the expansion of the Potrero Power Plant.

I received a call from Mike Thomas at Communities for a Better Environment informing me of their important contribution to the campaign to oppose fossil fuel driven industries in our city. He stated that the letters from Thurgood Marshall High School made a substantial impact on the Bay Conservation and Development Commission's decision to unanimously oppose the expansion of the plant. This was an important vote, as the BCDC was the first City Agency to oppose the plan.

Thank you again for your heartfelt and honest response to this significant environmental justice concern. Without your back-up, we might have had a much tougher fight on our hands. Let no one say that today's youth are uniformed or apathetic! Thurgood students are leading the way to a better, healthier, and safer world.

Reading these letters underscores for me the importance of designing curriculum around "the commons." Whether it is a natural resource, such as the San Francisco Bay, or an educational resource, such as open access to strong academic high school curriculum, Lance Powell's skillful pedagogy offers a strong model for challenging students to develop a point of view about public resources and policies. Indeed, it has been argued (Barber, 2003; Carlson, 1997) that public schools are a central place to develop the type of democratic citizenry capable of working across differences toward a common good. By understanding the interdependence among people and between people and our environment, and being able and willing to deliberate about the nature of the common good, students will be better able to protect the commons both while in school and after they graduate. By engaging this way, students are, as Sandia pointed out at the top of this chapter, able to feel they are part of the communities in which they live, and feel efficacy by contributing to their protection.

4

CULTURALLY RELEVANT PEDAGOGY AND ACTION FOR THE COMMUNITY

Derrlyn Tom at Mission High School

If you're in a classroom you learn a lot, but if you're out in the community you learn even more, because you're in an environment where people have different struggles every day. It's like learning from the outside of school. To me, I'm learning more from the outside. I'm learning more outside about science than in school.

—Antonio, 10th grader

Choose one. You need to finish one. I'm asking you to do something. To take action and do something.

—Ms. Tom

Derrlyn Tom—from Mission High School—was a science teacher recommended to me by the community-based non-profit organization Literacy for Environmental Justice (LEJ; along with Lance Powell; see Chapter 3). Thrilled to be conducting fieldwork in The Mission—my favorite San Francisco neighborhood—I eagerly agreed to Ms. Tom's suggestion that we meet in her classroom for an informal get-acquainted visit the week before I was scheduled to spend five days in her classroom. Feeling my typical nervousness of going to meet a total stranger, I arrived early, settled myself into a wonderful café across the street from the school, and contemplated the impressive school building. Mission High School has stood on this site—across from the lovely Dolores Park—since 1898 and was, in fact, the very first public comprehensive high school west of the Rocky Mountains.

Upon entering this ornately decorated building, its long history is immediately reflected in the numerous framed portraits of each graduating class lining the hallways. The pictures from the previous century of mostly all white faces offer contrast to the vibrant ethnic and racial diversity of the contemporary Mission High students walking the halls. Much like at Thurgood Marshall Academic High School, I met a significant number of first generation immigrant students from China and Southeast Asia; but Mission High School also had a very large number of African American, Latino, and Pacific Island students as well.

Being a total outsider to the San Francisco Unified School District, I was only minimally aware of the significant perceived status differential between Thurgood Marshall High School and Mission High School. However, that distinction was quickly painted for me in interviews with students who frequently explained that Mission High School had a reputation as a school for "dummies." When I asked a student, Kim, for the roots of those negative ideas, she explained, "If you lived here, you would know that Mission is like the worst school in San Francisco." Tagging on to Kim's comment and using the language of "accountability," Robert explained, "They say it because in our academic testing we have the lowest—what do you call it—yearly progress."

However negative some students' sense of the public impression of their school, throughout my visit, youth, teachers, and school administrators were eager and quite able to counter this deficit framing. Students proudly shared that Mission's mock trial team had recently won the citywide competition. Most of the teachers and the principal with whom I spoke were enthusiastic about their jobs, and all the students I interviewed and observed displayed enormous energy and reflected strong desire to personally and collectively contribute to the improvement of their high school's image and of their communities. The overall tone in the building and during class discussions, focus groups, and interviews was one of youthful optimism and deep commitment to school and their academic and vocational futures.

Meeting Derrlyn Tom

Ms. Tom—who told me in the interview that she is Hawaiian/Asian and in her sixth year of teaching—was waiting in her bright and cheery classroom and greeted me with a degree of formality. In her Hawaiian shirt, jeans, and hiking boots, Ms. Tom (as I called her throughout our time together) struck me as both energetic and serious. A bulletin board outside her room offers a colorful collage of photographs taken from numerous field trips around the Bay; a world map is prominently mounted in front of the room and has yellow sticky notes marking tectonic plates; posters hanging on walls throughout the room include Fossils through Time, Bay Area Earthquakes, "Be Healthy, Stay Strong," a detailed map of San Francisco, and the Bill of Rights. A Syracuse Cultural Workers Peace Calendar listing important dates to social movements and activists rounds out the display.

Just as Lance Powell's pedagogy was designed to center on student voice, so too, Ms. Tom regularly signals to students the importance of their voices. As she introduced me to the six members of her "transition class"—students recently released from incarceration—she said that, although I am at Mission to observe her, "It is really your voices that we all need to hear." Tied closely to her continual urging of students to share their ideas and her pedagogical moves, which make space for student voice, is her obvious commitment to constructivist learning theories. Unlike any other teacher in the study, Ms. Tom, made comments while teaching about students' schema and background knowledge, and to me during the interviews about how she scaffolds instruction. For example, when introducing the journal prompt of the day to her ninth graders, she told them, "You have a different schema than I do, and I can learn from you. You've had different experiences than me … it's about you and your voice, not mine, because you hear my voice all the time. When you write in your journals, I can learn from you."

A visible manifestation of this constructivist approach to teaching and learning was her consistent use of rubrics and her scaffolding of large projects by itemizing all the steps on direction sheet handouts. Ms. Tom seemed highly aware of students' zone of proximal development and English language proficiency; I watched her go from an honors class, in which she used quite sophisticated oral vocabulary, to her transition class, where she used much of the same vocabulary but paused frequently to carefully illustrate and define some of the key words.

Culturally Relevant Pedagogy

Ms. Tom's obvious commitment to constructivism (although she never named it to me in any conversation or interview) was equally matched by her commitment to culturally relevant pedagogy. Although Ms. Tom never used this term either, I was struck by the presence of all the components of culturally relevant pedagogy in her practice. Culturally relevant teaching, as explained by Gloria Ladson-Billings (1994), "is a pedagogy that empowers students intellectually, socially, emotionally, and politically by using cultural referents to impart knowledge, skills, and attitudes" (p. 18). In looking back on my time spent in Ms. Tom's classroom, interviewing her, and speaking at length with many of her students, it is easy to view this teacher's practice through the criteria Ladson-Billings explains as central to culturally relevant teaching. Therefore, in this chapter I introduce Ms. Tom's social action project-based teaching through the lens of culturally relevant teaching and show how she

1. Organizes social action projects to create a strong academic program and support students for academic success,

2. Builds curriculum and instruction around cultural competence and community connections, and
3. Builds critical consciousness as a centerpiece of curriculum and instruction.

What follows is a detailed description of one class period that I use to introduce Ms. Tom's pedagogical moves—particularly in regard to culturally relevant pedagogy.

A Class in Action

Not a minute was ever wasted in Ms. Tom's class, and the "Do Now" greeting students on the board was often a journal prompt. In this morning's ninth grade Integrated Science class, Ms. Tom had written on the board:

> We will celebrate Cesar Chavez's birthday on April 1st (Monday). His work and his continued struggle for the rights and dignity of all migrant workers (the people who pick the food) and as a co-founder of the United Farm Workers (UFW) will be remembered. Cesar Chavez died in 1993, but his memory and his fight (*la lucha*) live on. How will you remember and celebrate this day and this man?

Students enter the room and begin writing immediately. I wander among the desks and ask permission to read over their shoulders. Quite a few of them write in their journals that they would like to find out more about Cesar Chavez. I am in awe of these 14- and 15-year-olds who are clearly quite motivated to pursue learning beyond classroom assignments. A Latina named Daniela writes:

> Something that I would do is to try to see who is still involved in UFW and maybe I would be part of that because there's still migrant workers who are struggling for their rights. I could tell my friends that don't know why we have Monday off. Maybe in this break I could learn more about Cesar Chavez.

Ms. Tom then tells the class about a big march coming up on Sunday that is in honor of Cesar Chavez and she explains that Mission students went last year. She takes a breath and explains the connection between the journal prompt and the video she is about to show: "Let's talk about Cesar Chavez's struggle. He fought his whole life for farm workers' dignity. He's gone, he died ten years ago, but we're still struggling for some of the same things he was. When you think about something you believe in and you're committed to changing, it may take a long time. It's not going to happen overnight."

Clearly, this is a discussion not a lecture because Daniela raises her hand and says, "You were telling us about another leader of the farm workers who wanted to go to school and couldn't."

"You're right," comments Ms. Tom, "Dolores Huerta. She wanted to go to school. Isn't it amazing, some of you take it for granted. I take it for granted too. I take many things for granted. I drink coffee every day. And I have to ask myself: Does the person who picked the coffee beans I drink get the money I paid for the coffee, or does it go to the company that exploits the workers? Exploiting them by not paying them enough money to feed their family or have the children go to school. There's a way to tell if the coffee you buy, if the money goes to the workers."

"Do you buy that coffee?" asks a boy from the back.

"Yes, I do," says Ms. Tom, "And I'm glad you asked. If you look at the package of the coffee, if it has that label Fair Trade Coffee, then you know the workers get a fair wage."

At this, the room begins to buzz with students' comments and questions about fair trade coffee. One question is louder than the others, "What if it doesn't?"

Ms. Tom elaborates: "Fair trade coffee is a little bit more expensive. It's more costly to produce it, because they're doing it for themselves. It's a business, to make sure they can feed their families. You have to be willing to pay a little bit more. You have to really think about what the families are being exposed to. Some of the things we're not even aware of, like our strawberry pickers who are exposed to pesticides."

Ms. Tom quickly starts the video *Transfair Fairtrade* and makes a link between the coffee growers in Central America and the migrant workers that Cesar Chavez helped organize. While showing the video, she makes quite a few explanatory points along the way. She particularly underscores (with a smile and a chuckle) when the farmer/peasant/cooperative worker said, "Science is great," as he showed the machine that pulps the beans. Some of the students seemed quite interested in the picking of coffee. She explained that the mules were used as the farmers didn't have trucks. But students are watching carefully, and when a truck did appear after the beans were taken from the cooperative to the city, Anthony says, "I thought they didn't have trucks?"

The film ends, students pose many questions which Ms. Tom answers, and then she switches gears and tells the class that they are going to finish the lab they had started writing the day before. Nailana, an Indian American girl I had interviewed the day before, interjects, "Can we just celebrate Cesar Chavez's birthday today?" Ms. Tom is firm in her rejection of this attempted student diversion: "I've gone to a lot of trouble to prepare the materials. And it would be disrespectful of me and my time not to use them." There is no more discussion of that idea and the class moves on to the lab, which uses gelatin to explore plate tectonics. After finishing the lab, Anthony and a few other students tell Ms. Tom that they really want to see the end of a video about earthquakes they had been watching. Ms. Tom turns on the video for the whole class to watch.

Indications of Culturally Relevant Pedagogy

In this short and very typical class, Ms. Tom packs a lot in and maintains active engagement of her students during the entire ninety-minute block period. Looking closely at the classroom talk and the activity structures, it is easy to see all the markers of culturally relevant teaching. First, she maintains very high expectations for engagement with academic work and plans so that each learner will be involved in individual (journal), small group (lab), and large group (discussion and videos) learning activities. She collects, reads, and responds to journals on a regular basis, providing ongoing feedback to students' ideas. Ms. Tom further signals the import of sticking with the learning agenda by rejecting Nailana's suggestion to make a party to celebrate Cesar Chavez's birthday.

The second aspect of culturally relevant pedagogy visible in this vignette is that of cultural referents. A large number of students at Mission High School are Mexican, Mexican American, and Chicano/a, and integrating the work of Cesar Chavez and Dolores Huerta (as co-founders of the United Farm Workers) into her science class is a wonderful example of making sure students have knowledge of the accomplishments of a majority ethnic group in their neighborhood, city, and state. Ms. Tom provides additional cultural connections as she mentions the community march that marks Chavez's birthday and signals the possibility that they themselves might want to attend. In this way, Ms. Tom is connecting her students to a rich aspect of their ethnic history and also to its contemporary movements and local organizing. She even provides them with a vocabulary word for this—*la lucha*—in her written journal prompt. From these small pedagogical moves, students have the chance to participate, and indeed, many are like Daniela who writes, "Maybe I would like to be part of that."

The third aspect of culturally relevant pedagogy visible in Ms. Tom's classroom is that the curriculum is designed around critical consciousness. Some science teachers may take the stance that science curriculum and instruction should be limited to academic facts, skills, and concepts. Yet most teachers quickly understand that the knowledge of most worth is entangled with matters of power, identity, morality, and decision-making. For a quick example of the political and moral nature of much of science, one need look no further than the advanced science knowledge of the Nazi regime or of the U.S. eugenics movement. Clearly, science teachers have almost daily opportunities to support students to investigate the connections between scientific development, personal well-being, and human rights. Indeed, throughout my brief time spent in her classroom, Ms. Tom made many connections between science and health and science and human rights. She seemed highly motivated to help these young people use science for the improvement of their own bodies and the health of their communities. This, then, is a view of science in the public interest; science for the people: science to be used by people to achieve a better life and stronger communities.

The final noteworthy aspect of Derrlyn Tom's practice of culturally relevant pedagogy encompasses all three markers; that is, she herself embodies and practices the tenets of academic success, cultural and community connections, and critical consciousness. In her exit interview with me, she expressed satisfaction that her students can have a scientist who is a woman of color as their teacher, that she strives for helping her students learn about solidarity among people of different ethnic and racial identities as they seek to improve their communities, and that she shares with her students her decision to protest the School of the Americas.[1] It was clear to me that her embodiment of these tenets of cultural relevance was not lost on students. Notice, for instance, how upon hearing about free trade coffee, a student immediately asks, "Do *you* buy that coffee?" And as 10th grader Enita made crystal clear in an interview,

> I really like Ms. Tom for going to Georgia to protest because she's over there defending people's rights and her rights too.... I always think about, you know, my life. And being a Latina in the United States makes you think a lot. And it's good to know that people that are not the same race as you are thinking about your rights, too, and defending you as a human being, not as a person from another country or wherever. And it made me change the way I thought about that. And it gave me the chance to defend my rights.

As I watched and listened to Ms. Tom's enactments of culturally relevant pedagogy for social action, I became increasingly aware of how her curriculum was organized around "community." And by "community," she meant much more than merely a neighborhood.

A Curriculum of Community

A key component of culturally relevant pedagogy is the relationship teachers foster with students and families. From this perspective, low-income communities are not viewed as sinkholes of despair—as is portrayed by authors such as Ruby Payne (2001) and her "culture of poverty" (for a critique, see Bomer, Dworin, May, & Semingson, 2008). Instead, teachers help students see their communities as filled with resources, with visionaries, and with people who understand oppression and who struggle for a better world. For Derrlyn Tom this showed up in many ways—in her collaborations with community-based organizations, her use of curriculum designed around field trips, and her design of an interview assignment for students as part of community-action projects.

Working with Community-Based Organizations

Many resources upon which Ms. Tom's pedagogy is based are provided by community-based organizations (CBOs). She teaches her students to interface with them, and her curriculum is interwoven with them. This strategy was highlighted for me by reading the fine print on the eight-page bi-fold publication written, illustrated, and produced by ninth graders. Titled in graffiti-style lettering *Mission H.S. Making Changes*, the black and white newsletter offered a compilation of articles, essays, photographs, and illustrations stemming from the environmental and political projects that students, teachers, and community organizers had been doing about the effects of the power plant on the San Francisco Bay. Tucked into the bottom right corner of the second page were the acknowledgements thanking no less than seven non-profits (see Figure 4.1).

Although she is not listed as the architect of this multi-pronged collaboration (and she insisted with me that the students and other teachers and community organizers should receive all the credit for the newsletter), Ms. Tom's touch can be seen in the small tag line: "A project that brought ninth grade students, teachers, and community organizers together." It was evident to me, after spending only a week in her classroom, that Ms. Tom carefully crafts her curriculum so that people collectively engage in social action.

Ms. Tom also wanted me to underscore for other teachers who might read this book that much of her community-based work is made possible from small grants she writes each year. She handed me the brochure from the San Francisco Education Fund and explained that she is able to use some of the funds from the annual grants to pay for the substitutes for her other classes when she takes one class on a field trip. She elaborated on this strategy: "If you have your own money source, if you can get your own money source, you don't need to ask for certain things from the administration." Indeed, in a subsequent interview, the principal underscored this point and said it was easy to support Ms. Tom's community-based curriculum because she asked him for permission, rather than money.

A major part of Ms. Tom's rationale for bringing in community-based organizations can be seen as interwoven with her culturally relevant style. Specifically, when I asked her how she had come to have so many collaborations with community-based organizations, she explained,

> I do this every time someone wants to work with my students. I want my students to realize how special they are because people want to work with them. People really want to come in and be their allies, their advocates. Because in the long run, that's my hope: my hope is that they'll keep those connections when they're working and continue that work ... beyond just ninth grade.

Noting as she does, the power of community organizations, I was not surprised when she told me that she was one the designers of the San Francisco Teachers for Social Justice. Derrlyn and another teacher dreamed up the idea when

---

Change and Making Change in Frisco

A project that brought ninth grade students, teachers
and community organizers together

Mission High School
3750 18th Street, San Francisco, CA 94114
(414) 241-6240

Special thanks to the San Francisco Education Fund
for providing the funds to fund our fun!

Thanks and solidarity to our community organizers
and supporters:
LEJ: Dana, Marshawn, Akua, Antonio
INS Watch: Elly, Ruby
Third Eye Movement: Jasmine, Jesse
Mission Science Workshop: Dan
Ollin: Antonio, Marisol
PODER: Oscar, Gerry
ZEUM: Susan

Artist in residence: Lani
And, Victoria and Heather, you're both the greatest!!!

Teachers: Thomas Quinn, Lorena Soto, Derrlyn Tom,
Jill Parmeter, and Jennifer Fong

FIGURE 4.1 Acknowledgements in 9th graders' newsletter

they met in jail after being arrested at a protest of Prop 21.[2] Teachers for Social
Justice has turned into a very successful organization that in a addition to many
other activities, hosts an annual conference for local educators. Lately, the conference has even been attracting a national audience.

Field Trips

A central strategy of Derrlyn Tom's pedagogy community-based curriculum is
field trips. Angela, a 10th grader whom I interviewed and asked to reflect on
what she learned in science in ninth grade, connected field trips with stimulating her interest in science:

> Ms. Tom made science class fun. I never liked science, I never did. But
> with Ms. Tom it was different because, you know, to learn something it
> wouldn't just, you know, be all in books; we would go on a field trip and
> learn.

Javier, another 10th grader, elaborated on the role that a field trip to the power
plant played in igniting his interest about the environmental effects on the Bay:

I think it's better for us to go out there and see what's really happening, to take a bigger part about it. I wasn't really interested in the PG&E plant, it really didn't interest me. But when we went out there and saw the community, I got interested.

Field trips are an obvious pedagogical tool to help students find relevance and connection with the curriculum. Yet field trips take a great deal of advance planning: for logistics (funding, permissions, and itineraries), as well as for the structuring of student learning. During my week at Mission, I was fortunate to be invited to accompany Ms. Tom and twenty-six of her ninth graders on a half-day field trip to the San Andreas Fault: where the Pacific and Atlantic tectonic plates meet. The non-profit organization Mission Science Workshop leaders drove the vans. The trip was designed to complement the in-class study of plate tectonics, and Ms. Tom structured the learning, including explaining how students could earn "points" by finding geologic evidence. I was fairly amazed at the high level of interest the students all showed for finding fossils and seeing evidence of plate tectonics in the striation in the rocks. Students found bi-valve fossils and also snail fossils, as well as various assorted fossils that no one could identify with any certainty.

The science learning took an unplanned zoological turn when the students came across a stranded elephant seal pup. Kim, from the Mission Science Workshops, called a marine animal rescue operation in Sausalito, and they came with a truck, put the pup in a cage, and explained it would be cared for and released. Some of the students had been very insistent that they couldn't just leave the seal pup stranded alone on the beach, and many were visibly relieved when it was rescued. The workshop leaders and Ms. Tom said they will make sure to stay in touch with the animal rescue organization and plan another field trip for when it is released back into the ocean.

This spontaneous real-world problem of the stranded seal offers an important illustration about the pedagogical power of both field trips and social action projects. Even though the field trip was as well planned as any field trip I have ever seen in my thirty-two years of teaching, it still offered an opportunity for learning that exceeded the curricular and instructional plans of the teachers. In the real world, new problems present themselves to us every day. If school curriculum is to truly prepare young people to assume full responsibility in our world, it is opportunities to engage in real-time authentic problem solving that offer students the chance to be full participants. Students were able to demonstrate their concern for the seal pup, learn about what to do to best help a stranded seal, and then witness a swift rescue. By being offered the opportunity to later observe its release back into the wild, these students are able to be active participants as problem-solving agents of an interconnected world. Ms. Tom's field trips are truly a window into the world and help students view learning as happening beyond the four walls of the classroom.

When reading the ninth graders journal entries about Cesar Chavez's birthday, I had been so struck by their interest in spending time over the weekend learning more about him and the United Farm Workers. I was intrigued to study their curriculum to try to unpack what helped them view learning as happening both inside and outside of the classroom. Clearly, field trips were an essential aspect of this, and in my final interview with Ms. Tom, I was eager to have Ms. Tom talk to me about her thoughts on field trips. She told me what sparked her commitment to getting students into the community:

> In high school I had an amazing physics teacher who took us out all the time. So when I began teaching here, I knew I wanted to make sure the curriculum for science would be part of what was relevant to them. In other words, I needed to make sure that there was something in their lives that made them feel that they could either do something about, or be proud of, or make a change. So that's where my activist side came in; I try to put those two together.

The idea to connect out-of-school learning to social change is fundamental to understanding pedagogies for social action. In addition to field trips, Ms. Tom's students also got into the community through required community projects.

Community Projects

When I visited, students were in the midst of a multistep project called, "Change and Making Change in San Francisco." Students work in small groups and start by identifying the community they are researching. Ms. Tom used class time one day to explain the requirements of the group project: (1) determine all the issues in your community; (2) interview people from a community-based organizations and find out the services they provide; (3) analyze your data and present it to the class; (4) make a plan of action. She tells them that their plan of action can be inviting a speaker to come to school, creating a petition, designing a poster or flyer contest, and writing letters and/or presenting data to lobby city officials. "Choose one," she tells them. "You need to finish one. I'm asking you to do something. To take action and do something."

The rubric given at the start of the project (see Figures 4.2 and 4.3) includes all different sections for each of the parts of the data collection and also products.

Students get credit for skills, such as "sequence and order of slides" in PowerPoint, for meeting deadlines, organizing the materials, as well as strong connections made between the explanations offered in the essay and the evidence available in the taped interviews.

Ms. Tom provides the presentation outline to students in advance: "(1) Community issues: What are they? Who decides? (2) Community solutions. What are they? Who has the answers? (3) Our groups' solutions/actions: What can we

D. Tom
9th grade Integrated Science
Spring semester, 2002
Community projects

Change and Making Change in San Francisco

Community _____

Group members _____

Interview at Mission High School with _____

   • *3 interviews in the community*

Not	1	2	3	4	5	Good
Evident		Needs work		2 out of 3		

Ms. Tom's comments

Our comments/reflections

Grade for 3 (4) interviews _____ **/100**

   • *Essay*

Not	1	2	3	4	5	Good
Evident		Needs work		CD and CM		

1 2 3 4 5   handed in on time, title, typed, double-spaced, 2 pages

1 2 3 4 5   clear introduction, topic sentence, details

1 2 3 4 5   explanations (CD) are from the interviews (on tape)

1 2 3 4 5   sentences provide commentary (CM) to explain details about the topic

1 **2 3 4 5**   essay written in a logical, easy-to-follow order

Grade for essay _____ **/100**

FIGURE 4.2 Derrlyn Tom's rubric for "Change and Making Change in San Francisco," page 1

- *Interview with CBO*

Name of community based organization (CBO) _____

Contact person _____

Date of interview _____ (before April 4th)

Turn in cassette tape to Ms. Tom by _____

Not	1	2	3	4	5	Good
Evident		Needs work		OK		

Ms. Tom's comments

Our comments/reflections

Grade for CBO interviews _____/100

- *Power Point Presentation — 3 main parts*

1. Community issues: What are they? Who decides?
2. Community solutions: What are they? Who has the answers?
3. Our group's solutions/actions: What can we do to help or educate our community?

Date of presentation _____

1. Number of slides _____   _____

2. Sequence and order   **yes**   **no**   _____

3. Creative, yet factual   **yes**   **no**   _____

Grade for Power Point _____/100

FIGURE 4.3 Derrlyn Tom's rubric for "Change and Making Change in San Francisco," page 2

do to help or educate our community?" In this way, Ms. Tom's commitment to the careful scaffolding of constructivist pedagogy meets her social action pedagogy. This is a very important intersection to note and may help many teachers break down the steps in a large social action project in a sort of "task analysis" style. Without this step-by-step advance organizer, many students may flounder and be unable to direct their learning to the actual content of the project. By being so clear in regard to her expectations, Ms. Tom is helping structure students' success, and thus build their skills for social action.

Community Interviews

Just as journal writing is a frequent genre in Ms. Tom's classroom, so too, is interviewing people: both peers as well as community members. Accessing the resources of community-based organizations is central to the community project, and Ms. Tom carefully scaffolds her students' connections with and knowledge about these organizations. A primary tool to do this is the community interview.

Ms. Tom does not reserve this sophisticated pedagogy for her honors class, but assigns it to all students, including her ninth graders and her transition class. She has tape recorders she acquired by writing a grant and loans them out to students for the day their interview is scheduled. She further facilitates the process by providing students a letter they can give to interviewees to explain the project. Below is a letter ninth graders were using as part of their "Change and Making Change in San Francisco" project. It was printed on school letterhead and says:

> To Whom It May Concern:
>
> My ninth grade students from Mission High School are conducting a survey around community issues. I asked them to interview community members on the issues or concerns you think affect your community. My hope is for my students to learn something new and different about communities they know very little about. They will ask you to contribute your time and to allow them to interview you on tape. Then they will each report back what they learned and ways we can help or support all communities, whether they happen to be particular neighborhoods, particular lifestyles, particular cultures, or particular beliefs.
>
> Thank you for your cooperation and generous outpouring of time and understanding. If you have any questions, please call me if you would like to know more about this project.
>
> Thank you
> Derrlyn Tom
> Mission High School teacher
> (Phone number)

The evidence of high academic standards—an integral tenet of culturally responsive pedagogy—can be seen even within this genre of interviewing. Ms. Tom signals the seriousness with which she views the interviews by stating to her ninth graders that she had been up until one o'clock in the morning grading their tapes. Not only are the interviews required, they are also graded. A rubric is used and specific academic standards apply to this oral genre.

I got a hint about the potential of the interviewing process to help shape critical democratic skills when I interviewed Barbara Chang and Jorge Gonzalez. They were currently 10th graders, had taken integrated science with Ms. Tom the previous year, and generously agreed to reflect on their experiences of being in the class. They both mentioned interviewing community members as one of the highlights, and actually had conducted their interviews as a team. Neither one of them had ever conducted an interview before and said that they were nervous because they "didn't really know anyone [in that community]." Barbara found the entire process "kind of weird" because the two women they interviewed did not agree with each other even though they "asked them the same questions." Jorge elaborated: "Yeah, that was sort of surprising for me. I didn't expect everybody to have the same point of view, but I guess I sort of thought that because they were both Latina that they would say the same things."

Listening to Jorge and Barbara's surprise about the community members' different viewpoints offers educators a glimpse of the importance of learning an essential concept central to democratic deliberation: that reasonable people often disagree about the roots of a problem or its solution. This understanding that problems do not often have binary solutions, and that people can hold a range of viewpoints on any subject, typically gets more developed as children and youth mature. By requiring students to interview more than one person, this assignment helps them become more aware of the complexities inherent in deliberative democracy. This understanding is central to what Parker (2003) calls "enlightened political engagement."

The final important detail I almost did not learn about how Ms. Tom structures the interview process is that for Jorge and Barbara's class Ms. Tom provided most of the questions for them to ask in the interviews. This is a significant pedagogical decision and is worth analyzing. Some teachers may require interviews as part of a project but want the students to come up with their own questions. But because generating interview questions requires a great deal of knowledge about both the structure of questioning (open-ended vs. close-ended, for example) and about the subject matter, Ms. Tom helped scaffold the students' academic success by providing questions. Students were free to add some of their own, but by providing students with good questions, the teacher was setting the students up to be able to actually use the information from the interviews as a basis for their long-term, multi-step projects. This issue of teacher authority has long intrigued me (see Oyler, 1996). To actually share authority for knowledge construction as a democratic process sometimes requires the teacher to assume more authority, rather than to abdicate total authority to the students. By claiming and asserting expertise (as a formulator of questions), Ms. Tom made it possible for Barbara and Jorge to feel competent and confident as interviewers.

The Bay Project

One day after school, Ms. Tom invited me to accompany her to a planning meeting of teachers working on the Bay Project with organizers from LEJ. I had already met one of the LEJ organizers when she came earlier in the week to work with one of Ms. Tom's classes on making a model of the watershed for the students to use in subsequent educational outreach. I realized from the meeting that the LEJ organizers were working on the same project as Lance Powell (see Chapter 3), but the two teachers ended up engaging in different forms of social action and advocacy.

Literacy for Environmental Justice was formed to address the ecological and health concerns of southeast San Francisco, in particular the Bayview Hunters Point neighborhood. The specific project that Ms. Tom tapped into was explained to me by Jenn Franek, the program coordinator for The Living Classroom, which was started with a power plant company education grant from a $13 million consent decree based on litigation related to the "peak plants" that spew carbon emissions. Jenn explained to me that the southeast quadrant of San Francisco had been bearing the brunt of the industries: both power plants, the Naval Shipyard (with its hazardous waste), and the sewage treatment plant that processes 80% of the city's solid waste. She describes the rationale for working in public schools, particularly with students of color:

> It's all concentrated in that one part of the city, and there's no one saying, "Wait, I know what this is doing to us and I'm not going to stand for it." There are a lot of health concerns in the area: elevated asthma and breast cancer rates, elevated prostate cancer rate—over four times the Bay Area average.

The Bay Project is Ms. Tom's primary focus for social action projects and she explained to me that she entered into the project as a learner, intent on finding out what was going on in her community.

> When I first started doing the Bayview Hunter's Point project, [which involves] the PG&E power plant ... a lot of it was because I ... needed to know these things ... as a concerned citizen, as someone who lives in San Francisco. So for me ... it was my own self-education. I needed to ... really understand ... really in context what was going on in the community where so many of my students come from. And every year there's so much more I can learn and so much more I can do.

It is clear to me that for Ms. Tom her curriculum is centered around scaffolding students' commitment to their communities. To do this, she begins by learning what are the most significant community issues. Her understanding that social action must proceed from the felt needs of the community can be seen in her inquiry-based design of the Change and Making Change project.

Educational Outreach About the Bay

All of the interviews I conducted with students centered around the Bay Project. Much of the classroom curriculum was interwoven with this long-term collaboration with LEJ. Overall, the primary focus of the efforts in Ms. Tom's class seemed organized around education and outreach. They engaged in many different strategies, including studying about the fish and pollution in the Bay, making models of the San Francisco watershed, writing letters to elected officials, planning and implementing peer education, and helping with the restoration of the salt marshes at Heron's Head Park.

When asked to explain the Bay Project, ninth grader Daniela talks about the educational outreach and tells me about a survey and a skit they created:

> What we're doing is about the pollution in the Bay, and there are so many people who fish in the Bay, and they don't know the fish is polluted, and they can get sick. So we're trying to send a message out there to people to not eat the fish because it's polluted. So we did a survey on that and went out and met the fishermens and asked them if they knew about the pollution in the Bay and if they are still doing it. What we did is just went up to the people, and we said, "Can we have a little of your time?" And the survey took approximately three to four minutes. And we did a skit for students in other schools. Yeah, that's what we're doing.

Trang adds to Daniela's list of activities: "Also, we're trying to get bigger signs [to post in the fishing areas], and universal signs so everyone can know that the bay is polluted."

Power Plant March: Youth on Fire Celebration

A significant high point in the Bay Project was the march on the power plant— the Youth on Fire Celebration. Photos from the march were displayed on a bulletin board outside Ms. Tom's classroom, and quite a few poems, articles, and essays in the newsletter focused on the march and rally. The excerpt below is from a longer essay written by a ninth grader:

> On Wednesday, May 16, 2001, Mission High School participated in a protest in Bayview/Hunter's Point. We were there to protest and march against the PG&E Company. Bayview/Hunter's Point has the most people with problems such as asthma and breast cancer. These people are

sick because of the pollution caused by the PG&E power plant. When we got there, students from Mission High School put on costumes. The costumes were a representation of the people who are affected with these diseases caused by the power plant. The students were also wearing masks that represented that they couldn't breathe in this area. There was not as many people as I thought were going to be there, but we made up for it with a lot of noise. One of the things we wanted to happen was to shut the PG&E plant down.

I was holding the banner that said "Youth on Fire" with my other classmates. I love when I go and protest about something I want to change in a community. People from this community shared their situation in Bayview/Hunter's Point. Most of them spoke about the different problems people have in this community at a rally at the end of the march. Students from Mission High also got up and told their stories.

In an interview, Sahar—a first generation Indian immigrant—recounted her recollection of the march:

We were at the front of the march; youth were leading it. We had on white suits and medical masks. We made a banner so people would get the point; kids came from another school too, so there were lots of us, we saw it was other kids too who knew about this and were doing something about it, it gives you hope when other people are there too. We chanted, "Shut down the power plant!"

When I asked Sahar what her parents think of this, she said that her parents just came to the United States and don't know about the issues here, "They're more focused on family. But my mother was a scientist in India, and when I told her about the issues, she said it was good for me to go." Sahar seemed eager to continue her educational outreach and told her supervisors at the credit union where she works about the issues, and her brother and sister and friends. Just as with the Nova High School case and the Tar Creek case, students did interviews with the media as well, and were invited to come to the Channel 4 television studios for follow-up interviews about their participation in the march.

Always very curious about the possible negative repercussions of including protest marches and rallies as part of the regular school curriculum, I asked the students to share their thoughts on integrating protests into the public school curriculum. "Is there a reason more teachers should do this sort of thing?" I asked, "Yeah," one girl told me, "I think they should do it because it's something about the community so it's better to get ourselves involved in all the problems." Michael chimed in with more details that helped shed light on issues of imposition and student choice:

It's good as long as the teachers aren't forcing you to come to it. As long as they don't make it a requirement. Like the kids make the choice. We learned about what the power plant was doing to the community, in the Bay Area in general; like how everybody was affected even though we don't live in that area. And so, the teachers, they're like, "We're going to go out to a field trip to protest about it," and all the kids were like, "Yeah, we want to go too." So they didn't make it a requirement, it wasn't like you were going to drop some credits or something like that in your class if you don't go. If other teachers did that, that would be good, too, because then the kids learn about what's going on and they can help make a change; their input, like what they think about it, would be included too.

In considering the possible learning outcomes for students, Enita assured me that

It's a good thing because it's like a chance for us, for youth, to let our voice be heard, you know? Because we're...it's not one or two, it's many students and when they come together and they protest for something it's very, I believe it's very strong, it's a strong voice, and sooner or later it will be heard and that's good. I think that's very positive on youth.

Michael—one of the few white students in the class—said that participating in the rally had a significant impact on him: "After going to the PG&E march, I started going to political rallies and stuff. I brought my friends with me too. I'm like, 'There's this really cool rally and it's like forcing people to look at us, and pay attention to the issues, and it's really cool.'"

Connecting Student Agency and Collective Responsibility

In this era of top-down accountability systems, Common Core standards, high-stakes testing, and public scrutiny of teacher effectiveness, it would be understandable if some educators felt too pressured by basic expectations to add on the extra work of integrating social action projects in the curriculum. We can learn a lot from Ms. Tom who does not see social action projects as dichotomous with the standards-based science curriculum. Although some teachers posit that they can't do projects, or can't integrate social action projects, because they need to "cover the standards," Ms. Tom doesn't pose these two sources of curriculum planning against each other: "Am I concerned about the standards? I am. If I don't teach the standards to my students, it's a disservice to them when they start to find what the colleges are looking for."

Indeed, she has ongoing systems for tracking assignments completed and all the steps of every project have points that are included in the six-week grading cycle. And in the best tradition of the culturally responsive teacher, she is clearly a "warm demander" (Irvine & Fraser, 1998; Vasquez, 1988) who holds very high academic and behavioral standards and "communicates both warmth and a nonnegotiable demand for student effort and mutual respect" (Bondy & Ross, 2008, p. 54). Ms. Tom expects her students to meet her half-way and then reassures them she will be there for them. She expects students to show responsibility toward their own learning and development. While I was visiting, a student came in during his lunch hour to discuss problems he was facing with this project. Ms. Tom explained to me her thinking about his visit:

> Like with Mark, if he didn't come and talk to me about his project I would have never known; I wouldn't have been able to help him. But the fact that he made that first step, he took that first step to come and talk to me today, means a lot. And I told him that. I always say to students, "I'm going to always want to help you. If I can, in whatever capacity, I'm always going to do that. But I'm not going to offer it unless I know you really want it. I mean, there's no point in me saying, 'You need this?' When that's not where you are or what you want. But if you know that I'm going to be here ready to help you or you ask me if you can come and get some help, then I will always be there. So I need to know from you when you come in." And I said this at the beginning of the year, "When you come in and say, 'Ms. Tom, I need help,' or 'I need ...' whatever it is, or 'Can I just come in and use your phone?' Whatever it is, it's the fact that you come and approach me. Because me chasing after you makes us both feel so bad."

This focus on the student-teacher relationship with the student expected to assume active agency is a starting point for the relationships Ms. Tom wants her students to develop in the world beyond her classroom. These relationships are based on mutual respect, and this message is overt, as I learned as I listened to some negotiations about field trip permission slips.

It was the day before the field trip to the San Andreas Fault. Ms. Tom advises the students about wearing long sleeved shirts and bringing plenty of water as they will be in the sun. Students ask if they can bring their permission slips tomorrow, or if she will accept a phone call from a parent. Ms. Tom quite calmly says, "No. Phone calls are no substitute for the permission slip." She tells them that it is a common courtesy to have returned the slips since she went to all the trouble to make them and to have organized the field trip. In this small interaction of preparing to go on a field trip, Ms. Tom can be seen acting as an "other mother" (Henry, 1995): telling them how to dress and how to prepare. She is not a teacher who assumes that the students should know this information. She wants them to be successful so she takes care of them in advance. And her expectation for their behavior (get the permission slips in) is couched in relational terms, rather than in compliance with an external system.

Community and Critical Consciousness

As pointed out earlier, the third tenet of culturally responsive pedagogy, and inextricably tied to social action curriculum, is that of critical consciousness (Freire, 2005). In explaining the centrality of critical consciousness to culturally relevant pedagogy, Gloria Ladson Billings (1995) lays out the relationship between critical consciousness and engaged citizenship:

> Students must develop a broader sociopolitical consciousness that allows them to critique the cultural norms, values, mores, and instruction that produce and maintain social inequities. If school is about preparing students for active citizenship, what better citizenship tool than the ability to critically analyze the society? (p. 162)

As can be seen throughout this chapter, Ms. Tom's pedagogy is designed to foster community consciousness among her students. This includes strong attention to relationships of solidarity across racial, ethnic, and neighborhood lines, and to critical consciousness around power.

> It's very important that they understand in regards to having community how you make an education benefit you personally, but also your community. I think that's so important. I try to make sure that they understand when we're in class together and they all want to yell at the same time because they all have something to say, that we need to listen to each other as a community. You know, if we can't respect each other as being part of the community, this is where things break down. It's just all those different social skills; I try to really make them understand and see why that's powerful. And, again, where that lies in terms of your collective voice, I mean, your voice as a *collective,* the voice that says, "This is what *we* want and this is how we feel about it," and *why.* You know, people are more apt to listen to them rather than all shouting at once about what they individually want. So, I really do appreciate when they have something that they really want to understand. And, again, but it's more of the social skills than the science skills, if they are going to be life-long learners, it's what I keep trying to instill in them.

In this detailed description of her pedagogy, it is evident that Derrlyn Tom connects student voice and agency with collective responsibility and community action. Thus, in her ninth grade integrated science curriculum, she understands that teaching the social skills of democratic participation and debate is as essential as the science content knowledge. In fact, if her field trip and community-based projects are taken as major evidence, it seems that most significantly she wants her students to ask, "What problems does my community have and how can we help in creating solutions?" Certainly, this is what most socially engaged scientists must also ask.

That such questions are fraught with dilemmas of power and privilege is the final critical piece in understanding Ms. Tom's teaching. She actively urges them to investigate the structures of power and decision-making. Although I was able to listen in to her classroom dialogues for only one week, I heard a consistent challenge to her students to carefully analyze relations of knowledge and power. Two examples help illustrate this important way she helped students develop critical consciousness.

For a "Do Now" in class one morning, the ninth graders were answering questions about a recent article from the *San Francisco Chronicle* (Gledhill, 2002) on a report linking academic success to health care. Juliana says to the class, "You know they're taking money away from the children's fund?" Before any student can offer a reply, Ms. Tom quickly asks, "Who is they?"

Then, later in the week while discussing a different newspaper article with her honors class, a student recommends, "They really need to get the message from us." Ms. Tom agrees with the suggestions but challenges the student to elaborate on his ideas: "You really have to think about who it is when you say, "they." Who do you mean by "they"? If we are going to save our community, we really need to know exactly who needs to get the message."

Listening to Ms. Tom's pedagogical dialogues, which are designed to foster critical consciousness, I was struck by the centrality of the individual teacher's own critical consciousness that shapes the questions in the first place. Later that day, Ms. Tom began reflecting on how unpacking "they" is so central to her teaching.

> We need to identify who "they" are so we can actually tell them why we feel this way, and let them hear our voices.... But it's hard, it's hard, because the way San Francisco is set up, it *is* a segregated city. The boundaries have been defined and you don't cross those boundaries. It's like going through The Mission and knowing that if you're Latino you only stay on one side of The Mission and the territories are really defined you don't cross them. And that's the same in regards to the city. It's extremely defined by these ethnic boundaries. I mean, I had twenty-six we took out to Russell Rock yesterday. My hope is that, yeah, they enjoy the beach as often as they want because it's not that far, really. But then again it is because in a student's mind, like Dandre, Presidio is hecka far. And you know what? I agree with him. To these kids, that's like a world away, it's so far. And when I have organizations that call me, I tell them the same thing, because that's what my kids say, "It's too far." It's just too far, you know. Help us build a park up on this side where they live, in their community. Sure, they can go to The Presidio and help with the restoration and feel good about themselves because they help the environment, but they don't live out there, they live out here. And they're entitled to the same thing.

In this excerpt from our final interview, Ms. Tom shares an important analysis of her students' race/ethnic and class positioning specifically in relation to the social action and field trips she plans. Through this excerpt we are offered a glimpse of the central role that critical consciousness of the teacher plays while planning community-based curricular engagement and social action projects, i.e., social action projects are conducted in social contexts, and these contexts occur in locations where identities intersect with privilege. Specifically, in this conversation, Ms. Tom was discussing why she did not sign her students up for a field trip to participate in restoration work at The Presidio, which is in a wealthy and predominantly white side of town. Knowing that many if not all of her students experienced that part of San Francisco as "hecka far" away, Ms. Tom told the non-profit that her students would not participate.

In this way, we can see that the teacher's own critical consciousness plays a very key part in shaping both the community-based opportunities that she extends to students as well as shaping the dialogue that occurs inside the classroom. For Ms. Tom, she most wanted her students to have a critical analysis of power and who wields power. This lesson was not missed by her students and was summed up quite eloquently by Jorge who described the work the class had done around the power plant and why it matters that students in school learn the skills of speaking up and fighting for their communities.

> It's the low-income community where the power plants are. There wouldn't be a power plant like in the Marina, in the wealthy end. They might actually say something. And because they have money they can pay them off. And the reason I think they go to the low-income neighborhood is because they see them not being able to do anything about it. But I think you can if you put your mind to it. Yeah. And if you have a lot of people and you have evidence that what they're doing is bad, you can change things.

It was quite powerful to hear Jorge explain how important it is to provide evidence when petitioning for change, as that was a key feature required in the Community Change projects. Here Jorge was, a year after taking Ms. Tom's class, and he had obviously walked away having learned the two central lessons I observed her teaching: (1) look for evidence about what problems exist in your community and (2) work with others to collectively advocate for change.

"It's Better to Know What's Really Going On"

I was struck throughout my interviews with many students at Mission High School with the knowledge they had regarding the environmental and health problems facing their communities, ranging from lead poisoning to elevated cancer and asthma rates. Asking, as I did at each school, again and again about students' views on what they think about using real-world problems as an organizing center for the curriculum, I never had a student say that learning more about the problems of the world depressed them. I often probed to ask students if it sometimes got too overwhelming. Sahar offered this answer to my queries:

> I think it's a good thing to know what's going on. Realizing it makes you aware of restrictions, and if there's anything to do to help, you will. Before finding out about how things are, you may be happy, but that's just ignorance—you don't know what's going on. It's better to know what's really going on.

Sahar's explanation of moving from ignorance to critical consciousness, coupled with Ms. Tom's pedagogy, reminds me so much of Paulo Freire's (2005) list of components of "critically transitive consciousness," (p. 14), which among many others include: "depth in the interpretation of problems," "rejecting passive positions," "soundness of argumentation," and "the practice of dialogue."

All of these components of critical consciousness are well illustrated in Ms. Tom's teaching. And it is the active presence of these elements in the classroom which help foster social action that is not dogmatic—or as Freire terms it "polemical." Concerned, as I am, with matters of teacher imposition, I think this list is very helpful for teachers who want to design curriculum around social action but who do not want to be telling students how to think or what to do. Ms. Tom's model of continual dialogue and insistence that her students carefully unpack relations of power provides us a chance to see and hear what Freire's list can look like in the classroom. Couple this pedagogy of critical consciousness with high academic standards and cultural connections, and we have a portrait of what culturally relevant pedagogy combined with social action projects offers to young people. This then, is an invitation to see the world in all its complexity, to analyze how it came to be this way, to listen to others who have ideas about amelioration, and to engage in collective action to make the world a better place.

5

EMERGENT AND INTEGRATED CURRICULUM

Brian Schultz at Byrd Academy

Just 'cuz we nine, ten, eleven, twelve years old they think we can't do nothing. But the adults is the ones who do the most problems. And around the world, kids try to do good things for the school community and all that.

—Byrd Academy, fifth grader

Unlike the other teachers in my study, Brian Schultz—a white, fifth-grade teacher at Byrd Community Academy in Chicago—did not set out to create curriculum around a social action project. Although his seven-month-long activist project was the most intensive one in this book, as Brian explains, "It kind of happened accidently to some extent." What started as a small curriculum unit based on materials from The Center for Civic Education, blossomed into a huge project of students trying to get a new school built—one that had been promised to the community six years earlier by the Chicago Board of Education.

I found out about this case one Sunday night while listening to one of my favorite radio shows, *This American Life*. The episode—"Desperate Measures" (see http://www.thisamericanlife.org/radio-archives/episode/263/desperate-measures)—opened with children describing the massive indignities of their decrepit school building and their heroic efforts to demand change. I called their teacher the next day, and he suggested I put my request for a weeklong visit in writing and address it to the students. The children and I corresponded; they posed numerous questions to me and then told me they would take a vote and get back to me. A few days later, I was pleased to find out that the sixteen students had unanimously approved my visit, and I scheduled my trip for May.

The Dilapidated School

Upon my arrival at the school building, I notice a large billboard in the vacant lot next door. It bears the emblem of the Chicago Board of Education and proclaims in large letters for all to see: "Future Home of the New Byrd Academy." Architects drew up the building plans six years previously, but no new school is yet on the docket for this Chicago neighborhood. Year after year, Mr. Gartner, the school principal, goes to the Chicago School Construction Authority hearings to testify to the urgent need his school faces. Yet, year after year, there is silence. No one can tell the community the status of the new school.

The vast majority of Byrd elementary students live in the Chicago Housing Authority Cabrini-Green Homes. These are, of course, among the most notorious public housing high-rises in the United States, for their levels of violence and lack of safety for residents. Not having visited this neighborhood in many years, I am shocked when I drive to the school and find a large supermarket chain store and a Starbucks. Having lived in a low-income neighborhood in Chicago for many years, the presence of a real supermarket immediately signals to me that Cabrini-Green is undergoing massive gentrification. The presence of the Starbucks seals the deal. Thus, I am not surprised when I find out from Mr. Schultz that the Cabrini buildings are being razed. Indeed, during the week I am visiting, three children come in with the devastating news that their families received a letter informing them that their building is the next one scheduled for demolition.

The school building is in shameful shape, and could provide a photo documentary to accompany Jonathan Kozol's book *Savage Inequalities* (1992). Windows are riddled with bullet holes and are opaque rather than translucent. Classrooms are dim due to florescent lights that no longer function. Thermostats are broken, meaning that children wore coats and mittens most of the winter; the outside of the building is filthy, exhibiting over forty years of accumulated city grime.

The children at Byrd are all African American, and some are the third generation of their family to live in Cabrini-Green "projects"; indeed, some of the children in this fifth grade classroom have grandparents who attended Byrd Academy when they were in elementary school. Having taught for many years in low-income, African American communities in which many of the children live in substandard government housing, I do not use terms such as *inner city*, *poverty stricken*, or *at risk youth* to describe this setting. Yet I am fully aware that for children growing up in neighborhoods with concentrated poverty, by fifth grade many will have had to develop sophisticated coping skills such as navigating through competing gang territories and learning to read complex communication systems to facilitate their safety. And they will have undoubtedly overheard many adult conversations planning short- and long-term financial and physical survival. Furthermore, they have most probably withstood years of subpar schooling and yet still come to school each day not defeated by life.

However resilient the children and their families may be, the challenges for students and teachers in this school are very real: average daily attendance rates at Byrd Academy are low; quite a few children have been retained, sometimes two or three times; a number of Mr. Schultz's students clearly struggle with reading and writing. In my interview with Ms. James, the assistant principal, she explains that most of the 381 children in the school have witnessed shootings and killings, and "we never get counseling like you see on TV." Violence and threats of violence are persistent, and during the week I was at the school one of Mr. Schultz's students was suspended by the school administration for five days for threatening a third grader with a plastic sword.

Yet when I arrive for my visit at the school, none of these issues is visible. I sign in at the office and, after a short wait, two very tall and very serious children (a boy and a girl) arrive to escort me to their classroom, providing a small tour of the school's deficits along the way. Students, they tell me, eat lunch in the hallways, as there is no cafeteria, nor is there gymnasium, nor an auditorium.

Meeting Brian Schulz

Entering the dimly lit classroom, I immediately note the strange windows: they are made from some opaque plastic material and are impossible to see out of, which makes their bullet holes that much more obvious. The classroom looks more like a workspace for an Internet start-up company than an elementary school classroom. There are none of the traditional markings of bulletin boards with fancy borders, or carefully hung charts directing children about how to accomplish some task. Instead, there are piles of papers around the room, thick binders that turn out to be project portfolios, desks scattered in seemingly random working groups.

Brian Schultz turns out to be one of those teachers whose blood pressure never seems to rise, no matter what is going on around the room. He has fourteen boys and only two girls, and wonders if he was given some of the children who are known to be less compliant. Brian, however, rarely mentions behavioral concerns to me during my visit; instead, he sings the students' praises and explains to me all they know, and all they can do. The students explain to me that there is no free time in this classroom and that their teacher "expects a lot of us," but it's because he "really cares and knows we can do it." As I'm transcribing the week of recorded classroom talk, I notice how Brian consistently uses direct speech acts, redirecting students and prompting them to focus on the task at hand: "Put the glasses down, the stapler away, and pay attention." As has been noted by numerous scholars (Bondy, Ross, Gallingane, & Hambacher, 2007; Delpit, 2006), many white and/or middle-class teachers do not easily master this important skill and thus often miss the opportunity to convey to their students their specific expectations.

This is a classroom where students do not have assigned seats—Mr. Schultz wants children to be able to work with different partners and in flexible small groups depending on the task at hand; he believes in letting problems arise so students learn to negotiate and problem-solve directly with each other. This is, of course, quite a contrast to the high-control tactics gaining momentum for low-income African American children and youth and popularized in the national media by such films as *Waiting for Superman*. In these "high-control" schools, the adults make most decisions, and it is the students' job to comply with the systems designed to focus and control their learning. In contrast, students in this classroom shared authority for many classroom process and content decisions. An example of the process authority students hold for making decisions about who does what, when, where, and how in the classroom (Oyler, 1996) happened during a class session run by a man who had been recruited to help the class put together a DVD of their work. At one point during a presentation by the guest, a student, Diminor, got up to turn the lights off. I thought it was so instructive that he felt ownership of the classroom and didn't need to seek permission either to arrange the lights or to get out of his seat. This would never happen in a high-control school, where students (particularly low-income children of color) are thought to require external systems of regulation.

Student Decision-Making

Brian's pedagogy could not be more different from such high-control systems. Instead, his approach centers on student decision-making. This style, of course, requires much prompting and support for children to be successful. Mr. Schultz provides continual reminders throughout the day, for example, about the need to listen to the person who is speaking and not interrupt. In this way, good behavior is not enforced through "power over" systems (Kreisberg, 1992) but is emphasized to foster respectful relationships, which enable students to work together more effectively to accomplish shared goals. When it comes to starting new activities, Brian gives students much more leeway than I would have patience for. I watch—a little bit in amazement, actually—as slowly but surely, in each and every activity, every single child *does* get down to work. It just takes a few of them much longer than I think I would be willing to wait. However, Mr. Schultz appears unflappable and is calm and even in his tone, no matter how upset or frustrated the children act.

Throughout our time together, Brian continually insists that the project to get a new school built "is theirs: they own it, they make the decisions, and it has to be that way." This orientation is not lost on the students, and when I asked one boy in an interview what advice he would have for teachers attempting projects such as this, he offers: "Talk to your kids about what they want to do because this is a lot of work and you just gotta be patient to get where you're going." I realize that Brian's classroom management style is intricately interwoven with his approach to the social action curriculum. He tells me that "Giving space to the students is my number one job," and I see evidence of that in the pedagogical decisions he makes for the project as well as in the micro-interactions during class time. Listening to the dialogues he has with students, I am reminded of Caroline Pratt's book title, *I Learn from Children* (1948), and indeed, I am not at all surprised that when Brian publishes a book about the project (Schultz, 2008),[3] he includes Pratt's simple title as the epigraph.

Another aspect of Brian's pedagogy, which he points out to me as integral to his democratic classroom, is the regular use of the Junior Great Books program, which features grand conversations—students sit in a circle and discuss their interpretations of short stories and books. Brian explains that he likes this curriculum in which "there are no right or wrong answers and so ... I use it as tool to teach them how to debate and have conversations with each other." Indeed, throughout my interviews and observations, and subsequent follow-up conversations with him,[4] Brian continually stresses the importance of students having choices and making decisions; teachers must "give the opportunities" and the "tools to make decisions" and then "they're the ones [the students] that own the decision they've made."

Supportive Group Process

Unlike most of the other teachers in this book, Brian did not have any prior experience as a community activist. Rather, much of the process aspect of his pedagogy can be traced to his work with Outward Bound and adventure education.

> The idea is that they're all united on one shared experience, and the shared experience is that they come to a lousy school building.... One thing with Outward Bound and adventure education was the idea [that] why you learn so much about yourself and about your role in the group was because you were sharing it with the whole group and you all had to go through the same experience.... Everybody has their own experiences when they were out on the trail, but the idea was that you had something to tie you together. And that was the same sense here.

Brian did his master's project on the effects of ropes courses on group dynamics skills, and it is evident in my week at Byrd that students are functioning more as project team members than playground rivals. He is keenly observant of group interactions, making certain that I notice how well the students work together:

> I can't believe that they are so willing to help each other out, whether they're interviewing a state senator and they're teaming up, or they've divided the questions, and one kid loses where he's at and the other kid's

leaning over, pointing it out, or picking it up in mid-sentence to help him or to coach each other, or the fact that four kids can be assigned to one digital camera and they take turns and pass it around.... The sharing that goes on around here, the helping, and the assistance is amazing.

I saw this ethic in action on the third day of my visit when the class spent a very long time deciphering an article that had been written about them and published in the *Orlando Sentinel* (Brady, 2004). After having read the article in partners and made comments in the margins, the class then took turns reading it out loud together. Although a couple of the children struggled to decode certain words, and many children needed lots of teacher support on pronunciation of words, I heard not a peep of criticism or impatience. Rather, they would chime in and offer assistance or just wait patiently. I asked Brian how he had managed to create such a supportive stance toward working in heterogeneous groups, and he explained that he encouraged team work and would make clear to students that "There are going to be people better than you and weaker than you and that's okay. Let's all work it through together." Brian talks about how some of the students would probably be floundering in a traditional curriculum because of skill deficits, but that working together, students can share their strengths and that children naturally gravitate toward working with those who can help them be successful in finishing tasks.

Project Citizen

These sixteen ten-, eleven-, and twelve-year-olds spent from December through June on a campaign to advocate that the Chicago Board of Education make good on its promise from six years earlier to build a new school for their community. Unlike the other educators I described in previous chapters who had identified an issue (if not a plan of action), Brian launched this project by implementing the first lesson in the Project Citizen manual, a curriculum created by the Center for Civic Education. The project began with this simple prompt: What are some problems that affect you and your community?

After about an hour, students had brainstormed eighty-nine problems and a significant portion of them revolved around the dilapidated school building: from getting doors on the bathroom stalls to fixing the heat in the building, to getting better windows. The Constitutional Rights Foundation Chicago came to the school and taught a simulation lesson, designed to help students analyze the roots of problems, rather than only focusing on the symptoms, and the students quickly decided they wanted to advocate for a new school building. Brian felt strongly that he did not want to be the one steering the project, or pushing it along, so he waited for some student-initiated activity. After some time passed and little action had been taken, one student got some momentum going by interviewing a teacher who was a member of the local school council.

He shared the interview information with his classmates, including a list of other people the students could interview, and they soon hosted a classroom interview with the local school council president.

Brian skipped the next pre-planned lessons in the Project Citizen manual, and began supporting the students as they started working on the sections of the portfolio for Project Citizen, which would also be presented to a panel of judges later in the school year: (1) a statement of the problem; (2) alternative solutions; (3) a class policy; and (4) an action plan. Students were excited to start gathering background information, including articles from the Internet on the history of the promise of a new school building and interviewing a range of people. Brian then photocopied a chapter on organizing techniques for citizen movements he found in *Civics for Democracy: A Journey for Teachers and Students* (Isaac, 1992). The chapter is divided into specific techniques across twelve categories, including individual action, forming a citizen group, public education, research, direct action, citizen lobbying, the courts, initiative and referendum, community lawyer, shareholder activism, the media, and fundraising.

Taking Action

Students discussed and debated various strategies to put into their action plan, including the feasibility of going on strike. Brian reports that although he was intent on having the children lead the decision-making of the project, he was relieved when they were persuaded by a student argument against a strike (i.e., they'd probably have to make up the missed days and come to a hot school in the summer). Instead of striking, the children decided to write a letter documenting all the problems of the school and do a mass mailing to everyone they thought was a decision maker or who could influence a decision maker. As Reggie explained to me, "We thought about the biggest people for our project to influence."

They collaboratively composed a two-page letter, including the powerful line, "We do not think you would let your kids come to a school that is falling apart," and invited people to come and see the school. They asked people to copy them on any letters they sent to the school board or to the mayor so they could include the letters in their Project Citizen portfolio. The children used the Internet to find addresses for a hundred different officials, Board of Education officers, and media outlets and addressed the envelopes twice: the principal required them to re-do many of the addresses, because they were not properly spaced or neatly written. Responses began to drift in, but in mid-March they increased to a flood when *The Chicago Tribune* picked up the story (Zorn, 2004).

Brian reported that students' enthusiasm and energy for the project went through ebbs and flows, but that receiving encouragement from people they interviewed or who wrote them letters often buoyed their spirits. For instance, one letter writer called them "young warriors" and compared them to students in the civil rights/Black Power movements who had formed the Student Non-violent Coordinating Committee (SNCC, pronounced Snick). It also was quite exciting for them to see themselves on television and in newspaper articles; in an interview Dyneisha told me how great it felt to be walking down the street and have people stop and compliment her after seeing her on the television news.

The children were thrilled that people seemed to be listening to them; it certainly increased their sense of self-efficacy and also underscored for them the injustice of their daily inequities. When Tyrone explained to me how this project mattered to him, "We fifth graders and people think only grownups can do the job but little kids can do the job too. We can see things that's messed up." Growing in confidence, a few of the students created a photo documentary and took it to public places and got people to fill out a survey or sign their petition. Tavon's grandmother, with whom he lives, told me in a long interview at her dining room table how incredibly proud she was of him standing outside of the Dominick's supermarket lot and getting sixty signatures on the petition.

Mr. Schultz insisted that the students be the ones to schedule the interviews, tours, media visits, and guest speakers. They kept a calendar on the wall and voted on all decisions about who could come to the classroom (as they did on my request to spend a week with them). Some children had a very hard time getting on the telephone to talk to strangers. To provide support, the class would write out a script and then practice it. Sometimes, in the middle of the conversation, the phone would be passed off to another student or to Mr. Schultz.

In a focus group over lunch one day, I asked five children about some of their successes. They told me that a state senator came for a tour of the school and to be interviewed, and they mentioned a long list of other people they have tried to influence, including aldermen. They also told me about their ongoing efforts to get a response from the Board of Education. To be honest, up until this focus group conversation, I was listening with more than a tiny bit of suspicion to Brian's insistence that the children were making all the major decisions of the project. Having taught elementary age children myself, I was sniffing around for some evidence that he was exerting a fair amount of influence to which he was not willing to own up. My doubts on the depth of children's knowledge and understanding were shattered when the conversation turned to the people whom they thought they most needed to reach:

Reggie: We can't never get through to Arne Duncan.

Celia: Who is he?

Tavon: The Chief Executive Officer of the Board of Education in the City of Chicago.

Dyneisha: We called him and he has his own planner. And he put down three weeks ago Wednesday but he never called us back or nothing.

The conversation continues, and I gently question them, probing to see how sophisticated their knowledge is regarding the structure of the Board of Education. It turns out that they are preparing testimony for the Chicago Public Schools Capital Improvement Plan (they know the full title of that committee) and that they regularly call Arne Duncan's office in an attempt to have him come tour the school before the meeting where they think the fate of the school may be decided.

Later, when I interview the principal and the assistant principal, it turns out they too are waiting to hear from Mr. Duncan's office and have been attending Capital Improvement Board meetings for many years. In fact, the architectural drawings for the new school building have been hanging in the lobby of the school for years, yet no one from the central office has been forthcoming with any information. I am beginning to agree with the person who called these children "young warriors," and I jot in my field notes that after only five days with the children, "I have such warmth in my heart for them." And I have a sneaking suspicion that they will lose.

Preparing Public Testimony

When I arrived for my visit in May, students were busy preparing their statements for the formal hearing that is part of the Center for Civic Education's Project Citizen curriculum being held the following week at a local college. Students from schools throughout the Chicago metropolitan area would be attending. Brian explained to the class that there will be legislators and attorneys serving as judges, and that the students will present to four panels of judges with (1) their problem, (2) the alternative solutions, (3) their class policy, and (4) their action plan. In small groups, they children wrote summary statements for each of the panels. The children are excited about the event, and one child explains to me that her mother is going to try to get time off from work to be in the audience. Throughout my visit, the children are working hard on practicing their statements and trying to commit them to memory. Because the statements are co-written, some of the students have to speak words they have trouble pronouncing, and one day's lesson included practicing words, such as *advantages, exist, issue,* and *alternative.* Brian is coaching them on pronouncing the words, and at one point during a child's practice he says, "Everyone: say it all together: "alternative." Students respond back in unison: "alternative," and I am reminded of all the research documenting the powerful effects of call and response and choral reading for many African American children (Foster, 2002).

Class is ending for the day, and Brian advises the students to go home and practice their statements with an adult. And then he—just as Lance Powell did (see Chapter 3)—paints a picture for what they can expect at the hearing, including all the details about taking the train downtown to Columbia College.

They will take their display boards and a huge binder of materials with them to submit as part of Project Citizen before the hearing.

In this way, Project Citizen provides an authentic audience to help structure the students' work. Just as with Tar Creek (see Chapter 1), I am reminded of Bomer and Bomer's (2001) advice of the importance of constructing public spaces receptive to student voices. Although in the case of Tar Creek, Ms. Jim went about creating those spaces herself, in this case, the curriculum came with a built-in audience. It is important to note, however, that Brian downplayed the importance of the judge's criteria to the students, saying, "I don't think they really care about the judges. And I certainly don't. That's not the idea of the project."

I think what he meant here was that the most important audience for this project was the community. In their interviews with me, it was very clear that children were highly motivated by the knowledge they were taking up this social action project on behalf of their community. This was echoed in the interview I conducted at Tavon's house with his grandmother and uncle. Sitting underneath beautifully framed photographs of Martin Luther King, Malcolm X, and W.E.B Dubois, with his grandmother telling him, "I think that's beautiful," Tavon explained that "Mr. Schultz taught me to stand up and make the community and school a better place." Everyone in the room paused for a moment, moved by this young boy's dedication to his community and his growing conviction that through collective action he and his classmates can struggle for equity and justice. Leaving their home, exhausted and exhilarated, I think, "Yes, this is what schools can and should be teaching."

Integrated Emergent Individualized Curriculum

There are three features of Brian Schultz's emergent curriculum that are important to explain, as they were both central to the project's rapid expansion. The first is that the curriculum was integrated, the second is that there was room for individualization, and the third is that the schedule was flexible. All of these features interacted, creating a workshop type classroom atmosphere in which, as the children repeatedly told me, they never have any free time, and they learned to focus.

Individualized Learning

Brian began the year by negotiating with the principal for daily access to the "tech lab," a room with enough computers so that each child had his or her own. He had noticed that no class was signed up to use the lab during the first hour and twenty minutes of each day designated as a school-wide literacy block. Brian decided he could more easily individualize student literacy learning with the support of technology. He had recently connected with the Northwestern

University developers of the Collaboratory Project (see http://www.icollaboratory.org/), an on-line space that allowed for data collection, research, resource sharing, on-line publishing, collaboration, and communication. Students readily embraced the on-line space for their reading and writing, and then began using it for Project Citizen. For instance, while deciding on their action plan, the students used threaded discussions in the Collaboratory space to debate the pros and cons of different tactics, such as going on strike.

Because Brian recognized the wide range in literacy skill levels in his students, he teamed up with a professor from a Tennessee graduate school of education who recruited volunteers from her literacy class to be on-line mentors to students. In this way, each student received individual and very quick feedback about their work. The effects of this on the students' writing were powerful. "All of a sudden," Brian relates, "I have fifth graders writing five to seven drafts of the same essay based on feedback they are getting. Last year I couldn't get my kids to write a second draft."

This sort of creativity regarding gathering outside resources is so similar to how Rebecca Jim, Joe Szwaja, Lance Powell, and Derrlyn Tom also worked. In this way, the curriculum is not static or received, but is dynamic and continually enriched by the gifts that people bring from outside the four walls of school. Yet merely planning such collaboration is still not enough. When some of the graduate school mentors did not follow through with their commitments, Brian did not want to leave the children of those mentors stranded. So, he recruited his mother and his wife to fill in as on-line mentors. Likewise, he drew upon a vast network of professors and colleagues at the university where he was enrolled in doctoral studies to invite them into the class to be guest speakers. Thus, the classroom curriculum is a continually expanding web of human resources, enriched by the cultural and social capital (Bourdieu, 1986) of the teacher.

Integrated Curriculum and Flexible Scheduling

By using social action to tackle real-world, authentic problems, teachers are automatically entering the territory of integrated, if not interdisciplinary curriculum. (For the important distinctions between the two, see Lindquist, 1995.). In Brian's words, "Real problems happen naturally and don't divide up into reading, writing, and arithmetic at 11:00 until 11:45." Thus, when a student in the class proposed that they needed "those pizza things," the students learned to create charts and graphs from data; and of course, first they needed to create the survey. In this way, social studies, math, and literacy were called upon, and new skills from each area were integrated. It is important to note here that these subject areas were not integrated by the teacher in his lesson plans, but rather required the learner to integrate the knowledge systems as they worked on the project. Brian explained this to me as "inverting the curriculum based on their interests and then meeting all the disciplines." It is what John Dewey (1902) called "moving from the psychological to the logical" or using student inquiries as the starting point and then helping learners draw upon the knowledge systems of the world. This then is where the teacher's more expert knowledge enters in as crucially important. Brian elaborates on the teacher's role with emergent, inquiry-oriented, project-based curriculum:

> I can always be aware of all the different places students can go to get knowledge and giving the space to students is my number one job. I can provide that opportunity to students and then go, "Oh wait, we can think about this in terms of math and what the state is saying what we need to know at a fifth grade level about math."

Brian supplements the content, concepts, and skills that emerge from the project-based curriculum with individual binders that contain specially tailored worksheets and assignments. He uses the standardized tests as a starting point to decide what they need to learn and then creates these "learning books" for them that students work on individually in a self-paced and low-stakes environment.

However, the bulk of the students' reading curriculum for the latter part of fifth grade emerged from the needs of Project Citizen. As I noted earlier, I observed how the students tackled the difficult text of a newspaper article about them. Because the classroom schedule was fluid, the day the *Orlando Sentinel* article (Brady, 2004) arrived, the students were able to spend an hour and a half reading the piece in groups of two and three and then as a whole class. At that point Brian taught the difference between a news article and this piece, which was a "commentary," and then proceeded to help them unpack the sophisticated metaphors and messages of the author.

Teacher: So, let's look at this. The very first paragraph. Darnell, I'm looking at you and I need you looking at me. Or looking at your article. It says, "For educators there ought to be an annual SPOOSE award." What does SPOOSE mean?

Student: Silk purse out of sow's ear.

Teacher: You're right. But what does that mean, Tavon? That's kind of a weird thing to say isn't it? Crown and Malik, I've had to ask you repeatedly to stop. What do you think that means, Tavon? "Silk purse out of a sow's ear?"

Tavon: I don't know.

Teacher: Break it down. What is silk, Darnell?

Darnell: Like clothes; a sow is a pig.

Teacher: So what do you think that means? "A silk purse out of sow's ear?" Who thinks they/

Student: Something out of nothing.

Teacher: That's exactly right. The idea is here that the writer of this article is saying there should be a silk purse out of sow's ear, or a some-thing out of nothing award. For our class. Crown, can you read the second paragraph?

In this very short excerpt of classroom dialogue, it is easy to understand how so many of Mr. Schultz's students made gains on their standardized test scores at the end of fifth grade. By reading about themselves, they were highly motivated to persist with difficult text well above their "independent reading levels." Students are able to make important connections to text and really see themselves and their lives in print. And then later in the article:

Teacher: So what does that mean, though, "For starters average daily attendance is 98%." What does that mean for you guys? Crown, what does that mean for you, that your average daily attendance is 98%?
Crown: That I come to school every day.
Teacher: That you come to school every day. So is he saying that's a good thing?
Students: Yeah.
Teacher: If you think about it, before you were in this classroom, did you come to school all the time?
Crown: No.
Teacher: I mean how much school did you miss last year?
Crown: A lot.
Teacher: So why do you come now?
Crown: Cuz of this project.

Emphasis on Focus

Just as I heard the word *voice* continually while visiting Lance Powell's classroom, in Brian's class I heard the word *focus*. The idea of focus was stated in different ways over and over: "I wanted them to be focused. They had to be focused on what they wanted to do, what they wanted to accomplish." And when I asked individual children what were some of the most important things they learned in fifth grade, I heard: "We learned how to stay focused" and "The main thing is, we gotta stay focused." When I asked the same children what advice they have for teachers who take up large community action projects as part of school-work, I heard in a variety of different ways, "Tell them don't give up."

This habit of persistence and ability to focus on goals is central to any learn-er's future endeavors. The assistant principal, an African American woman who had been at the school for a number of years, spoke with me at great length and related:

The learning aspect of this [project] is enormous, and I don't think the kids will fully understand it until they get a little older and are faced with some dilemma of their own and they'll reflect and say, "I remember when I was in fifth grade, this teacher I had helped us work through this problem that we had." And they remember they had a plan. And that's basic. We all need plans before we do anything. Our kids are so used to diving in.... What they're learning now will stay with them forever.

I credit the flexible schedule and the integrated and emergent curriculum as primary tools in helping the students hone their skills at planning and focusing. Brian explains to me his belief that "It's being able to focus and analyze that makes a difference.... A lot of it takes time and if you can give that space and time, things will happen. That's a big lesson."

He was remarkably able to give them space and time, and was much looser than any other teacher in the book regarding pushing his students to complete tasks. I think a large part of being able to give space and time was the rest of his classroom set-up and curriculum. When Project Citizen waned, there were always the Collaboratory projects, the individual lesson books, and the *Junior Great Books*, so he didn't need to force the Project Citizen curriculum along. He could allow it to emerge: "You have to be willing to have down time when things aren't going well.... This year I allowed for weeks at a time where there was that dead time [with the project].... In any kind of learning you're going to have peaks and drops, you have to embrace them both."

Wins Along the Way

On the second day of my visit, Brian and I are waiting in the classroom for everyone to arrive for a field trip when Shaniqua runs up, exclaiming with excitement, "Did you see the new water fountain?" I comment on how great it is that the Board of Education is responding to the students' campaign, and she counters, "Yeah, but we wanted a new school." Much later, after a long walk and exhausting (for me) day at the zoo where students meet with a scientist who also works to solve big problems, we walk into an appreciably brighter classroom. In our absence new florescent lights have been installed. Although the opaque windows with random bullet holes still filter some of the light, the students had two more "wins" for their list of improvements to the school. I ask the students what other improvements they've seen, and a boy takes me to see the soap dispensers for the bathroom and the new library tables and chairs.

The next day, in an interview, the principal explains that it is the students' project that has generated the rash of recent maintenance:

> This project ... has forced others to make decisions that probably would not have been made for awhile. I'm talking about new lighting fixtures. Well, they had talked about new lighting fixtures for six years. But all of a

sudden it's being done. The bathrooms are getting new fixtures and doors for the stalls. The new windows, fencing, painting. I think the outside pressure that has been generated from the project has brought the change.

The renovations clearly please the children and offer tangible proof of the efficacy of their campaign, but even so, Brian shares with me his plans to "get some closure" on the project within the six weeks left in the school year. At the start of my visit, he elaborated on this point, and it clearly worried him:

> That's been a theme throughout the project because every other person who hears about the project says, "What's going to happen if they don't get what they want, what are they learning then?" And people write to them and say that if you fight for something you believe in, good things will happen even if it's not what you actually ultimately wanted. So I really picked up on that and tried to focus on having wins all along the way. So they have some kind of take-away that they can actually show and share and be proud of all the work they've done.

I realize that my interviews and focus groups with the children may offer a chance for them to orally rehearse their "wins" and thus serve as reminders to help cushion the blow of what the adults fear will be a school closing within a year or two. One of the most vocal students, Dyneisha, advises me that

> Even if we don't get a new [school] at least we tried and learned how to keep confident in ourselves. And we getting the word out and we fifth graders. And we still looking for people to come and talk to us and they be thinking that these kids really improved and can do something with their lives.

This confidence is visible to the adults who have watched them throughout the year. Ms. James, the assistant principal, describes the growth she has seen:

> As they've developed with this, we've seen their confidence grow. When they first started coming down with the various people who've been in and out, they were tentative, they wouldn't speak out. Our kids are basically very shy. They're a terror with each other, but when they're with strangers, they turn in and they don't always speak up and express themselves, they hesitate. This is due to a lot of things. This may be the first time some of them have ever engaged in the interviewing process. But as the year evolved, I noticed they got a little more confident, their body language was more positive, they held their heads up a little higher, and they even know it's time now to go into the next phase of this. They don't know where the end may be, but the learning aspects are enormous. It will help them throughout their lives.

Closing the School

After I returned home to New York City, Brian and I kept in touch. In early June he emailed me with an update. On June 7th, members of the Board's Capital Improvement office came to the school to announce that $4 million of renovations had been approved. But later that same day, a different Board of Education office called the school principal to tell him that Byrd would be closed permanently in two weeks. Brian explained, "The students have been really frustrated, angry, and disappointed." He went on to say that he was extremely proud of their perseverance and so pleased that they are already writing about the skills they had learned in the project and can transfer to new situations. "What was most interesting to me was that so many of them focused their writing on their concerns for others. They are concerned about 'the teacher losing their favorite school' and about the principal and assistant principal 'not having the school and the kids they have worked so hard with.' Their compassion and selflessness never ceases to amaze me!'"

I immediately drafted a sort of condolence and encouragement email to the class and quickly received a reply back from a child with whom I'd made a small connection because I had helped him memorize his speech for the hearing:

> Dear Celia–
>
> How are you? This is Tyrone Isaacson from Mr. Schultz class. Thank you for the letters. They were very helpful because it will help us not give up when we need it. When you were here you helped me a lot on the speech and I did good but that is not the point the point is you were a great help.
>
> Thank you,
> Tyrone

This is what I wrote in my journal on Monday June 7, 2004:

> I feel bad. I feel bad because we have been working on Project Citizen for six months and that is a long time for sixteen fifth graders. The project is trying to get a new school but Friday we found out that we was not going to get a new school so Mr. Gartner and the assistant principal Ms. James have been mad. The person that been mad the most was Ms. Johnson she is our lunch lady and she have been here since it open and she feel bad.
>
> I also been happy because I got to go place with Mr. Schultz about it and I get to stay focused and get to write letters to people that wanted to interview us and who wanted to see what we did in the class. Project Citizen is a fun thing because you can make things work.... You don't never have to give up because they say you won't get your goal. That's why it is fun.

In this journal entry and email, Tyrone provides evidence that people, through organized and focused effort, "can make things work." As Ms. James, so eloquently explained,

> They always say from the mouths of babes, right? Our children needed this. I think it's benefited the whole school. We're not supposed to be about going about trying to solve problems of this nature in elementary school. But what they're learning this year, will stay with them, I hope through college and through life. Because they're learning how to solve life's problems that they're going to be facing and they're learning that in order to solve problems, one must research, write, talk, edit, interview, critique, evaluate, and then go back and then maybe move over to another plan. If A doesn't work, let's try B. And this is what we all do and what we come to school to learn to do, but we don't usually get it until high school, or even college.

These fifth graders' campaign to get the school they deserve had other potential outcomes besides just the learning of the individual children. The principal, who is fiercely committed to the Cabrini-Green neighborhood, explained that

> This project [has] provided us [with] a model for a middle school that we are very serious about that doesn't exist in this area. But people beyond the neighborhood won't see it as a Cabrini-Green school, but a Near North school. We have hatched this around, but we would not have moved as quickly as we have. We have to attribute it to the fallout from the project that so many people are talking about it.

Entering the Fray

Getting "so many people talking" is quite an accomplishment for a class of fifth graders. They were willing to enter the fray of political engagement, shine a spotlight on educational inequity and abuse, and stand up for what they knew they deserved. Their teacher, too, deserves recognition. Not an adventurous, outspoken activist, he was repeatedly accused of "having an agenda." But although helping serve as project manager for this "citizens campaign" (Isaac, 1992) was not his own idea, he was a fierce advocate for his students' right to a quality education:

> I always throw the question back, "So what's my agenda then?" I certainly do have an agenda: I want these kids to learn and to love learning. I want them to learn how the systems that they live in work, so they can work them back. That's really what they're trying to figure out: How can they have a place in this world? How can they effect change? I think that the system is completely unequal and there needs to be equity.

And so we are left with questions of efficacy, and teacher authority, and the enormity of allowing children to tackle matters of justice that the adults around them seemed unable to solve. What is learned when a project of this scale ends in "failure"? Were there enough "wins along the way"?

The people closest to the case—the school leaders, the families, and the children themselves—certainly seem to think so. But before closing the story of this remarkable tale of young and determined children who learned to focus their energy and their outrage and work collectively for justice, I turn ever so briefly to the important research conducted by Kahne and Westheimer (2006), two university professors who have contributed so much to our understanding of community action projects and civic learning. They studied different programs designed to engage youth in community-based projects in order to promote democratic values. The research was designed to examine students' attitudes toward political engagement in different kinds of programs. Their findings point to the importance for educators to look at both internal and external political efficacy. Internal political efficacy relates to one's sense of one's own ability to participate in the political process; external political efficacy is a person's sense of how responsive institutions are to citizens' needs. In the Kahne and Westheimer study, the students who worked side-by-side with government officials confronted little conflict and developed strong and positive internal efficacy. However, they did not demonstrate increased interest in political issues or in being part of a political engagement process. However, in the program that involved *challenges* to government and policy—working outside the system—the high school students often experienced "high levels of frustration and a growing sense of hopelessness" (p. 291) but a *heightened* interest in "talking about politics and political issues" (p. 293).

The researchers use Walker (2000) to discuss the "service/politics split" and point out that if students are involved in non-controversial activities that allow them to see results and "get things done," they may come to understand civic engagement as a "results driven activity" that does not challenge institutions and power. They may have an increased sense of internal efficacy, but not be that interested in engaging in participatory political life. Hence, their research underscores that "exposure to certain kinds of constraints, although frustrating, can also help students learn about the ways power structures, interest group influences, and technical challenges can limit the ability of concerned citizens to bring about change" (p. 290).

They warn us that as educators we are often making the choice through the curriculum to emphasize projects that lend themselves to internal efficacy, but

> that such activities will not provide sufficient preparation for the often contentious and difficult challenge of working to understand and change the social, economic, and political dynamics that surround complex issues such as poverty, caring for the environment, or racism. If teachers

and students decide that such problems are hopeless, or, alternatively, that it is easier to pursue a vision of citizenship that avoids conflict, the full promise of democracy will not be realized. (p. 295)

Although the young Byrd activists did not win their perfect solution of a new school, they certainly experienced a high degree of external efficacy in that they secured a large and wide audience for their pursuit of equal opportunity to learn. They learned that such struggles are "a lot of work" and "you gotta be patient to get things done."

It is the collective pursuit of systemic change—and the teaching and curriculum that support children and youth to learn about change and also work for it—that I am so interested in understanding. In this case—with a teacher only in his second year of teaching elementary school, who did not originally see himself as an activist—we can learn that even young people have a thirst for justice, an eye for equity, and a longing to make contributions to their communities. And, at the end of the day, it is the teacher's job to help children learn, as Tyrone did, not to give up. I am certain that the great scholar, poet, and singer Bernice Johnson Reagon, whose wisdom leads us into the next chapter, would be inviting us to sing to Tyrone and to all our children, from the song she wrote: "We who believe in freedom cannot rest until it comes." ("Ella's Song," 1983).

6

EDUCATION FOR ACTION

Eric Rofes at Humboldt State University

By participating in this class you will come to understand the value of skill development for community organizers who are working with movements of people who aim to change the world. You will also understand the value of organizing skills to your home, your workplace, and your life.

Students will become better able to reach individual and collective organizing goals and learn ways to strategically bring about change. Effective organizing is more than charisma, charm, and smarts: it's about roll-up-the-sleeve skills, working with people across differences, and not backing away from difficult, sustained work in the service of creating a more just and equitable world.

—Education for Action syllabus

We teach people how to run a business, we teach people how to be a social worker, we teach people how to do everything, why don't we teach people how to be organizers?

—Dawn

Professor Eric Rofes writes the evening's agenda for his Humboldt State University students on the whiteboard in alternating colors:

Grassroots Fundraising
    Administrivia
    Fundraising Focus
    Team-teaching Groups
    Coalition Building
    Class Projects

He then uses an overhead projector to prominently feature a quote from the evening's reading:

> Coalition work is not work done in your home. Coalition work has to be done in the streets. And it is some of the most dangerous work you can do. And you shouldn't look for comfort. Some people will come to a coalition and they rate the success of the coalition on whether or not they feel good when they get there. They're not looking for a coalition; they're looking for a home! (Reagon, 2000, p. 346)

Eric (no one ever called him Professor Rofes during my visit) is a presence: filling the classroom space with his warmth and his seriousness, striding to the front of the room with intensity and clarity of purpose. Dressed in blue jeans, he is a tall, broad-chested, bear of a man, sporting a short, neatly trimmed beard and mustache. This is an undergraduate class at Humboldt State University in Arcata, California, titled "Education for Action: Skills-building for Community Organizers and Social Change Activists." Eric designed the class because he thinks that university courses often help students do a fairly good job of analyzing what is wrong with our culture and what needs to change, but they do not typically provide students with any skills to actually help create change. Now in his fourth year as professor at Humboldt, he explains that by the end of his first year on campus he had quickly gotten a

> reputation as someone who was an activist. And the head of Women's Studies and the head of Ethnic Studies both approached me at the same time and said, "Listen, women on this campus and students of color on this campus really want to make some change, but we don't offer them anything that gives them the skills. Could you create a course that does that?

How important Eric's course is was underscored by Dina, a first year Latina student whom I interviewed. After her first semester of classes in the Ethnic Studies major, she became quite depressed, and her professor recommended Eric's class. She echoes the professors' points: "Those kinds of classes are giving all the problems and … everything that's wrong with America, but we're not really getting the tools of what to do about it."

The class meets once a week from 4:00 p.m. to 7:00 p.m., and so, during the other four days of my visit, I shadow Eric as he goes from meeting to meeting, and I interview students currently enrolled in the course or who had taken it in one of the other previous two years it had been offered. Eric explains that he has experimented with the action component of the class requirements and that this year is different from either of the previous years. He hints at some sort of "issue" that arose in relation to the social action project with this class, and by the end of my visit I have put the story together from a variety of perspectives. He explains that he's very interested to see how this year's version of the class works out, and shows me the "Early Semester Feedback Form" he is distributing in class tonight so he can survey the students (see Figure 6.1).

How Eric Rofes Teaches

Calling a student feedback form a "survey" should have been my first clue that this class is based on an organizing model, rather than a traditional educational model. Much that I end up learning about Eric's teaching and about his approach to teaching with social action projects is hinted at in the wording of this form. For Eric and for this class, the words *organization* and *organizing* are key. This survey's wording makes it clear that class sessions have organizational structure about which someone has made conscious decisions; and teachers, texts, and courses are all assumed to have strengths and weaknesses that can be discussed and debated. As the lead organizer for this class, Eric is demonstrating the necessity for participants to evaluate their experiences and for the facilitator to make adjustments based on these evaluations.

Emphasis on Structure

Eric clearly uses methods of popular education that rely on significant input and decision-making by students. However, this is not to suggest that Eric is a "loosey-goosey," abdicate authority, everyone-do-their-own-thing kind of professor: quite the contrary. And he makes this perfectly clear at the start of the evening's class in two ways. First, he is not pleased that not all students have been doing the readings, and he tells them that is why he is giving quizzes on the readings; if everyone has completed them, the class will run better and people will get more out of it. Second, he asks, "Who has the email address redlibre123? I need to be able to reach everyone in the class via email and yours keeps bouncing back." A young, white woman raises her hand and explains she doesn't often check her account. "Can you make arrangements with another student to print out the emails and give them to you in timely way? Will that work? You absolutely must be looped in to the communication."

"Structure" is the word many students use: Eric is all about organization and structure. A master's student in the class—David Riesenfield—elaborates:

> [Eric] has a very rigid structure to his class, more rigid than most people I know at the university. But inside that rigid structure it's very fluid, in the sense that people can really work with it and make it their own. That is what he's giving them to use, I guess.

Another student explains to me, "It's just such a well-rounded atmosphere in there. The class is such an open place. Like open with structure."

In many ways the class is similar to many well-facilitated community action groups in which I have been active over the years. Each class session always

*EDUCATION for ACTION / Spring 20*03

Early Semester Feedback Form

This brief survey is intended as an early semester "check-in" to gather information about how you are experiencing this course. I want to know what works and what doesn't work; what could be changed or improved, and how the course seems to be meeting your needs. Please answer the following questions. There is no need to sign your name, but you may do so if you see a reason.

Consider these issues and others when answering these questions: **The course design ... Eric's teaching skills ... the textbooks and readings ... the way each class is designed ...Eric's one-on-one communications ... the syllabus ... the activities featured thus far ... the classroom and materials ...our discussions**

- How do you think this course is going? What are its strengths and weaknesses?

- How does the organization of each class session feel to you? Can you suggest things you like or things that might be added or changed?

- How is the reading going for you? What are the texts' strengths and weaknesses?

- Are there topics we don't seeem to be covering that you'd like to see covered? If so, please name them here:

- Please comment on the strengths and weaknesses of Eric's teaching.

- Is there anything you'd like to see changed? Also, add any other additional comments here:

FIGURE 6.1 Eric Rofes's early semester student feedback form

begins with the agenda on the board and a time for class members to share announcements about local events. And just as skilled facilitators do in meetings, Eric keeps a speakers' list, saying for instance, "Katie first, and then Dan," as he calls on students during class discussions. And, again, just as a highly skilled community organizer or popular education facilitator, Eric is precise, methodical, and observant, setting exacting criteria for classroom process.

Use of Small Groups

The night I observe Eric's course, at one point he asks students to move into small groups for discussions about fundraising:

> I'm going to ask everyone to put yourselves into groups. I worked hard on this: deciding how big the groups should be today, and I decided five. So, I'm going to ask: You, Katie to form a circle here. I'm going to ask Leah, you're over here. One, two, three, four, five. James, you're in this group. Move the chairs around, one, two, three, four. You three and you five.

He then starts giving students an introduction to the task they are to complete and notices that not all the groups have five members. He interrupts his explanation of the task related to fundraising and says, "How did your group get to be six? Did I count wrong? Somebody needs to be over here. Someone shift over here. Okay."

I smile to myself, as this has happened so many times in my own teaching—even adult students want to be with their friends or are loathe to move—but Eric notices, and it matters to him. Group dynamics and participation structures are part of what he is teaching, and he conveys this to students directly when he says: "I worked hard on deciding how big the groups should be." Organizers, it is clear, must pay attention to details related to group interactions. Later, in our second interview, he shares with me how groupings matter a great deal in this class in particular. He wants people to learn to work together across differences, identities, causes, and perspectives:

> I assign people to groups. Because otherwise the more experienced students, either from environmental groups or the women's center would cluster on their own. We do a lot of talking about this. We did a whole session two or three classes ago about recruiting people to your organization or your cause and how that dynamic of the "in crowd"/"out crowd," how real it is, and how it keeps people away.

In the class session I observed, students worked in three different small groups, for fundraising discussion, team-teaching planning, and project-organizing time.

Eric next provides written prompts for the questions students are to discuss about fundraising and also says the first question out loud: "What's been your experience as a fundraiser, and what did you love and what did you hate about it?" After a quick small group discussion, he asks for examples from the groups. As the class moves from question to question, they alternate between having a discussion in the small group and then processing these discussions in the large group. Clearly, maximizing participation matters to him and near the end of the discussions on fundraising, he asks, "Other tips from people who haven't shared much maybe?"

Struck by the connections I see in his teaching to some of the best facilitators of community organizing and consensus-decision-making groups with whom I've worked throughout my adult life, I ask him in the second interview about this link. Eric agrees and says it is not without tensions:

> I bring popular education processes into my teaching, and struggle with it, because what I often get from students in their evaluations is that it's not seen as learning. They see it as me abrogating my responsibility as a teacher. And so now in all my classes I talk about why we do group work. Like with the fundraising discussion in class. You know: "What have you learned from that?" and "Share that together and then bring it forward to the whole group to process." I talk to them at the beginning of the year about why we're going to do that and why that's a form of learning, and that that's not because I'm lazy that day but it's because I believe that's where education takes place.

Next, the students divide up into different small groups: these are their "team teaching" groups in which they have all read the same book.[5] According to the syllabus, each group will be

> given a two-hour block of class time to teach the rest of the class some of the key learnings from their text in an interactive and enjoyable manner. The team teaching will be assessed with a focus on the group's planning and organizing skills and will be assigned a single grade.

I listen in to one team teaching group as they discuss how to model their lesson on Eric's approach. One student proposes: "We could do case studies. Like how Eric comes in and gives us stories from his experience and you get an idea of how things worked and how they didn't." Another student agrees:

> It's effective to hear his personal stories; his are always - - - they make what he's saying so concrete and real. They're definitely not frivolous. Sometimes personal stories in the classroom seem really, like, flaky and what's the point. But his are all really concrete. What actually works and doesn't work in reality.

Eric's integration of personal stories from his own organizing experience plays a central role in the next section of the class, which is devoted to a discussion of the reading assigned for tonight's class.

Discussion on Coalition Building

The class moves from small groups back to whole class discussion to unpack the assigned reading. It is a classic piece on coalition building—a speech by someone very well known in progressive movement circles: Bernice Johnson Reagon, singer, scholar, and founder of the woman's a cappella social justice singing group, Sweet Honey and the Rock.

There may not be a more fitting person to teach students how to work in coalition than Eric Rofes. He is a man who is knowledgeable about feminisms and who talks about working in "co-gendered" groups, a white person who is devoted to multiracial organizing no matter what the issue, and a gay activist who brings feminism and anti-racism into gay/lesbian/transgender organizations. In the course of this interactive discussion, he explains complex issues of working cross-racially, working across class lines, and working in co-gendered groups, and also demonstrates knowledge about the history of disability rights organizing. Sprinkled in the evening's class are frequent personal stories that illustrate a point a student or he has made. The stories are not self-congratulatory and often highlight an important lesson Eric learned.

The discussion on coalition building begins with Eric asking students to share what points stood out for them from the reading. A small part of the classroom talk is offered below to provide a taste of the rich discussion and how Eric pushed people. We can also learn from Eric's long history of working in coalitions:

> Tony: You're going to have to do work with people that you don't necessarily get along with that well, in order for it to work for everybody.
>
> Dave: I'm seeing an interesting recurring theme that we're seeing in all the readings we come across. The idea that we can't go out looking for the milk and cookies comfort in these groups. It's going to be blood, sweat and tears every place you go and not to expect it's going to be a cushy, fun-loving ride every step of the way. Seems like that's what a lot of the authors are coming at. It's a lot of hard, hard work.
>
> Eric: What's that work about? When you say it's hard work, make that real.
>
> Dave: What it is is essentially taking people's differences, whether it be differences of opinion on an issue or finding similarities between people, and often it's really difficult to find those similarities.... but it seems like on a root level, it's just finding those similarities and finding those small ties between vastly different groups so that we can get together and be unified as a very powerful force.
>
> Eric: The whole question of comfort is at the core here. I think this is coming from a particular political moment when she's essentially saying ... when you put yourself in a group of people that seem different from you, and they might be racially different, it might be co-gendered, it

might be people of different ages, or some other difference. And it felt totally comfortable and cool. Bernice would probably say, those are people of great similarity. They might *look* like they're different in all kinds of ways, but they might all be middle-class-educated people. And so the differences might be minimized there. And if it feels great and comfortable, she would say, you might not really be facing the differences you're working across. Or people might be holding back parts of themselves, both stylistically, and maybe politically in order to have that feeling. But real coalition work, she argues, is working across those differences for a common end. Go back to what we talked about. What it was like for me during AIDS activism to being doing AIDS work with people from the Catholic Church? And these were people who both stylistically and politically were real different, but we were both working for homeless people with HIV and there weren't a lot of people working for homeless people with HIV. Can you let go of that other stuff? Can you feel weird with these people who you think might not want you to exist at all and still work on a project with them? To me, it raises a really core question, which I want to situate historically. Are we going to win on our causes if we work out of a womb-only model [this is reference to the reading]? If it's only the twelve of us who are just like each other, is that going to win votes or win issues activist-wise? Now help me situate this historically. Where did she speak this, and what's this situated in? Do you know?

Situating activist work historically is critically important to Eric, and throughout the single class period he makes it abundantly clear that the activists of today are in a different place vis-à-vis coalition work than they were during Eric's youth. Later, he shared with me that he had been criticized by some former students for teaching "old style" organizing methods and so was very excited to be using the newly published book, *From ACT UP to the WTO* (Shepard & Hayduk, 2002), which offered an important counterpoint to his beloved *Organizing for Social Change: A Manual for Activists* (Bobo, Kendall, & Max, 2001).

While I listen from the back of the room—fairly transfixed, I must admit—Eric moves from discussion format to a short lecture,

> If you are in a coalition where there are disagreements, do you skewer each other or do you find ways to disagree? Put the issues on the table, but leave each other standing okay. To me, these are real questions about the ethics one plays when working in coalitions. I want to go from this particular moment of Bernice Reagon's which is 1981, lesbian feminism, West Coast Women's Music Festival. Fast forward to our book on *ACT UP* and those first couple of chapters.

He launches into a call to action: for people to actively confront issues of racism, sexism, and classism. Throughout the discussion that follows his brief lecture, he works to help young activists at this predominantly white college analyze the importance of power and identity politics related to race and class, along with the intersection of gender and sexuality. Many of them are environmentalists, and a young white woman explains that at a conference she recently attended, there was an all white panel on eco-feminism. Eric replies:

> It's a great example. Because our ethics matter. I don't know if I was raised out of guilt or anything, but the whole question is, if you are a white woman asked to be on a panel on eco-feminism do you ask who's on that panel with you? And when they say "Three other white women," do you say, "Is this about white women and eco-feminism, or is this about women and eco-feminism?" [student laughs]. And if it's about women and eco-feminism, why is it all white women, especially since so much about eco-feminism has come from women in third world countries? So raising that question, raises the ethical question.

I am enthralled by the intensity of this discussion and how seriously so many of the students are engaging with the complex issues around coalition work. How, I wonder, has Eric managed to so seamlessly combine being an academic and an activist?

In our final interview he tells me that he welcomes conservatives to class— and indeed on the syllabus he lists "people working for a conservation political lobby" as one constituency for which his class is designed. He tells me stories of working well with Republicans and Libertarians when he was a visiting professor at Bowdoin College, and somewhat regrets that such students are not present in this class: "To me it would be a livelier course if those folks were there. They, too, have activist projects. I mean, to me, I'd feel comfortable training anyone in these skills."

Portfolio Reflections

Because he wants to keep the students' focus on self and group evaluation of their group action/organizing projects, he does not grade or evaluate the group work. Instead, each student is required to submit a portfolio with at least five reflective pieces evaluating the organizing work they are engaged in—or observe—during the semester. This portfolio counts for 50% of the course grade, and Eric encourages students to submit the pieces for formative feedback before the end of the semester. David Riesenfield explained to me that Eric had very high expectations for the portfolio reflections:

> It's a very introspective look at my own activism. And that's kind of hard. I never thought it would be so hard. He wrote on my paper, "You didn't really look inside yourself on this one." He was pushing me to think.

Eric is so able to push his students to think and reflect on their organizing practices because he also pushes himself. (At the conclusion of this chapter I enumerate some of the activist–sustaining practices in which Eric engages.) He had a very sophisticated explanation of how he handled the "issue" related to the class activist project.

The Projects

It is now 7:00 p.m. and Eric wraps up the interactive lecture on coalition politics and signals that it is time to meet in action project groups. I watch as the class divides into two: the group on the "Graduation Pledge" and the "Food Not Lawns" group. Having a hint from our first interview that Eric had originally wanted the whole class to pursue the Graduation Pledge Project and that he was overruled (in a sense) by the half of the class who ended up in Food Not Lawns, I move my chair into that group.

Focus/Goals

As with all prior segments of the class, Eric structures the project time for the evening:

> I'm going to ask you to move into your class projects now. And I'm going to ask each group during the time remaining to try to come up with one or two objectives. Make it specific and achievable this semester. So it shouldn't be, "Get rid of everyone's lawn in Arcata and replace it with sustainable agriculture" [laugher]. It should be something really narrow that your team is aiming for. Come up with steps and a timetable for the rest of the semester and look at who does what. You can flex it if it's useful, but I would like to get some semblance of what each group is aiming for by the end of class today.

The idea of specifying goals to focus the energy during social action is a centerpiece of what Eric teaches and what students report to me as a key learning during almost every single one of the eleven student interviews I conducted. Just as students at Byrd Academy had told me they learned "to focus" (see Chapter 5), I also heard that same idea at Humboldt. Maria, who has been working with young girls on how to be activists at a summer camp and who took the class last year, explained: "We were at the building stage with the activist work. Everyone had great ideas and nowhere to go with them, so this class gave us more focus." And later the same day, Jermaine told me she had learned what was most essential is, "You have to be really focused."

However, the most elaborate and powerful student story I heard was from Tony who teaches first-year English composition classes at Humboldt while he works on his master's degree. When asked what he is learning in "Education for Action," Tony tells how he is applying Eric's teachings about focused and goal-oriented activism:

> The thing about this class that's meant the most to me is the way it's already affected my life outside of school. There was a campus walkout a few weeks ago. And my students all wanted to go. They wanted to walk out of their classes and go to the rally. I got some e-mails, "Can we go? Will you excuse us from class to go to this?" And I said, "Sure, if you can tell me who the target is? What are the goals of this rally? How will you know if the rally is successful or not? If you can tell me these things, I'll let you go. Not only will I let you go, I will go with you." And nobody could tell me.… That's where Eric's class is really, really helpful because that's what he's always focused on, "What are you objectives? What are your goals for this? Who is your target? Who are you trying to make uncomfortable? Who is it that can give you what you want?

Of course, the work of agreeing on the answers to the key questions about organizing that Eric (via Tony) outlines here is enormous. In more than a few interviews, the students chuckle knowingly as we acknowledge that one of the hardest aspects of social action projects is working with other humans. "That is why," explains student Christa Harrison, "we need something that we can work on all together in this class so we can learn how to organize with people."

Indeed, for most all of his classes, Eric organizes these goal-setting interactions through project work.

> In all my teaching I've often been about producing things. In my middle school teaching—I was a sixth, seventh, eighth grade teacher for five years—we did three book projects with kids that became published books [Rofes, 1981, 1984, 1985a]. That really started me on this idea that … projects, whether it's higher ed or elementary ed, around something that's a central interest to the students could have value. And that's how I made my early name as a teacher; besides losing a job when I came out as gay [Rofes, 1985b].

Eric describes his role with group activist projects as that of an observer and a supporter, because he wants to give them enough space to work together (without him) and learn from their mistakes. He explains to me that the next week's class session is on "Critiquing Organizing Work," where he helps students learn to engage in systematic evaluation of their work.

The Issue

At the start of the semester, Eric sent his syllabus to me in preparation for my research visit in mid-March. On the syllabus I read that the class would be engaged in a "unified class project." However, when I arrived on campus Eric told me that I would not see students working on a joint project as the class could not agree. Knowing that my research questions centered in large part on issues of teacher power and imposition, he said he wanted me to glean the details of what happened from students and would fill in from his perspective at our closing interview. He did tell me that he found the classroom process challenging, "I ran it democratically and it was very long; it took us two extra sessions to decide what we're doing. But now we know what we're doing." Students were eager to talk to me about what had happened as many of them experienced the process of deciding on what organizing project to take up as "very tense," "very emotional," "really heated," "a potentially explosive situation."

The story actually began when Eric was planning the class and decided to organize the class around a single project. This was the third time he was teaching the class, and, in previous iterations, small groups of students created organizing plans that were hypothetical, and could perhaps be used in the future. This year, however, he wanted the class to dig their collective teeth into a concrete and local project: the Graduation Pledge. Upon graduation, some students signal their commitment to social and environmental responsibility in the workplace by signing the pledge, which reads: "I pledge to explore and take into account the social and environmental consequences of any job I consider and will try to improve these aspects of any organizations for which I work."

The Graduation Pledge was started in 1987 at Humboldt State College (not a university then) but had languished in recent years on the campus, although simultaneously it had spread to other campuses (see www.graduationpledge. org). Eric thought the class could breathe new life into the Pledge in time for graduation in May. However, led by one woman in particular, some of the students in the class did not think the Graduation Pledge was radical enough; the statement offered only a bare minimum of what they wanted their fellow students to be working toward. As Tony explained, "They didn't feel like it was going to really change the world this month. They wanted to change the world this month."

At the same time that the project was being critiqued, students also raised issues about classroom power. Some of the same students pushed the class to create an alternative classroom space not dominated by the hierarchical constraints of a professor who came in with his own agenda. One student explained to me:

> Some of the students had this idea of the "professor as oppressor." Yeah, it was interesting because I thought that [Eric] had wisely chosen a small enough project that with thirty people working on it we could have made some really concrete progress and had feelings of success and you know, "Look what we did?"

Eric encouraged me to interview some of the students from the Food Not Lawns group who had most vocally raised the issues of power and politics. To a person, each student explained how impressed she had been with Eric's facilitation of the class conflict. One student who joined the Graduation Pledge group said she had learned important lessons by watching the negotiations over three class sessions:

> I just kind of sat back and watched Eric facilitate in awe. He did not engage. He didn't enter the drama. I think that's one of his phrases. Like he just looked calm, he didn't take it as a personal attack; he facilitated the alternative that he hadn't planned for in a really amazing way. I was like, okay, in twenty years I hope I can do that. You know?

Hearing so many of the students talk with great respect about how the negotiations around deciding on the class project(s) were handled, I felt hot on the trail of my questions about teacher authority and social action projects as part of the regular school curriculum. I was chomping at the bit to sit Eric down for the exit interview and hear his explanation of how he had thought about and facilitated the difficult class sessions. Rather than paraphrase his account, I offer it as interlude in (not its entirety) but at some length.

〜〜〜〜〜〜

INTERLUDE: Eric Rofes as Reflective Facilitator of Power and Authority for Social Change

It was a really hard two sessions. I realized I was going into difficult territory, which I hadn't anticipated. I immediately did Midwest Academy: What is my goal here? What do I want out of this? Rather than say, "This is how I'm going to get what I want." What do I want out of it?

And what I most wanted out of it was not a unitary project, although that's what I thought I wanted. I wanted students to do something that they found meaningful and make sure it was somewhat activist based. So I actually wrote my goal out on the lesson plan. And when the discussion opened up and it started to become really intense, I was pulled to go into that intensity. And I would keep referring to the goal, how important it was for me.

I was very well aware that if the teacher played heavy I would get exactly what I didn't want, especially because I know my own experience holding power and the box that I'm in, and what that sets off for people. I can't come from that butch, sure of myself, confident, smart, Jewish male energy.

I've actually learned this from lesbians [Hollibaugh, 2000]; I mean, I have to come from my femme space ... It's knowing when to come from my butch power and my femme power. And the exact thing that triggers my butch power, which is about control, I have to downshift and come from my femme power, which is to be gentler, use humor, let go of the results, and still shepherd things through. And it was by shifting into my femme power ... my voice is different, my hand gestures are different, my body gestures are different, and it worked.

I hated those two sessions because I wasn't getting what I wanted and I hate not get-
ting what I want. I'll be honest about that. And I was really outraged by one student's
conduct.... And yet, I wasn't going to give her the power by attacking her. I just hated
the whole process and the fact that the majority of the students went with her. I felt awful
about it, but I knew I did the right thing; that it looked like I lost face, but I saved face
by just staying and doing it.

I learned how to do this in career organizing.... I learned if I tried to control with that
traditionally masculine energy, I get attacked. And if I downshift and let other energy
flow, and use humor and gentleness, I get a different outcome.

Certainly, most of us who take up the challenge to teach with social action
projects do not have the organizing experience and depth of insight to match
Eric's. (I for instance, am not so able to summon my "femme power.") However, Eric's lesson for us is about his commitment to the deliberative process
of collective organizing. A very key take-away for students in this class was
the idea that to make change in the world, people have to come together and
focus on specific goals. By demonstrating how to facilitate a group through a
decision-making process—that did not end up with Eric's original plan being
adopted—he gave his class of thirty students an invaluable lesson on group
process for collective decision-making. The class ended up voting to split into
two groups—the Food Not Lawns group and the Graduation Pledge group.

Food Not Lawns

Concerned that only 15% of food eaten in Humboldt County is grown in
Humboldt County, and claiming "unless you want to do cartwheels all day, a
lawn doesn't do you much good," students in this group wanted to organize
a project much bigger than just a one-semester class project. One of the lead
organizers said during small group work—as they were attempting to specify
their objectives as Eric had asked both groups to do: "I was just thinking that
we want to dedicate at least a year to this." During small group time they also
discussed whether to let in people from outside the class and decided they
should let anyone join them who wants to. In the words of one group member:
"I say we rage it!"

In class that night, during the hour allotted to the group work, various students tried to focus this group of ten on the task Eric had laid out for them—
come up with an objective or two and outline some steps. Some students were
clearly less interested or less able to focus on goals than others. Much of the
conversation was a hodge-podge of ideas for activities in which they could
engage, and no one was yet displaying practices of facilitation that they had
"covered" in class. Clearly, this was the messy work that Eric had told me they

needed to be immersed in. One student finally emerged as a facilitator—not by group agreement, but out of tangible frustration with her colleagues:

> Which brings me to our objective. Our objective is to organize a network in the community, so the people that are already involved in this kind of work can network with each other and we can bring these skills and beautiful knowledge to community members who might not be connected with it yet and we can make it in our consciousness that we build in this community. Consciousness of where our food comes from.

The group agrees with this articulation, but no one writes it down to turn in to the professor at the end of the class.

One woman keeps pushing for a timeline and the other student who'd laid out the agenda tries too: "The next question has to do with what we're supposed to figure out today. How are we going to make our project public so we can get more support? Let more people know about it?" This bid to get the group focused also falls flat. By this point, I want to be a member of the group and help them get organized. I write in my field notes that they may end up spending this entire semester brainstorming and never get around to any planning, even though Eric has given them a very specific strategic planning task. I wonder in the margins of my notebook if some of the students are perhaps consciously or unconsciously resisting Eric's "assignment." Indeed, after class, Eric shared the results of his survey of students course evaluations at mid-semester, and one student remarks that the "hierarchical structure is oppressive."

By the end of class the group has decided to do a bicycle tour on Sunday afternoon. Their plan is to go around to all the different projects that demonstrate practices supportive of using lawns to grow food and that could be networked together. They have figured out how to get free rental bicycles from the library and a time to meet. The previous week they had created subgroups (infrastructure, design, government), and at the end of class, Julie asked the group: "Who will bottom line each group?" (Who will be left making sure the subgroup is organized.) Students provide the names of people for each group (either themselves, or someone who is absent that evening) and the students pack up their bags to leave.

I am left to ponder the outcomes for this small group work time: They have divided up the work and have organized a next step for an activity. But they have not engaged with the focusing task and goal setting that their professor assigned. Despite Eric's overt efforts, they are clearly more interested in activities and action than in strategic planning. I am reminded of many organizing meetings I have attended where we get more excited about planning the actions, than by organizing our overall goals and strategy. I leave the small group thinking how useful this class would be for so many activists working for social change.

Alive with the Struggle

Along with the necessity to engage in strategic planning (What is the goal? What are our targets?), Eric's other major lesson relates to cultivating lifelong activism. He tells me that he wants to "model for students how to hold activism in one's life over the life course, for the long haul." Although he did not specify this to me, there seemed to be three categories of advice related most directly to long haul activism: skills building; movement building, and embracing inherent non-perfection.

Skills Building

For the class I was part of, the skills-building focus of the evening was fundraising. "Get yourself to some of those workshops on fundraising," he tells students, and then provides a couple of examples of sessions they can attend in Northern California. "They're the best things to do. Do them over your career as an activist." In the interactive lecture, he outlines how complicated it is for most people to talk about money and deal with money, but that if you want to be part of community-based organizing, you will have to learn the skills. And, in true Eric form, he has a story to bring home the point:

> Two basic skills organizers can develop that will hold you through multiple issues and multiple projects you're working on: one is basic writing skills and two is basic fundraising skills. And I gotta tell you: I know all these people who avoided one or the other until they were in the 40s or 50s and then wish they had developed their skills earlier on. I have to say, I don't like fundraising. I still hate making asks. I had to make an ask this weekend. I got it. I asked for a thousand and I got a thousand.

Students loved hearing his stories and viewing his artifacts. If the skill for the evening was writing press releases, he brought in press releases he had written and then the subsequent newspaper articles that covered the event. When the skill was proposal writing, he brought in successfully funded proposals and also proposals for work-in-progress. While I was there, for example, Eric shared with me a proposal in progress for a North Coast Community-University Center for Organizing. Students were able to see skills in action—not just read about them in a book. And then he would sit, side-by-side with students in their project groups and coach them through putting out a press release for their actions. "We want," explained Christina, "to soak in his knowledge and squeeze everything we can out of him while we're doing this project so we can learn to apply all the skills he's developed over his lifetime of activism."

Movement Building

A long-time supporter of the Highlander Research and Education Center in Tennessee (see Adams, 1975; Bell, Gaventa, & Peters, 1990; Horton, 1997), Eric was determined that his students learn to "resist the kind of Martin Luther King heroism model, which is all they've gotten before this class usually." While listening to Phil Ochs protest songs in his pickup truck on our way to dinner after class, Eric explains that it is in social movements that he has found much meaning in his life. In class that night, he offers students some concrete tips: Keep a private file of successes that help you "realize the world has changed and you've been a part of it or you've lived through those changes." Eric drives home the point that liberation and rights movements "do not happen biologically. The state usually didn't lead it. There were people themselves who led those changes." It is a rallying call to lifelong movement building, "It kind of gives you the hope to go on," he concludes.

Accepting Non-Perfection

A constant theme I heard across my days of student interviews is how Eric taught them that they shouldn't strive for perfection. During the class I observe, he models mistake-making. The class is in the fundraising portion of the agenda, and Eric is describing his current dilemmas about funding for the Gay Men's Health Summit he is organizing with a collective for May. "And now," he says, "I'll tell you the horror story of today. Real life organizing. An Eric mistake." The class laughs at his introduction, but the story involves a serious issue of funding for scholarships. He tells me later that this is one of his challenges as an academic who is also an activist. He had received the news of a budgeting snafu early that morning, and because he had a fully scheduled day on campus, he was not going to be able to devote time to solving it until much later in the week.

Eric's advice about accepting imperfection in themselves and in the world resonated with the students. Tony told me, "Eric was saying you can't just … expect the world to be perfect. I need to hear that … I feel like … I'm a failure until the world is perfect, so it's difficult." In Eric's words:

> Some of us did this work in our 20s thinking that oh, racism will be over in our 30s. And in fact, this is going to be with us forever, and the question is whether you're going to think of this as a struggle or as failure. And a lot of the dynamic of people leaving activism as they get older, 30 or 40, or something like that is from thinking that unless the world is perfect, you've failed. And boy, during this current era we're living with, if you have that attitude, you are withdrawing right now. You need to be in for the struggle and see social change as a series of things that hopefully moves in the right direction. I feel we need to stay in touch with the value of being alive with the struggle.

Collective Organizing for Social Change

It was with Eric Rofes at Humboldt State that a big piece of what I was seeking to understand in this research project fell into place. It was what Eric's class was designed around: organizing. It is the human organizing aspect of community action projects in which I am most interested because students are invited to plan unique engagements with people and the world. That is, when projects require organizing, students are in the position to be making decisions about what the problem is, what some solutions are, possible avenues to pursue, activities to plan, and actions to organize. They are not just showing up for volunteer hours in a soup kitchen where someone else has already done the organizing. They are not just going to a nursing home to sing songs and cheer up the elders. They are not just tutoring at a learning center for children with disabilities.

Eric drew a sharp distinction between service projects (helping people), advocacy projects (professionals who help people who cannot help themselves) and community organizing which centers on getting people together to "do for themselves." Eric told me:

> I want them to be activists and when they propose projects, this came up last year, that are, you know, Kiwanis Club stuff ... I'm glad they're doing Kiwanis Club stuff and the same skills can apply to Kiwanis stuff, but I want them to be aware how that's not social change activism. Activism involves looking at relationships of power and pushes to change the status quo.

Organizing projects that seek to change the status quo: that is exactly what I have been seeking to understand. I feel so fortunate to have watched Eric Rofes in action and thus gotten so much closer to concluding my fieldwork.

As I wrap up this chapter, I want to call attention to two very basic elements of Eric's pedagogy for organizing social justice activist projects. David Riesenfield summed up Eric's method quite elegantly: First, "Eric lays out a smorgasbord of things for us, and then lets students make decisions as to how they're going to use them." And then, "He leaves space for many points of view and for people to work on all different things together."

Postscript

It was with a deep sense of loss that I heard in late June 2006 that Eric Rofes had a heart attack and died. He was only fifty-one years old and still had so very much to teach us. In his final interview, he told me that he had built his life around the four things he loved: teaching, writing, researching, and organizing. I feel blessed to have seen his integration of these four activities in action.

Across these four activities, Eric quite openly shared much about himself, his stories, and his practices. These practices were rooted for Eric in a deep and abiding confidence that people—when they came face to face with injustice—would be moved to take action. He devoted his life to teaching people how to organize these actions, so I think it only fitting to conclude with a series of quotes from his students about what they learned in his class. I think Eric would be pleased to read this list:

> Jermaine: Change takes a long time and you need to be patient and not expect things to happen overnight or in a year; you have to really make a plan, it takes a long time, and you need to really organize it every step of the way.
>
> Maria: It takes a lot of time, but it also takes a lot of thought. Good intentions alone won't do it. There has to be a systematic plan, strategy, and a carefully defined destination.
>
> David: It's so cool because now I'm getting these tools and all these things and when I go and put together a group of people, whether it be students, or other teachers, or whomever, and whether it be in my neighborhood where I live, it's going to be so useful to be able to say, "Ok, well, let's figure this out folks. Let's sit down and meet every Tuesday and figure out who we're actually going against, or who can work with us, and how we can utilize all these resources and all these different things. And I think if we all, what, thirty-five of us from this class, go to thirty-five different places, with the tools we get from this class we can put together cohesive networks of actions. People want to act on things and we can help them do that.
>
> Dawn: It's people organizing that changes things. To sustain the work over the long-term, you need to cultivate a life devoted to activism and develop your organizing identity. The bottom line is that people have to make that commitment. One of the first classes, I remember Eric talking about how you've got this life ahead of you, and you have to figure out how you're going to live your life and what is going to have meaning for you. He talks about how organizing has brought a lot of meaning to his life and that it certainly isn't easy but that the rewards of fighting a good fight are worth it. Fighting for what you believe in and what you believe is the right thing, and speaking out when you feel like there's an injustice. Eric is a good example of how after thirty years of organizing, he can look back and feel proud of what he's done. And that is all that I think most people want out of their lives.

7

BECOMING AN ACTIVIST TEACHER

Barbara Regenspan at SUNY Binghamton

Monday class meetings will specifically support students to become increasingly conscious of what it means to be/become a responsible social activist who is also a teacher. We will study the lives of characters in books who evolve into activist-teachers and we will continually analyze our personal and political connections with these characters, at the same time that we reflect on our own teaching and activist pursuits.

—from the class syllabus for Social Action as Curriculum

What sparks a teacher to integrate social action projects into the regular classroom curriculum? What experiences help teachers take a leap and create opportunities for their students to actively shape the future of the world through community and civic engagement? The teacher of my final case—Professor Barbara Regenspan—created an entire course for her teacher education program around social action and curriculum. As a central requirement of the class, each student designed his or her own social action project to carry out in a classroom that semester, as well as a paper on some issue or theme from the project. This chapter explores Barbara's pedagogy, her students' projects and stances, and concludes with an exploration of the role compassion and radical acceptance played in Barbara's pedagogy to promote social action.

Barbara Regenspan integrates individual or small group social action projects into her undergraduate and graduate teacher education. Having met her at a conference, and having engaged in provocative conversations about curriculum with social action projects as part of required work in teacher education programs, I was eager to visit her university class at the State University of New York, Binghamton, where she was teaching at the time. As a professor, also, of graduate preservice education, I was excited to be working with someone who had designed an entire teacher education course around social action. Called "Social Action as Curriculum," the class was required for all elementary education students in the master's program. The year I visited, it was the first time that the social action course was being taken concurrently with the second semester of student teaching, and was the fifth time that Barbara had taught it.

Unlike my field work for the other research sites in this book, the proximity of Binghamton to my home base enabled me to spread my visits over three months. For my first field visit, I drove from New York City to observe Barbara's three-hour class. The students were reading Barack Obama's *Dreams From My Father* (1998) and were discussing questions that Barbara had posed in a study guide. It was a few years before Barack Obama was elected president of the United States, and at one point in the discussion, Barbara shares that she is brought to "the verge of tears" by a certain section of the text. It is a part of the memoir when Barack writes of a deep encounter that he has with a person in the community. It is my first hint that in addition to a focus on preparing teachers to be activists, this case may offer me insight into the emotional component of social action work as well.

Social Action as Curriculum: The Course

I quickly found out that the elementary education program has an explicitly social justice focus, and it was assumed by program faculty that students had signed up to become "social reconstructionist" teachers. Teacher education programs with a social reconstructionist commitment have been in existence for almost eighty years now (Zeichner & Liston, 1990) and are designed to prepare teachers to create more just outcomes for people through attention to matters of diversity and equity in curriculum and schooling. Faculty collaboratively designed the SUNY-Binghamton program, but Social Action as Curriculum is clearly Barbara's course. Barbara explained its origins:

> I came into this job knowing I wanted to do a class like this. Drawing upon the dialectic of freedom and seeing … the push for action, seeing that if they were going to seize the dialectic freedom during student teaching it had to be around social reconstructionist thinking … I define social reconstructionist as what we have to do to reconstruct our disappointingly inequitable social worlds.[6]

The idea of teacher as agent of social change is one which resonates with most of my preservice students. As I explained in *Learning to Teach Inclusively* (Oyler, 2006), of the hundreds of student teachers with whom I've worked over the years, not one of them states that they wish to teach so as to preserve the status quo. Most all of them want to "make the world a better place," yet often are not very confident that they understand the relationship between social change and classroom curriculum. Because Barbara's course is explicitly designed to link community activism and classroom teaching, I was eager to see the projects and interview students about their learning.

In their final semester of their master's program, students were very confident about their understanding of the program's goals and this course. When asked to define social action, students had no difficulty. As one student stated:

> Social action to me means that you're constantly looking critically at what's going on in the world around you and trying to address the issues, positive and negative, and valuing community and people in a way that works to benefit everybody.

"The projects," Barbara tells me, "can be something they are already doing. They're welcome to use anything in their current situation, but they have to use the course to buy extra energy and extra infusion." She worries, however, that it is all just "bits and pieces" and "doesn't go anywhere." Students were very clear about the expectations:

> She wants us to think of projects we could do that would change our society in positive ways. What are some things, as teachers, we can do to go outside of normal teaching activities? And what are some things we can do to make them not just for the kids but for our community, the parents we work with, or even if we're going in with the kids, some activities we can do with our kids that will make them think about their society and how can they go home and make their environment a better place. That seems to be the whole theme of this class.

However clear their definitions of social action curriculum, there was a wide range in the actual projects the students worked on. Some of them reminded me of what Eric Rofes (see Chapter 6) called, "Kiwanis Club" projects—or projects that required organizing skills, but were not efforts that challenged the status quo. The projects all involved learning, and all involved community, but they were not necessarily much beyond what many teachers would do who do not consider themselves activists. I knew the book the class was reading by Barack Obama centered in large part on his community organizing and I suspected Barbara would help me sort through these issues. How did she help scaffold students' social action projects? What was she aiming for? By the end of my visits, I had some very illuminating answers.

Visiting Class

The class of fifteen students sits seminar style with Barbara and her co-teacher at the front of the room.[7] The co-teacher leads a brief meditation, and while I am a meditater, I wonder if I would ever feel comfortable doing that in my own classroom; again, these questions I have center around imposing or integrating my own world view and practices into the teacher education classroom.

Invitation to an Encounter

Barbara opened her section of the class with an invitation for students to engage in a specific instructional event—Tar Beach in Iraq—and by the end of my time with this class, I realize moves like this are central to her pedagogy: Curriculum planning is all about imagining possibilities. Because this process of curriculum planning—particularly with a focus on aesthetic education—is so central to Barbara's teacher education work, I quote her at length here. She is sharing with the class an idea she has from the Teachers for Peace group she is part of:

> You all know *Tar Beach* [children's book by Faith Ringold, 1996], right? We took *Tar Beach* and we generated photographs from the Internet of Iraq, and we said, "Identify with Cassie Louise Lightfoot but envision her in Iraq." Now we weren't specifically relating it to the war; we weren't envisioning her as flying over Iraq during the war. But what might her story be?... I sent a description of the meeting, to Bob Peterson of *Rethinking Schools*, you've read some of his articles, and he emailed back; and he said, "Now I want one of your students to do it in a classroom and then let's hear what happens." So if any of you want to take that on, if anyone's in a position to try something like that out in a classroom or wants to brainstorm with me how to make it possible, what might have to be tweaked, I'd even help you get photographs. I know what the good sites are because I spent a lot of time Friday finding some good pictures. And we have good art materials, so you can even take those.

Although no one immediately took Barbara up in her lesson suggestion, this example is emblematic of what she offers throughout her teaching: opportunities to engage directly with the lives of characters in books as a vehicle to propel students to more deeply examine their own lives, their own priorities, and their own consciousness.

Discussion of Privilege and Power

Barbara's primary method for pushing for these close encounters with "the other" is through careful selection of texts—novels, memoir, art, poetry, research articles, teachers' magazines, and community murals. For primary course texts, she develops very detailed study guides. The night I visit class, students moved into small groups to discuss their responses to some of the study guide questions from *Dreams From My Father* (Obama, 1998). She prefaces the small group discussions with a reminder about why they are reading this book:

> What do you think happens to him? Don't forget, the questions are intended to get you personally connected, so take guesses based on the

constellation of emotional and political realities you're being presented with. Use your own experience. What might have happened?

Many of the questions—and much of the subsequent large group debriefing—centers around issues of privilege, identity, and positionality. In answering many of the questions, both students and professor made connections to their own life experiences. A very long and intense conversation ensues when Barbara poses a question that is not on the study guide but that she says is a "live question" in her life:

> How do you know that you're not patronizing people? What are the elements that let us know that Barack was never patronizing the people whose kitchens he was sitting in when he was listening to their stories?... There was something healing about the process and there was a real connection between himself and them that had nothing to do with the fact that he had more, in some ways, privilege, that he had more possibilities than those people. But how do we know that it wasn't patronizing?

Answering Barbara's question, a student gets right to the core of the matter and says, "He's really listening to them so that he can learn something." There is a moment of silence in the class, and it sinks in for me—and I imagine for students too—why Barbara is having them read this memoir during student teaching. To proceed with curriculum planning toward community engagement, the teacher must first be listening to children and to families and to the community. It is from a stance of listening-to-learn-from-and-with that socially responsive action can emerge. I understand that this, too, is intentional in Barbara's pedagogy when she offers the class:

> Barack is totally invested and that's when he realizes that the stories are sacred. It touches me on the verge of tears when I think about this. I think that where it gets me is the recognition that he sees the sacredness in their stories at the same time that he can give his own; that he can talk about his own life and realize that the dilemmas that he's facing about who he is and where he's going, that they're the same order of dilemma.

This opens a floodgate from the students to talk about dilemmas of power and positioning and identity in their own lives. The discussion takes a critical turn that I later find out is at the heart of Barbara's agenda: "Coming face to face with your own implicatedness." It starts when a student begins to unpack the central requirement of the class to link curriculum to community service:

> We started talking about just the reality of service in any form it takes, that the people who are performing the service also get caught up in a romanticized view of, "Oh, I'm doing such a great thing for people who really need my help." And like Tina was comparing it to her confirmation

group, talking about not recognizing the poverty in Binghamton but recognizing it in other countries. And it just seems like a much more fulfilling thing personally because the service part of it is for yourself; I mean you get something out of it. And it just seems like in a selfish way, not intentionally selfish, but in a selfish way you're going, "Oh, if I go to Central America to play hacky sack, it's much more important than if I go to play with the kids in the park next door." But it's just more of a fulfilling thing for yourself.

I am moved by the students' frankness and willingness to make themselves vulnerable to talk about issues of privilege and power from their own lives. I am intrigued and curious to see if and how this conversation will link to their own social action projects.

The Social Action Projects

The class segues to a time set aside for each student to explain what his or her individual project is. I am aware that Barbara—with her questions and suggestions—offers gentle nudges for many of the students to consider issues of their own privilege and also of the impact of the projects. I find out afterwards that each student has already had at least one individual meeting with Barbara to brainstorm and negotiate and firm up the project.

Barbara asks the students to say what they're doing for their projects, to share their ideas for the focus they are going to take for their final paper they will write about their project, and also to say "what you see as needing work, either because you want support from us or because you want to state what the challenge is going to be for you."

Peace Chorus

Timothy goes first and explains that his project is a Peace Chorus. He is working with young children in the local Saratoga Homes, a public housing project where one of the students in the class lives with her young son. He has a concert planned for the end of the semester for which he is sending out press releases. At some point in the discussion, the class decides to host a fair for the children in the housing complex on the Saturday when the chorus sings. They will use the community room, and each student will set up a table. I quickly realize this will be a terrific opportunity for me to see what each student has developed for her or his project and also will provide an opportunity to conduct both formal interviews as well as have informal conversations as I rove from table to table.

Barbara spends some time hearing from Timothy the "angle" for his final paper, and they end up in a discussion about the resurgence of anti-war music with the invasion of Iraq, the flap over the Dixie Chicks anti-war songs, and how music plays such an important part of Timothy's life. He explains to the class how important it has been for him to bring something personal to this project, and also how the personal helps make a bridge for him to the political.

International Child-to-Child Communication

Zena is the next student to discuss her project, and she says that she is still trying to sort out a plan. She knows that her goal is to expand her elementary students' perspectives on the world and she wants to create some contact with children living in different countries via some form of Internet communication. Zena explains that she has found a site that promotes exchanges for students in other countries who are learning English, so she is hoping that will work out.

Protecting Wetlands

Cathy is the next student to present her project, and there is much more back-and-forth between Barbara and her. She is already a teacher of a multiage class and the seven- and eight year-olds are in the midst of a large project related to wetlands. Cathy took the opportunity created by some recent school building renovations to get permission to have her class design a wetlands nature trail. She wrote a Learn and Serve grant (this is also what funded much of Rebecca Jim's Tar Creek work—see Chapter 1) to fund materials purchases. Cathy also contacted the Rogers Environmental Education Center, in Sherburne, New York, and some environmental scientists have been coming to her class to teach about the plants and animals of this wetlands area. The children are creating the text for the nature trail signs, and Cathy worked with the high school technology class to actually make the signs. Her students have been taking turns making public presentations about the project, including to the Board of Education, the Rotary Club, the Lion's Club, and to their entire school community. They are also giving tours to other classes in the school.

In a subsequent interview when Cathy tells me her goals, I hear her careful attention to issues of privilege and positioning, which are so central to the Curriculum as Social Action class:

> I've been really trying to get the parents involved; that was my big goal, too, besides letting the kids really feel like they have a responsibility to work in their community or to work on environmental kinds of things. There's a group of parents who might not feel as comfortable coming into the school, and I'm trying to get them to feel comfortable coming to our wetlands to help with something ... In a few weeks we're having a whole parent day, on a Saturday, where everybody can come and bring their shovels and their wet gear and start digging. And that way we're really getting a lot of parents involved that have some background, because they have outside jobs ... I'm hoping that they're going to feel more confident to come in and share that with our class and be part of our class that way.

By creating a space for some working class parents' authentic expertise, she is attending consciously to relationships of power in the school setting. She understands that many of her poor and working-class parents do not feel as comfortable or as entitled as the middle-class and educated parents do to participate in school activities. In fact, we have much research documenting this pattern (Heath, 1983; Jones, 2006; Lareau, 2003), yet too many interventions designed to increase family involvement in schools do not take relationships of power into consideration. Instead, parents are expected to learn behaviors that the middle-class school values (Auerbach, 2007; Lareau & Horvant, 1999). In contrast to this traditional (and deficit-oriented) model of teachers training parents, Cathy uses this project as a mechanism to have parents with outdoor experience and laboring skills be authentically valued members of the school community.

Later, in an interview, Cathy explains how thinking about social action influenced her science curriculum planning:

> We've done biomes before, but we've never done the wetlands as a biome. So when I started taking classes with Barbara and learning about social action, I really started focusing on the community around us. I threw out some of my desert and rainforest stuff. We have a forest out back and we have a river that runs through our town, so we focused more on the river, and the forest, and wetlands this year.

Cathy went on to say that the class helped her "voice more confidently" that she wants her curriculum to foster her students' relationships and connections with people besides just their classmates and teachers. She explains that it's a small town and, "In a few years these kids are going to be the adults of the town and it would benefit everybody if they cared about each other and especially about the land."

Parenting-Assistance Calendar and Soldier-Care Bags

Claire is the next student to explain her project, and she is working on two things: a home–school newsletter and soldier care bags. She explains the home–school newsletter first:

> For parents who have children between ages birth and five, every month teachers send home a newsletter with a monthly calendar where every day you write in, "Here's something you should do with your child." And I did two of those last year and I loved them because it's something every day that [they] don't need a lot of money to do. Because we have a lot of parents who don't know what to do with their kids, so once a week you'll write in, "Read your child a book." And then for one day you can write, "Whisper 'I love you' in your child's ear" or "Just sit with them

and hold them for one minute." I mean just simple, simple things you can do but things that parents need to know that they don't always know.

Listening to her, I am struck by the contrast between Claire's deficit construction of parents and Cathy's search for authentic participation based on parents' strengths. It is obvious to me that projects called "social action" are greatly influenced by the teacher's own critical consciousness. How, I wonder, will Barbara handle this? After all, they have just spent approximately an hour and half with her study guide questions that ask students to probe for questions of privilege and power. Barbara's only question about this project to Claire is, "Do they respond to the newsletters, do you know?" She is probing here for evidence of impact and take-up. It is a gentle nudge to pay attention—as they have been discussing in the Obama book—to the connections and stories of "the other."

Claire reports that, "Yes, parents love the newsletters," and then goes on to tell the second part of her project. Every month her first grade class focuses on a character education word, and this month's word is *cooperation*. All the students will bring in addresses for any soldiers they know who are in the war and they will create packages to send to them:

> "Hee-Haw for Heroes," which is where a child writes a joke, something just cutesy, something that's very elementary humor, send it out along with two tubes of toothpaste, "One for you and one to share." So if the soldier sees somebody who never gets any mail they can share it with them. Which we thought would go really well with cooperation and sharing.

When I hear her explanation, I am grateful to be sitting at the very back of the classroom, because as a researcher I never want to have my internal evaluations of things I hear leak out to my research participants. But I am holding my breath a bit, struck at this distant notion of cooperation with someone twice removed and also saddened at a character education curriculum with such a limited goal of one word a month. Yet even more than this, I wonder what Barbara—who has made her active membership in Teachers for Peace clear to everyone—will say. Does Barbara think a soldier care package is a good example of a social action project? Does it meet her goals? I offer the subsequent classroom dialogue to illustrate the very gentle nudging of Barbara's pedagogy, and of the way that the other students take it up, so it truly is a discussion, rather than just a back-and-forth between one student and the professor (see p. 181 in Appendix for transcription notations):

> Barbara: That's fine. I want the class to know that I asked Claire to connect with Christina. Those of you on the listerv will see her name.
> Student: Students for Peace and Justice list?

Barbara: Yeah. She's the head of that and she's in the Student Environmental Action League. She e-mailed me this morning that because the students have been very visible in anti-war work, they're being perceived as anti-soldier. And she wanted to be involved in some kind of care package arrangement. So she wanted to know if I had any connections with any schools that were doing it. She would like to shift the focus of it and have something about the promotion of peace go into the packages. And Claire was open to talking to her. So I'd like to put them together so that it has a little more - - - because, you know, ideally, there would also be thought about how to make care packages for Iraqi people.

Student: But with our district we thought that would be too controversial. We have too many parents come in that are very anti-Iraqi and to make/

Student: We're starting that. My friend, Athena and I are going to get started on the same thing.

Barbara: Oh, you're doing that in your/

Student: Yeah, she's a third grade teacher there and she came to me last week.

Barbara: About care packages for/

Student: Iraqi children.

Barbara: Yeah. It might be one of those cases where you can do more than you think you can; that you could take a risk that you don't think you can take, given who you are and how you're seen, how you're so highly regarded. But I think we might not have time for how long a discussion it is. We discussed these kinds of issues at Teachers for Peace.

In this exchange, Barbara signals that this topic is really complicated ("we might not have time for how long a discussion it is"). She also wants the class to know that she is nudging Claire to expand her thinking and open up to the possibility that the care packages could be oriented in some small way toward peace.

Yet I see something else important here, besides the professor's hopeful nudging, i.e., Barbara has made it abundantly clear that she is against the U.S. war in Iraq, but Claire still feels safe enough in this class to bring in her support of the U.S. military personnel. Admittedly, one can be against a government's war and still want to support the soldiers. Yet, as Claire already had her newsletter project, she did not even have to mention the soldier care packages. That she did, gives me an indication that students in this class felt quite free to negotiate their own meanings for this social action project.

Newcomers' Photography Project

Stacey is the next to talk about her project, which she is doing with Rose. It is designed to engage elementary children who are learning English in a community photography project. The two student teachers were inspired by the book *Material World* (Menzel & Mann, 1995) that documents statistically average families from thirty-two different countries and includes a big picture with each family's material possessions displayed in front of their home. They plan to work with the library in Ithaca to present a showing of the children's photographs about what matters to them in their lives. They explain the rationale: "Like I wrote in the letter about all the misunderstanding in the world right now, we need to understand others' cultures and where they come from, and different perspectives. Hopefully the library will see that this will be a beneficial thing to do."

I am reminded of the way that Rebecca Jim (see Chapter 1) created opportunities for the Miami High School students' social action work to have a public audience, and again of Bomer and Bomer's (2001) advice that unless teachers help create authentic audiences for the students' justice-oriented inquiries, that we are just teaching children to "talk to walls" (p. 157). Much of the scaffolding that Barbara does for her student teachers is help them develop those authentic audiences. Additionally, of course, it is those audiences who often learn from, and are moved by, the project content. In this way, the children become the teachers, and the community members are their students.

Becoming a Teacher-Activist

Tina was the next student to present about her work, which she called "a hodgepodge of things." She ended up writing her paper on her struggles to be both an activist and a teacher, particularly in light of her search for her first teaching position and not wanting to "burn bridges."

In class that night—with some prompting from Barbara—Tina talked about a curriculum unit she had developed with Stacey called, "Mahatma, Martin and Me." The unit is designed to help elementary school "kids organize community projects and ... help kids realize that they don't have to wait for the grown-ups in their world to act, that they can make changes in their own community ... and help kids coordinate community projects." At the end of the semester, Tina told me about presenting the unit at the Binghamton Area Reading Council. It was her first professional conference presentation, and she explained how she thinks about her role of teacher-activist: "If I'm doing this unit in my classroom, that's great, but to spread it to other classrooms, even if they just take a book or a single activity that we did, it's really important." She also shared with me that when she went to the conference she deliberately wore her peace button, and that she was very nervous about this, but that it sparked good discussions. Upon hearing this, I realized that for many young and beginning teachers, small acts such as wearing a peace button could be much more weighted than I realize. Schools, in so many ways, are designed to be conserving institutions, so for a teacher to engage in unconventional behavior can often take a fair amount of courage. (It still strikes me as sad, however, that advocating for peace is controversial and unconventional.)

Toxic Waste

Mark admits that his project is "still getting off the ground," but he has connected with a research team from the university that is studying a neighborhood with high rates of cancer and a toxic waste site. He has identified a fifth grade classroom to present information to and then plans to help the students do some follow up research about the links between carcinogens and cancer. He thinks he'd "Like them to maybe write some letters to who - - - - I'm not sure who we're going to be writing to yet. That's the last part." Barbara then asks Mark, "Is your hope that the teachers will develop a bigger curriculum around it?"

"Oh, I don't think so," he replies,

> "I don't have that hope. But if it happens, that would be great. I've talked to a few teachers about it, but I don't have any commitments yet, so I mean I can't say what sort of - - - what is going to spring from it, but that would be great. And this - - I mean this is-it's going to be going on well into May. It will be something - - - I'll have something for the first week in May."

Barbara very patiently gives him the name of the scientist who is a friend of hers and did "most of the work spearheading that investigation" of cancer and toxic waste. She writes down his contact information for Mark and says he would be willing to come and talk to the class. I wonder if he will manage to make anything happen by the end of the semester.

Kids' Leadership Retreat

Marge and Renee are last to present and one of them explains to the class, "Our project is kind of about perspective, too, in that within the four walls of the classroom the kids have perspectives of each other, misconceptions about who they are." They take turns describing their collaboration to plan a camping trip for Marge's student teaching third grade classroom of "high-needs kids." They explain that many of the children were put in this class because they have challenging behaviors. "Their needs are not being met," and they have designed a "leadership retreat" around an overnight camping experience with a ropes course and a conflict resolution curriculum. "Just an experience outside of school to see, hopefully, something that they will carry with them once they get back into the classroom and will carry over with them in the classroom." They explain that they do not know how they will gauge the impact of their project, and Barbara reassures them that they do not have to "prove anything in terms of carrying it over to the classroom." She shares some illustrative stories from her own experience working with teenagers in detention facilities and affirms that ropes courses and camping trips are powerful experiences in and of themselves.

Books for Kids

Trish is absent from class that night, but I find out in interviews with students and Barbara that she is working with children in her class to collect books for the waiting rooms of doctors' offices. She has found that many of the poor, rural families with whom she works spend a great deal of time waiting in doctors' offices, and they have to bring all their children because of lack of child care. She decided to solicit book donations, and then have the children in her class organize and inventory them before distributing them throughout the county. She ends up being very successful at getting donations of books and plans to bring many of them to the fair.

Gently Nudging Toward Expansion

I returned to Binghamton on a number of occasions to conduct individual interviews, check in with some students on their social justice projects, and then attend the fair, held at the community center of the public housing project. The fair included tables where each teacher had created something special for children to do in relation to his or her project; they had also prepared a lunch for the children and each other; and then they sang. Without a doubt, when the Peace Chorus sang "We Shall Overcome," it was the highlight for many in the audience, even if the local teenagers snickered the entire time.

The young children in attendance expressed much delight and amazement when they arrived at Trish's booth and found out that they each got to select five books to take home. I heard over and over from the children, "We gets to keep these?" Trish's thoughtfulness very much moved Barbara, and in our closing interview she reflected:

> Trish came to that situation with hundreds of books ... This is what really touched me, that she didn't come with two boxes of books and think, "Well, maybe very few kids will come, we'll just let them take one book." There was such a generosity of spirit about loading up her truck with that many books; it just killed me.

Barbara's attention to "generosity of spirit" made me think of when she shared with the class that she had been brought close to tears by a section of Barack Obama's memoir; I realized that here was educator who could teach me about the emotional/spiritual component of social action projects. No other teacher had moved into this territory. Later, when I had completed all fieldwork and I went back over the interview transcripts, I was struck by how in every single interview I had with students they explained (in one way or another) that caring about others was a centerpiece of what Barbara was trying to get across to them. One student explained it as, "She wants us to take responsibility for a wider and wider community."

This, then, is an understanding of social action as being guided by a deep commitment to, and responsibility for, others. I was intrigued by Barbara's explanation:

> Social action is the work that comes out of any level of increased commitment to the community or to social change at a radical level. But the only value it has is related to the extent to which there's been an opening up: an expansiveness. And then whatever piece of the expansiveness got acted on, that's social action.... The genuine expansiveness sometimes comes after the project is over. The project wasn't really so significant; it was sort of like foreplay. It is the *shift* that matters.

This "shift" toward which Barbara is working was supported by her availability and the emotional tone she set. Barbara's availability had two aspects: the many times throughout class and the semester that she shared her own experiences, feelings, processes, and reflections on her growth; and in very concrete ways by making herself available for individual meetings. This was similar to Eric Rofes (see Chapter 6); he continually encouraged students to come and discuss their organizing projects with him. Barbara, it turns out, had started meeting with students well before the semester even began so they could be contemplating and planning for their social action projects. She launched the work by inviting them to her home for a potluck dinner and brainstorming session. This initial individual negotiation turned out to matter to the majority of students with whom I spoke. One stated: "Barbara has a wonderful ability to allow everyone to be able do their own thing and so a lot of it is individually negotiated with her.... Nobody could do a project without getting it okayed with her, and yet what she would okay is a wide range of stuff."

This level of support was available to students throughout the semester. In class that night in March she closed by saying, "This is the period when I expect to be used as a sounding board and to help you pull things together. And to listen to doubts or worries about your projects. So come see me, okay?" Students mentioned to me that they appreciated how she knew it was hard to do everything they had to do with student teaching and that they always liked it when Barbara acknowledged that any effort they made was worthwhile. Even students who did not start off seeing social action as part of the teacher's job description felt supported to take some steps:

> At first I was very opposed to her, and I resented her sometimes. We have so much to do as teachers, how can you expect me to do this? But she says you can just start it simple. Have one member of the community come into your classroom. Okay, and then once you do that, then that's great because it's part of your classroom. And then after that person comes, how can you maybe make that an every month thing? Then can you do a project in your class that you can take to your community? So she makes it seem simple but you realize, wow, just by doing these little things you can have a social action project that can benefit your community ... I think, oh okay, that is something I can do.

Another student's comments echoed these sentiments as she explained how, in the course of the semester, she moved from a self-focus to a community-focus. This seems to me a powerful aspect of Barbara's pedagogy, which she launched by exploring characters in books.

> When I first started to take the class, I felt very frustrated because I thought, I just want to get my degree, I don't want to have to do these big projects.... And then the weeks have gone on and I find it's a great way to start thinking not just about yourself, which I think I was doing a lot of "This is me, it's my teaching career." I kind of realized as a teacher I have a responsibility not just to myself and to my kids, but to my community.

Barbara was successful in encouraging her students to feel responsible for other people and to deeply care for others because she demonstrated this same sort of caring and responsibility to them. It seems obvious that students will most easily learn these lessons of caring when they feel unconditional regard from the teacher. In this way they do not experience many contradictions between what the teacher preaches and what she actually practices.

I wondered, however, about the gap between the social reconstructionist goals of the course and program, and some of the projects, particularly the home-school newsletter and the one student who had not really taken the time to develop anything around the toxic waste site. How does she think about such cases—the former based on a deficit construction of poor families needing to be told by middle-class teachers how to parent; and the latter, a case of inaction and lack of initiative? How does she provide unconditional regard and at the same time gently nudge students forward? Barbara said that she is willing to accept wherever students are at:

> Just figure out what you can validate, completely honestly, make sure they've done enough to pass the course, and if it's pass/fail you're in great shape with a student like that, and then validate what's good from the

bottom of your heart. And don't criticize. And in years past, I didn't understand that. That's the mistake I make in life. I assume that people have been battered around by the world the way I have and that, okay, they'll get bruised but they'll be fine … And I completely underestimate other people's fragility.

That prompts some information about her spiritual journeying which Barbara credits as having changed her stance towards what she pushes for, and I think must be responsible for so much of the compassionate view and openness her students report to me:

> The spiritual stuff has made me much, much better at this; I've improved tremendously in the last two years. Because I listen better and I have much more compassion for them. But, as a result, I'm also less controlling of "Social Action as Curriculum." In years past, I would demand a project that could get us in trouble or that would be highly visible.

By creating this flexible and accepting space, Barbara made it less complicated for students to figure out what steps they wanted to take. There was no political litmus test or grand notion of radical change required of them.

Every single one of the students I interviewed talked about wanting to take some step to become an activist-oriented teacher. One woman told me that she is willing to take risks that she might not have imagined before taking this class:

> I want to bring things into the classroom that you might not necessarily think you can tackle in the classroom, issues in the community that some people might think kids aren't old enough to handle … I think that a lot of teachers might get scared: "I don't want to address that issue, it's too political. Adults should do the stuff in the community and the kids shouldn't have a role in it." And not being afraid of being labeled as the teacher who's doing all these crazy things.

It was Barbara's radical acceptance of wherever her students were in their movement toward critical consciousness that opened up space for them to take risks to bring social action into their classrooms. "In the end," Barbara tells me, "the bottom line becomes being as kind as possible to them in their own journey of developing their consciousness."

Students consistently expressed that developing their own consciousness was the project of this class. Barbara supported them in this work and gently nudged them to an ever-expanding awareness of others, particularly related to issues of privilege and identity. Even when students did not share all of Barbara's political stances, they understood and agreed with her project:

> And there are some things that she'll do that I don't agree with, that I don't like—like how she makes the war such a political statement in the

classroom. I don't agree with that. However, I have to give her credit, because she is constantly focused on how to make students consciously aware of what's going on.

The idea that teacher education can prepare teachers to look deeply into the perspectives of people in the community, and to become aware of "what's going on" for a wide variety of people, potentially very different from themselves, and to listen carefully to others—with a compassionate stance—is what grounded Barbara Regenspan's approach to teaching for social action. As I prepare to exit the field and end my data collection, somehow in the case of Barbara and her students I hear Marvin Gaye (1971) singing:

> Mother, mother
> There's too many of you crying
> Brother, brother, brother
> There's far too many of you dying
> You know we've got to find a way
> To bring some lovin' here today
> Talk to me, so you can see
> Oh, what's going on
> What's going on
> Ya, what's going on
> Ah, what's going on
> Oh, you know we've got to find a way
> To bring some understanding here today ...

CONCLUSION

Planning Social Action Projects

In the years between starting data collection for this research project and finishing writing the book, the landscape for public education—particularly for urban and rural working-class and poor students—has become increasingly contested. Whether through the influence of the Eli Broad Foundation (Ravitch, 2010), the Gates Foundation (Kovacs, 2010), or federal legislation and funding, a central focus for much of the conversation on public education has been reduced to student scores on standardized tests. Much of this emphasis has been propelled by the No Child Left Behind Act of 2001 that tied test scores directly to punitive consequences. How this single-minded focus on test scores has distorted the public-schooling process is not the focus of this book, but is extremely pertinent to this last chapter and to the work of teachers and school leaders who remain fiercely determined to educate children and youth to become active in shaping the future of local communities and our planet. Many people become teachers because they believe that classroom curriculum can provide students with both windows and mirrors: windows for students to encounter the world in all its complexity, and mirrors to look more closely at, and reflect upon, themselves (Style, 1988). Community-based action projects provide an ideal vehicle for not only learning about the world and one's self, but also for becoming an active participant in shaping the future.

The teachers and students in this book reflect some of the rich diversity of our country. They were: of many races and ethnicities (African American, Asian American, Latina/o, Native American, Pacific Islander, Southeast Asian, multiethnic, and multiracial); gay and straight; living in rural and urban areas and also small towns; both legal citizens and students without documents granting them full rights in this country; students with disabilities and those without. My cases include individuals of all socioeconomic classes; those born in other countries who immigrated to the United States and others who had lived in the same place their entire lives; those living in a Superfund site and others whose apartment buildings were being demolished by the local government.

It is across all these diversities of identity and life experiences and concomitant differential access to privileges and resources that we come together in public schools. The projects, teachers, students, pedagogy, and classrooms profiled here provide specific examples to answer Carlsson-Paige and Lantieri's (2005) question: "How can we make schools places where children learn to make choices that support the individual and collective good and actively engage in making a meaningful difference?" (p. 108).

In this Conclusion to the book, I summarize what I learned from the seven educators featured in the case chapters and their pedagogies that promote civic agency and community action. I include findings across the cases, a framework for planning classroom-based social action projects, tips from the teachers themselves, and challenges for educators to keep in mind when pursuing such projects. I end with attention to the central role of social imagination and the urgency to design curriculum around protecting the commons and advocating for human rights.

What All the Projects Had in Common

Looking across all the classrooms, teachers, and projects, there are many important points about teaching, learning, and activism that could be made. In selecting what to focus on here, I have chosen the findings most salient for educators interested in pursuing such curricula in their own schools: using the project method, learning organizing skills, caring teachers, and teachers as risk takers.

Teaching with the Project Method

The teachers and projects in this study helped students experience school as a place of learning, rather than as a place merely to complete assignments. Instead of mostly answering teacher-posed questions with single correct answers, these students were involved in asking questions, pursuing answers, and taking action outside the classroom. To accomplish this, all the teachers in this study utilized small or large versions of "the project method" (Kilpatrick, 1918).

Rather than organizing instruction around textbook chapters and worksheets, in a project-based approach to curriculum, textbooks chapters and worksheets are sometimes used—as resources to draw upon or to provide focused skills instruction—but the driving goal of the curriculum is to explore something that exists in the world. Thus, learning proceeds from inquiry, and content knowledge and skills are developed as they are needed. As any teacher will tell you, when skills and content are learned and then applied to solve a problem important to students, learning is greatly facilitated. Across all cases in this book, there are countless examples of such skill- and content-knowledge learning, from learning the chemistry needed for water sampling in Tar Creek, to learning how to make pie charts to represent survey data at Byrd Academy.

In the project method, the culmination is when students present their learning in some format; for instance, a poster, a play, a song, a skit, a model, a simulation, a letter, a book, a poem, a puppet show, a report, or an essay. Or in the case of projects in this book, students took action on their inquiries by creating public presentations, such as writing and circulating petitions, organizing outreach and educational campaigns, creating fundraising campaigns, conducting interviews, planning protests, leafleting, conducting surveys, and making public testimony. In large projects such as that of the fifth graders at Byrd Academy (see Chapter 5), the inquiry-presentation cycle was ongoing and overlapping, with many products being prepared and presented at once. But there were also examples in this study of simple and quick presentations, such as the letters Lance Powell's Advanced Placement Environmental Science students wrote to the Bay Conservation and Development Commission (see Chapter 3). More extensive writing also took place; for example, with the Tar Creek project at Miami High School, students in an English class wrote poetry (Kesson & Oyler, 1999) that was later published (see Chapter 1).

Most formats (or genres) for presenting knowledge become forms of advocacy when these presentations gain an audience. Whether it is first graders presenting a play about sweatshop labor (Epstein & Oyler, 2008), or Nova High School students presenting street theater about the World Trade Organization (see Chapter 2), classroom learning about social justice issues can become activism when the products are presented to an audience. Schools, of course, have ready-made audiences of other classes, and peer education is a much under-utilized form of instruction. Even if the student creators of an action project never have an audience beyond their own school, the effects of outreach and education can be powerful.

Learning Organizing Skills

Across all the cases, students learned a wide variety of community organizing and outreach skills. Such skills are crucial to community engagement and social change, and should be at the center of school curricula in order to properly prepare students to engage fully in democratic life. When writing about the importance of learning to take action for responsible global citizenship, Bryan (1993) urges that

> Students must be empowered with practical and strategic skills to resist and transform unjust social conditions…. Given our planet's present condition and dilemmas, it should be clear that students must do more than learn to *think about* social problems…. Students must also learn to *act* in

new ways to create preferable and sustainable conditions for humanity. (pp. 251–252)

In the classrooms in this research project, teachers scaffolded their students' skills and knowledge about such community action and organizing skills by making sure students had access to what Kirshner (2008) has termed "mature civic participation practices" (p. 94). Students gained access to these practices through a variety of texts and people.

Brian Schultz and Eric Rofes provided access to these practices of civic participation through very accessible organizing manuals (Bobo et al., 2001; Isaac, 1992; Shepard & Hayduk, 2002). These volumes offer detailed instruction in what Isaac calls the tools of citizens' movements. Shepard and Hayduk's *From Act Up to the WTO* was an important reading for Eric's Humboldt State University undergraduates as they had told him that they wanted to read about contemporary organizing strategies, and not just the techniques from the 1960s, 70s, and 80s (see Chapter 6). In addition to these how-to manuals, as we learned from Barbara Regenspan, students can also draw inspiration and knowledge from fiction and memoir (see Chapter 7). Her students read about the community organizing of Barack Obama (1998); they also read other writings by teachers and activists that offered compelling narratives to spark students' creativity and provide concrete examples of specific organizing techniques.

Additionally, all the teachers had guest speakers come to class and/or had students engage in community interviews. Guest speakers were particularly important to Brian Shultz who had the least experience with activism, and who had the most guest speakers of any teacher in this study. Community-based organizations and non-profits were an excellent source in providing guest speakers for all teachers in this book; sometimes the speaker was actually a guest teacher who arrived with materials, resources, and lesson plans. The other very important mechanism for providing students access to the practices of organizing and community engagement came via the community interview. Used in a variety of different ways by teachers in this study, it was most formalized by Derrlyn Tom (see Chapter 4). In conducting community interviews, students can study the range of adult thinking on an issue and can come to realize that people committed to working on the same issue do not always agree on the roots of the problem or the solutions.

Equally important, in the process of conducting interviews with community members, students are entering into formal conversation with people outside their familiar circle of friends, family, teachers, and schoolmates. For many of the students in this study, this was a unique experience and had the benefit of increasing their abilities to engage in oral dialogue so central to sustaining any democratic project. In the case of the fifth graders at Byrd Academy who repeatedly interviewed community members whom they had invited to their classroom, the assistant principal remarked on the students' increased confidence and body language when interacting with the visitors. Noting that many of the students at the school were very shy with people from outside their community, she took great pleasure in watching children hold "their heads up a little higher" (see Chapter 5).

Learning through Teachers' Caring

The students I interviewed in all the cases were extremely moved by their teachers' commitments to social and environmental justice. Recall, for instance, Enita, who said of Derrlyn Tom that she's "defending people's rights," and Thomas who said that Joe Szwaja teaches "from the heart." So in addition to the technical skills of organizing, students also learned from their teachers' commitments to justice, equity, and activism. More than all the other civic-participation practices, the most significant may actually be the stance these teachers modeled of civic agency. Students knew their teachers or professors had strong commitments to actively working for justice and admired them greatly for it.

Additionally, consistent across all the student interviews I conducted, the students spontaneously reported that their teacher was very caring toward them. These teachers demonstrated not only caring for the common good and social justice, but also for individual students. They seem to believe that through our investment in each other, we can make this world a better place. This is ultimately a very optimistic view of human life and one that signals a deep respect for individual people. Across all the cases, each teacher was acknowledged as one who really cares about students. In some cases this caring was expressed by teachers who held extremely high academic and behavioral standards, resulting in opportunities for students to learn habits and modes of interaction that will undoubtedly carry over into new social arenas.

Teachers as Learners and Risk Takers

The teachers in this study also had high standards for themselves and saw themselves as always learning. Derrlyn Tom said, "I want [my students] to understand that so much of what I'm doing is I'm learning as I do it, too." And Lance Powell explained, " I feel like I'm learning so much all the time. I'm still learning probably as much as the kids are collectively." Brian Schultz positioned himself as a white person learning from the African American families and community. Rebecca Jim—even at the end of her long career—followed student initiations for the Fish Dance and delighted in how much everyone learned. Eric Rofes—in almost every class session—shared with his students the recent lessons he'd learned about organizing. Barbara Regenspan shared privately with me how she had been learning to support the emotional aspect of working with teachers to develop critical consciousness and how difficult it is to ask people to confront their privileges and take a stand toward equity and social justice in school where so often teachers are asked to help maintain the status quo.

Across all the cases, the teachers were seemingly untroubled by taking risks and stepping outside the bounds of the traditional teacher role. These were teachers who did not mind expanding the carefully circumscribed role of teacher as dispenser of received knowledge and teacher as maintainer of order and wisdom. Instead, in every case, these teachers took chances and stretched the time and resource bounds of their positions. They seemed to be guided by their passion for the world and its people. They had their own clear vision of the role of teacher—and it was not as a tester of discreet knowledge on a standardized test or weekly quiz. Rather, it was as igniter of agency and of connection to the world. These were teachers who were focused outward on the world, and on the collective good rather than individual gain. Most of all, they were risk-takers who did not share with me any worries about what other people thought. (Of course, they may have harbored such worries and just not spoken with me about them.) They seemed perfectly willing to tread new ground. As one teacher explained to me, "I don't like the status quo; I just really can't stand that. And I know that's not what my parents wanted … that's not how they raised me … I was supposed to be good and follow the rules."

This commitment to taking a risk enables teachers to step outside the walls of the classroom and help students take deliberative action in the community. Such work offers a strong counter-narrative to schooling as a place to preserve the status quo and learn compliance with authority. As Howard Zinn (2002) notes

> This mixing of activism and teaching, this insistence that education cannot be neutral on the crucial issues of our time, this movement back and forth from the classroom to the struggles outside by teachers who hope their students will do the same, has always frightened the guardians of traditional education. They prefer that education simply prepare the new generation to take its proper place in the old order, not to question that order. (p. 7)

A Framework for Social Action Projects in the Classroom

By opening up their classrooms to a researcher, the teachers in this book all contributed to our collective understanding of pedagogical possibilities for integrating social action projects into the public school curriculum. Looking across the seven cases—and guided in part by the extensive literature on service learning—I have identified six aspects that form a basic framework for social action pedagogy.

1. The teacher overtly values equity, justice, and the common good. It is the teacher's commitment to equity, justice, and striving toward the common good that stimulates curricular planning of social action projects. As teachers are the gatekeepers for classroom assignments and also decide on most texts that are brought to students' attention, the decisions they make shape the direction of the project. Our planet has no shortage of local and global problems that need solutions, so the possibilities for organizing curriculum around matters of justice are limitless. Teachers who value equity, justice, and the common good also serve as exemplars for their students and offer reassurance to students that although the world's problems are large, it is possible, even desirable, not to give in to pessimism but to organize for more just outcomes. Finally, with an overt valuing of the common good, teachers present a mode of thinking and being that is counter to the individualist culture that circulates so strongly through much of contemporary life. As Gloria Ladson-Billings (2005) has pointed out,

> In less than 100 years, the economic pressures of our highly technological society [have] forced citizens to concentrate more on their own well-being and less on a notion of the public good.... The emphasis on *homo economicus* moved the society from one made up of public citizens to one dominated by corporate citizens. (p. 72)

Teachers who overtly value the common good offer a vision of public engagement directed to matters of justice and equity rather than individual gain.

2. The teacher designs instruction for student voice and decision-making.

By designing pedagogy to allow for student voice and decision-making, teachers create opportunities for education directed toward liberation rather than indoctrination. Without including specific pedagogical mechanisms for students to make real decisions about what they say and what they do, the teacher owns the action project, and students are consumers of his or her decisions, rather than agents of civic action. Although allowing for student decision-making can often slow down the movement towards action, engaging in such deliberation helps ensure that the students own the decisions and actions. Creating space and mechanisms for student input and decision-making does not mean that the teacher completely defers to students. This is a common misunderstanding of student voice and decision-making: that to promote it, teachers must step aside and not offer their input. This stance of stepping aside, however, is an abdication of authority (Oyler & Becker, 1997) and positions power as a zero-sum game, rather than as continually circulating in the discourses and relationships (Foucault, 1980) among teachers and students. Teachers should also understand that even when space has been created for student voice, and most decisions are actually made by them, the teacher still has much influence, stemming in large part from their commitments to equity, justice, and the common good. Finally, no matter how much the project is based on student decision making, the teacher is ultimately responsible for all actions students take, so the teacher must exercise wise counsel in mediating actions in the community.

3. The teacher helps students situate problems, building content knowledge and conceptual and socio-historical understandings.

Real-world problems are complicated. Most problems that lend themselves to activism and advocacy have complex histories and require learning new content and concepts in order to engage in problem solving and action planning. Many times the content and the concepts are brought into the planned curriculum by the teacher and are determined at the start of the unit or project. However, teachers can also use community-based agencies, community interviews, and guest speakers for curricular infusion throughout the course of the project. In this way, teachers are learning new content alongside their students; many times this content is brought into the classrooms by the students themselves. It is important to underscore that although many concepts and much content knowledge may be shared by all the students in the class, there is room for much differentiation in project-based work; therefore individual assessment of students' knowledge and understanding becomes very important.

Central to activism projects is a commitment to explore the root causes of the problem at hand. Helping students untangle complicated histories, competing interests, and even advertising, media, and propaganda is a critical undertaking. Teachers should not enter this terrain naively, as special interest groups and corporations may have powerful influence and reasons to protect their self interests. It is also important to acknowledge that people who analyze the root of problems are often criticized. I am reminded of Helder Camera—a Brazilian archbishop—who is quoted as saying, "When I give food to the poor, they call me a saint. When I ask why the poor have no food, they call me a Communist" (Rocha, 2000, p. 53). It is important for teachers to know in advance that helping students pursue root causes of structural inequality, injustice, environmental racism, or discrimination may not be acceptable to all members of the community. Thus, to protect the integrity of the project, it becomes important to bring multiple viewpoints into the classroom.

4. The teacher makes room for multiple viewpoints.

When teachers organize classroom instruction around community action projects that tackle complicated social or environmental issues, it is inevitable that there are multiple viewpoints on both the source of the problem and the solution. That is why many teachers who plan social action curriculum require their students to investigate multiple explanations for the problem and also what various people think are appropriate solutions before finalizing plans for their own action. In this way, the actions that are taken are deliberative. Students can listen to different opinions and come to understand that most issues have multiple viewpoints. Structuring the investigation of multiple viewpoints helps prepare students for pluralism and also for entering the democratic fray.

Teachers who organize classroom curriculum around social action projects must also be prepared to create opportunities to facilitate disagreements and differing viewpoints among class members. Students usually have to be taught how to debate and dialogue respectfully, and many students need to be continually reminded that people often disagree about important matters. Even when the class agrees on an activism goal, they may still disagree about tactics or strategy. Teachers must help students engage in the process of coming to a decision: either by consensus, by voting, or by dividing into smaller groups based on affinity of ideas.

When creating room for multiple viewpoints in the classroom and curriculum, it is important for teachers to help students think about the different outcomes that can accrue from different opinions, viewpoints, and orientations. That is, rather than merely strive for providing *a balance of opinions*, teachers should also help students analyze what the possible outcomes are for various perspectives. "That's just my opinion," and, "Everyone's entitled to their own opinion," are simplistic phrases that need to be challenged, because they do not require the speaker to spin out the possible consequences of their opinion. When bringing in multiple viewpoints to the classroom, teachers should help students ask, "Who benefits, who loses, who decides?" thus establishing critical analysis of competing viewpoints and interests.

5. The teacher enables students to learn skills of community organizing outreach, and/or advocacy.

The central premise of social action, advocacy, and activism is direct engagement with other humans to work towards improvement of the human condition and the common good. (One can also engage with other humans to create new products or new markets but that is most often undertaken with the goal of individual gain, rather than the public good.) Social action projects are most often aimed at structural change, including efforts to influence legislation or formal policies (school, school district, local municipalities, state, federal, international). Social action projects may also be directed towards the creation of programs, such as educational or outreach campaigns. Finally, social action projects may be directed toward organizing new groups, committees, coalitions, or organizations.

Within social action projects, teachers can provide opportunities for students to learn a great variety of skills, including, but not limited to:

1. Researching the issue and viewpoints on the issue;
2. Analyzing and reporting the issue;
3. Developing a viewpoint on the issue;
4. Creating an action plan with goals, strategies, tactics, timeline, and task analysis;
5. Creating a persuasive argument and a genre for presenting it (statements, poetry, essays, letters, posters, plays, street theater, leaflets, website, blog, mural, educational tours, research studies that include data presented with charts and graphs);

6. Presenting the persuasive argument to others: at the school, in the local area, to family and friends, to elected officials, to the media;
7. Reflecting on and analyzing the progress and results of the work and making plans for next steps.

Within these larger skills, there are a wide variety of sub-skills embedded at each step; for example, teachers can guide students to engage in dialogue with peers or conduct secondary and primary research. Students also have ongoing opportunities to learn and practice academic and artistic skills that are necessary for different genres such as oral communication, written expression, dramatic expression, visual artistry, or technological skills related to computing.

What distinguishes social action projects from volunteer-oriented service is that students are involved in learning some of the skills listed above and are making decisions about what actions are taken or what arguments are made.

6. The teacher creates opportunities for students to reflect and evaluate process and outcomes.

A key feature of service learning is the opportunity to reflect on the service and on one's learning. When service takes the form of social action, the "service" is expressed as community organizing, lobbying, petitioning, researching community opinions or needs, speaking with the media, offering public testimony, demonstrating, protesting, leafleting, picketing, letter writing, etc. Across all these possible actions, students' reflections and evaluations can and should be prompted, scaffolded, documented, and shared.

Using the recommendations outlined by Rahima Wade (1997) for service learning and applying them to community-based action projects, teachers can design reflection and evaluation activities for students across the following categories:

- The events of the week;
- An individual's own personal learning, preferences, and growth;
- The people with whom students are working, including the characteristics, needs, and beliefs;
- The act of community involvement and activism, including people's beliefs and values about community participation;
- Knowledge about the broader societal issue;
- The role and behaviors of community members in a participatory democracy.

Teachers can provide questions for student reflection within each area (Wade offers specific prompts within each of her categories, see pp. 99–102). Students' oral and written answers to the questions can serve as points of discussion to promote further reflection, and also can serve as data for assessment of student learning. It behooves all teachers committed to community-based activism projects to provide systematic and ongoing opportunities for student reflection.

Tips from the Teachers

Although I cannot possibly know or adequately represent all the motivations for the teachers in this book, I *do* know that they were all interested in helping other teachers engage their students in social action projects. Accordingly, on a number of occasions teachers offered specific tips and said that I should be sure to highlight them for other teachers.

1. In many of the cases, students were interviewed by journalists for print, television, or radio. Therefore, whenever students are going to an event where there may be press in attendance, teachers should be certain to get media release forms signed by parents or guardians in advance. One teacher in this study (who wishes to remain anonymous) learned this the hard way from taking the class to a demonstration where television reporters interviewed students. That night, on the local television news, the students were excited to see themselves. However, the next day, the teacher was called into the principal's office and told in no uncertain terms that before allowing students to talk to the press, parent/guardian media release forms must be collected.

2. As Derrlyn Tom points out, it is very helpful to write grants to secure external funding. She wrote grants that covered transportation for field trips, tape recorders for interviews, and money to pay for substitute teachers for when she went on fieldtrips. Rebecca Jim wrote grants for water testing equipment. As both women explained to me, it is much easier to get permission from school administrators to engage in actions when not asking for money.

3. Teachers discussed the importance of being flexible and contingently responsive in instructional planning. For example, the Thurgood Marshall Academic High School (TMAHS) ninth grade team switched its plans in order to take action on an authentic case (see Chapter 3). Authentic projects often emerge after teachers have planned their month, semester, or year curricular calendar. Because the TMAHS teaching team had co-planning time built into their schedule, they were able to decide to integrate an issue of local concern into their special urban challenge mini-unit. Helping students learn to deliver public testimony not only fit the larger goals of the curriculum unit, but it also helped students delve deeply into a matter that was so explosive that it provoked a student walk out. In this way, teachers were able to harness student concerns and teach them practices of "mature civic participation" (Kirshner, 2008). This sort of curricular flexibility may not always be present in schools where teachers are held accountable to a pacing calendar, a prescriptive curriculum, or collaboratively planned units of study. However, if opportunities do arise—from a local issue, strong student interest, or resources from a non-profit or community-based organization—there are often ways to integrate even small amounts of time for a project. Teachers need to be pro-active in

articulating how the action project responds to the goals and objectives for which they are accountable. In so many cases, the goals and aims of the curriculum are broad and basic, and thus the skills and knowledge learned in action projects often do indeed meet state and local standards.

4. All the teachers in this study describe how they worked to create and maintain open lines of communication with other adults in their school setting. They all had visibly strong relationships with secretarial and support staff, and they each had some strong peer relationships. At every single site the teacher had a list of colleagues and/or administrators for me to interview. In other words, engaging in social action curriculum was undertaken with a visible commitment to build respectful and communicative relationships with the people in the school or university community. None of these teachers exhibited a "lone wolf" perspective where they went off and did "their own thing."

Challenges of Doing Social Action Projects in Schools

For educators interested in designing curriculum around social action projects—which may be local or globally oriented—many challenges (and opportunities) certainly exist. I describe five of these challenges below.

Current Emphasis on Testing

Perhaps the largest challenge facing educators committed to civic education, community-based learning, and social justice-oriented curriculum is the narrowing of the curriculum that has occurred in the context of neo-liberal policies in education (see Lipman, 2011; Ross & Gibson, 2007). In this view of schooling, student learning is represented by standardized test score numbers, and much of what is tested is only limited aspects of reading, writing, and mathematics. Although many of these tests were supposedly developed to measure student learning of state standards, most exams only measure a fraction of these standards. None of the state achievement tests is designed to assess students' interest in solving local and global problems, nor do they measure students' skills at dialoguing across difference, sense of political efficacy and community-commitment, or knowledge of how to engage in advocacy or activism. By reducing "learning" to narrow test scores and by attaching punitive measures such as school closings and teacher evaluations to those scores, the public notion of what comprises a well-educated person is stripped of much of the content, concepts, skills, and dispositions central to preparing young people to assume full membership in local and global communities.

With the mission and purpose of public schooling so contested, it may be difficult for many teachers—particularly new ones—to carve out space for community-based activism projects. Yet, numerous teachers are doing just that. Teachers who make time for integrated projects—and who engage in dynamic assessment practices (Goodwin, 1997)—can plan for academic skill development in the context and alongside civic engagement. Academic skills and community-based projects do not have to be an either/or proposition. As demonstrated by Derrlyn Tom, high academic standards can be integrated with community-based learning. And as was seen in Brian Schultz's classroom, when he integrated his curriculum around the activism project, school attendance went up, and some of his students' test scores displayed dramatic increases. Most important, and across all classrooms in this study, students articulated a sense of efficacy and agency about community involvement. By learning some tools of civic engagement, students leave the classroom with specific strategies for tackling matters of concern.

One of the very best reasons to invest time and energy in activist projects is that students are almost always enthusiastic to participate. Young children through university students are typically very eager to begin this process by identifying social issues of concern to them. As Cathy—one of the teachers in Barbara Regenspan's master's class—explained when asked what advice she had for teachers,

> I just think it's not as hard as people think that it is. If you want to do a project and you're not sure about what to do, your goal should be to affect the students in your classroom. Because if you just have a conversation with your kids about, "Let's do something for somebody. What's something that we're worried about? What's something that we can change? What's something that we can help?" you're going to get twenty ideas in about two minutes. And then their excitement is just amazing, and you've kind of put that spark into them, and then they'll start thinking of other things, "Let's do this next." Then you've planted that seed in twenty kids and hopefully they'll take it on to the next year.… I think if people are nervous about it they should start off small because I really think it's … easier than people think and I think that the excitement from it is definitely worth it. And [the students' excitement] fuels you to keep going.

Under-Resourced Conditions

Although pressures on schools to raise standardized test scores are very strong, there are additional pressures that affect teachers who seek to plan classroom curriculum around community-based activist projects. These stem from limited resources. Since in most of the United States per-pupil funding is tied to local property taxes, most rural and urban schools experience significant resource hardships, and the K–12 schools in this research were no exception. Thus, each of the teachers in this book had to deal with limited resources, although none of them belabored this point during our time together—in large part, I think, because they were working very cooperatively with their administrators and did not want to be seen as complaining in any way. Still, Lance

Powell had thirty-five students in his Advanced Placement Environmental Science class, and walking among students as he supervised small group work required a lot of agility. Derryln Tom and Rebecca Jim wrote grants to fund their work. Brian Schultz and his class had broken lights in the classroom and, many days, no heat. Nova High School teachers consistently rummaged for materials and supplies and had to be thrifty in their purchases.

Whatever the circumstances, it is indisputable that limited resources do make teaching with community action projects more challenging than in well-resourced public or independent schools. Yet, as we discovered in the case of Nova High School, school funding itself can become a point of student inquiry. And as we saw at Thurgood Marshall Academic High School, students can also become involved in school district policies. One of the best sources to help compensate for school underfunding is the generosity of community-based organizations and activists who can be seen playing such a strong role in every single one of the classrooms in this book. Although some of the actual instruction I observed that was conducted by organizers and activists was sometimes weak—didactically passing on information rather than engaging students in interactive learning—they always brought a wealth of material and knowledge with them that the classroom teacher was then able to build upon. Also, it always struck me how terrific it was for students to see organizing and activism as possible career paths because of their interactions with these community workers.

Demands on Teacher Time

In addition to having limited resources, teachers also have to be organized and efficient when planning projects that involve the community. Getting students into the community or getting the community into the classroom (guest speakers) requires communicating with a number of people before or after school hours, or during an open prep period. Thus, teachers investing in community activism projects also have to use their time well, and plan ahead. Then, when field trips are arranged, substitutes are needed at the junior and senior high school level, and transportation and lunches must be figured out. It definitely takes a commitment of time, organization, and energy to bring the students to the community and the community to the students.

Another time-consuming aspect of teaching with social action projects relates to the importance of bringing in multiple points of view. Unlike teachers who use primarily one textbook in their teaching, teachers committed to helping students sort out complex social and environmental issues must seek out materials for students. These materials must be accessible to a wide range of readers and learners, so require additional teacher time to triage. Perhaps, for instance, there is a point of view on a topic that has not been discussed by the students, yet all the material the teacher finds is at a very sophisticated reading level. This might mean planning a special lesson aimed at teaching students how to tackle complex text, or it might mean asking a couple of advanced readers to develop a PowerPoint presentation for the class for extra credit. (Teachers taking this option would, of course, want to offer suitable extra credit options for all other readers as well.)

Dependency on Teachers' Critical Consciousness

Another challenge for educators interested in community action projects relates to the critical consciousness of the teacher. In every single one of the cases in this book, it was the teacher's commitment to equity, justice, or the protection of the commons that prompted the classroom curriculum. The challenge inherent in this is that cultural norms pervade all our public spaces, and schools are certainly no exception. Most teachers have grown up in schools that do not educate for critical consciousness related to matters of privilege, racism and white supremacy, collective action of oppressed peoples, globalization, gentrification, consumerism, environmental racism, imperialism, or capitalist supports for corporations. Yet, these are the very issues that undergird so many relationships and structures in local, state, and national political and social life. Therefore, when teachers educate for critical consciousness, their day-to-day classroom curriculum is shaped at least partially by the questions they ask and the resources they bring in.

If a teacher has particularly strong consciousness about how inequity is structured and experienced, then they will be attentive to these matters in their social action curriculum. Recall, for instance, Derrlyn Tom's decision not to accept a community-based organization's request that her students come and study/learn in a wealthy section of San Francisco, stating instead that her students' own neighborhoods needed their attention (see Chapter 4). Or Eric Rofes's strong feminist and anti-racist consciousness that motivated him to offer direct instruction in coalition politics (see Chapter 6). And Brian Schultz who made certain to tie his fifth grade African American students' appeal for a decent school building to the history of U.S. African American activists' struggles for educational equity in the previous century (see Chapter 5).

The fact that every teacher is limited by his or her own critical consciousness should be no deterrent to this work. Instead, this means that teachers need to network with educators and non-profits committed to socially just community action. In cities across the United States, teachers and activists have been creating groups similar to San Francisco's Teachers for Social Justice (see Chapter 4) and organizing annual curriculum fairs. For example, the New York Collective of Radical Educators (a New York City-based group) organizes ongoing Inquiry to Action groups designed to support teachers' curriculum development in their classrooms and also to support teachers who are activists for public education beyond their own classrooms. Some networks and support mechanisms can also be found online, such as the Education for Liberation Network "How Did They Do That? Project" (http://hdtdt.edliberation.org/).

For teachers interested in designing curriculum around social action, probably the very best set of resources is published by *Rethinking Schools* (http:// www. rethinkingschools.org). Their curriculum guides are extensive and their magazine routinely publishes articles written by teachers about exciting work they are doing in their classrooms, schools, and communities. They also have a lively listserv that is useful for teachers' networking.

The importance of networking and dialoging with other educators and with parents and community members is central to guiding the teacher in this social justice-oriented work. No matter how experienced a teacher, or well-grounded a teacher may be in collective organizing or in anti-oppressive education (Adams, Bell, & Griffin, 2007; Kumashiro, 2000), teachers with commitments to justice and equity know that lifelong learning is most critical. All social movements and all humans make mistakes, and we operate continually with limited knowledge and information. If we waited to act until we knew everything and could have guaranteed outcomes, we would never act. Therefore, we must collaborate and dialogue with others and learn together as we create school curriculum designed specifically to prepare young people to engage with the local and global community as deliberative civic agents. By working collaboratively with other teachers, students' families, and community members, our own critical consciousness can be honed. If a teacher's critical consciousness is well-developed, particularly in matters of privilege, power, and politics, then sharing such knowledge will serve to broaden and extend the social action work.

What is Acceptable to Pursue?

It is inevitable that as teachers, families, and community members discuss, plan, and implement community-based action projects, there will be points of difference and disagreement. Such disagreements may relate to the developmental appropriateness of particular curriculum. For instance, some early childhood and primary teachers subscribe to developmental theories that assert that young learners are "most at home dealing with concrete reality" (Carlsson-Paige & Lantieri, 2005, p. 115), so they cannot easily accommodate abstract and multidimensional problems. Other educators challenge such developmental theories of young children's readiness for matters of justice and equity and instead note the centrality of connecting children with people's narratives as a way to help them make sense of complex human dilemmas (Levstik & Barton, 2005).

Adult family members may also have differing stances on what they feel is appropriate for their children to know about war, injustice, and oppression. Some parents/guardians may not want the school to be where their children first learn about the world and its troubles. The best way for teachers not to be surprised by administrator, family, and community reaction is to forge strong lines of communication that allow for the adults to come directly to the teacher with concerns and for the teacher to proactively engage the other adults as she or he plans the curriculum. This is of extreme importance when working across linguistic, class, ethnic, and racial lines as matters of activism, relevance, and the role of teacher and the purpose of schooling are subject to both personal and community histories and experience.

An example of this comes from my own experience as a white teacher on the Southside of Chicago with predominantly African American teenagers. In 1987, my integration of political rap, house, and pop music into the curriculum led us to the album *Sun City* by Artists United against Apartheid. Given that my school designed integrated, inquiry-based curriculum, my class then ended up pursuing a study of apartheid. At some point in the course of the semester, I brought the class a leaflet about an upcoming march on Washington, D.C., that was being organized by activists working against U.S. support for the wars in Central America and for the end of apartheid in South Africa. When students found out about youth scholarships to support their travel, many wanted to attend the march, and my principal volunteered to chaperone with me. I knew that as a white person at a protest I am partially protected by my white skin, but my young African American students were in a different position. As excited I was to take them to a large march on Washington, I also wanted to make sure my students' families and school administrators were fully supportive. Buy-in from all adults turned out to be easy, and, for most students, the trip to D.C. was their first time outside the city of Chicago. (Before the trip, we did spend some time talking about the agreements of peaceful marches and also viewing footage from *Eyes on the Prize* (Hampton, 1987) about the 1963 March on Washington for jobs and freedom.)

Finally, a teacher's critical consciousness comes into play when pursuing potentially controversial actions because the more aware the teacher is of the politics and values inherent in the social issue, the more prepared they will be for controversy. Take, for instance, the students at Miami High School who initiated a boycott of the local poultry products because of their concerns about pollution from local factory farms (see Chapter 1). Rebecca Jim did not dissuade them from this action, and the students went to the local supermarkets with leaflets calling for consumers to boycott the products. The local paper wrote an editorial against the action, and the school superintendent accused her of interfering with commerce. Similarly, in many communities environmentalists have clashed with business and even labor groups as matters of job security sometimes conflict with environmental concerns. Rebecca Jim was not caught off-guard by the reactions of either the newspaper or the principal, as she had a firm grasp on both local politics and the conflicts between big business and environmental and health activists. She was knowledgeable, educated, and a lifelong community member.

The same political finesse was expressed by the other teachers in this study, whether it was Brian Schultz's concern about newspaper articles writing from a deficit perspective about Cabrini-Green (see Chapter 5), or the Nova High School administration proactively informing the Seattle School District of their students' street theater at the protests at the World Trade Organization meeting (see Chapter 2). All the educators in this research project had clarity about the politics surrounding their students' projects. They also—to a person—had confidence that their encouragement of multiple viewpoints and student-centered decision making protected them from potential charges of the teacher telling students what positions or actions to take.

The Role of Social Imagination and the Common Good

As I was finishing this book, I happened to catch W.S. Merwin on the *PBS NewsHour* soon after he was named poet laureate for the United States (Brown, 2010). He stated that the one aspect of human nature that distinguishes us

> from every other form of life.... is imagination.... the ability to sit here in [Virginia] and feel distressed by the homeless people in Darfur, or by the starvation of the whales in the Pacific, or by the species that are being snuffed out as we talk, or by the people who are suffering in Iraq and in Afghanistan.

At its very core, social action projects begin with this human capacity and appetite for imagination. As Maxine Greene (2010) continually points out, "Imagination allows us to bring alternative realities into consciousness, to look at things as if they could be otherwise" (para. 2). As seen in the day-to-day classroom interactions in these seven cases, students are often eager to tackle the problems of the world, and they will invest deeply when given opportunities to create a more positive future. This social imagination of which Maxine Greene writes and speaks is what fuels activism, advocacy, and volunteer projects.

Imagination can also fuel entrepreneurial efforts, and these should not be counter-posed with community action projects because many young people are motivated to create businesses that provide them security and autonomy. In fact, learning community engagement practices while in school may actually support responsible entrepreneurship. When we teach collective action and organizing skills for community improvement, we also teach an ethics of responsibility to the community and to the public good. In our capitalist economy, responsible entrepreneurs can assist community activists and provide resources for programs and projects that work toward the common good. It is wise to acknowledge that many young people are motivated to create socially just, environmentally sound businesses, and teachers committed to community-action projects may want to support these more individualistic leanings while simultaneously cultivating a commitment to the public good.

This research project was motivated in part by my questions about how teachers thought about their own political positions and how they negotiated their authority within social action projects that took students into the community. Yet, with the insights gained in these seven school settings and with issues of global resource commodification and distribution ever more serious, I realize that teachers committed to teaching for deliberative participation and civic agency have much to contribute. As most of the cases in this research illustrate, by organizing curriculum and community projects around protecting the commons—our land, our water, our air, our educational and recreational organizations such as schools, libraries, and parks—we have a wide range of inquiries and possible actions that could offer critical direction and help to the generations ahead. Such matters—although certainly political—are not partisan. Thus, teachers and students can avidly pursue solutions without too much fear of dogmatism or indoctrination.

In addition to protecting the commons, social action projects can also grow out of community concerns related to matters of human rights, equity, discrimination, and oppression. In fact, by protecting and defending marginalized members of the community we *are* protecting the commons. For as humans, what affects one of us, affects all of us. With inquiries and projects that grow out of human rights issues, teachers should carefully plan for hearing a range of community viewpoints with strong attention to guiding students to analyze competing interests and constituencies. Currently no human rights matter may be more contested than the issue of who gets to be a citizen, thus troubling many notions of citizenship curriculum. For teachers who work in schools with large immigrant populations, what should social action curriculum look like when some students sitting in our classrooms are not documented citizens of the country in which they are living? Yet, across many parts of the United States, youth are at the forefront of immigrant rights' struggles and campaigns, and their energy and insights should be incorporated into the classroom curriculum.

In schools without large immigrant populations, there are other groups who are often marginalized and less privileged. Gay and lesbian youth, transgendered and non-gender conforming children and youth, as well as the disabled are present in all communities. Likewise, many communities have many others left out of full promise of "liberty and justice for all" due to racial/ethnic/linguistic discrimination, homelessness, unemployment, or incarceration. Helping students free up their social imagination, and coupling this imagination with activist and organizing skills, opens a wide vista of opportunities for schooling to matter in the lives of both the students and the wider community.

When designing classroom curriculum around community activism on behalf of the community and the planet, the possibilities are as limitless as the critical social and environmental issues that continue to perplex our world's peoples. When teachers assist their students in tackling social problems through activism and advocacy, they are unleashing enormous energy and insight that can change material realities for generations to come. The classroom can be a site for not only encountering the world, coming to understand it and the world's people more deeply, but also learning to more fully care about and care for each other, with one eye always on matters of equity and justice.

AFTERWORD

Where Are They Now?

In addition to publicly sharing their pedagogical practices, the teachers profiled in this book also agreed to write an update for readers about their projects, experiences, and thinking.

Rebecca Jim

When the Environmental Protection Agency (EPA) designates a Superfund site, they develop plans with various actions components, each one called an operable unit (OU). For Tar Creek OU1 was the creek and what they did failed, but EPA closed that unit and is not planning to reopen it. OU2 is the yard cleanup where residential yards with high levels of lead are dug up and replaced. OU3 was a very small area that had some contaminated barrels of chemicals, and it was cleaned up in a few months. OU4 is the removal of chat piles and chat bases. There are lots of trucks hauling chat. Some of it is being sold for gravel, and I question the long-term safety of that action. The low-grade chat is being land consolidated and land is being scraped clean. OU5 is the cleanup of the streams and rivers. It will take thirty years, but will clean up Tar Creek and other contaminated streams and the Spring and Neosho Rivers, all the way to where they form the Grand Lake of the Cherokees. And the remediation may go on from there, as the metals have gone farther and that is the law, that they must follow the contaminants to where they come to reside.

There have been two buyouts. Oklahoma Governor Brad Henry used state funds for families with children six and under to move out, then later EPA funded the bigger buyout of most of the residents in Picher, Cardin, and Hock-erville, not for the lead contamination, but for the risk of cave-ins. Only seven families remain the most contaminated, living on risky lands, they refused to accept the buyout and leave.

Cathy Berger Kaye always told me that she would tell the story of what amazing work the Cherokee Volunteers did and what teachers and their students did in the Tar Creek Project, and she finally did it. In her new book, co-authored by Philippe Cousteau, *Going Blue A Teen Guide to Saving our Oceans, Lakes, and Rivers* (2010), each of the steps of service learning starts out with our project, using our work as a case study of sorts. What a surprise!

Our Cherokee Volunteers were interviewed by journalists from the *Washington Post*, the *New York Times*, and our area paper. They were depicted in films for the Kellogg Foundation and Nickelodeon. They have gone on to graduate and become leaders and parents, teachers and lawyers. They were incredible young people and will serve throughout their lives in ways that will surprise us all; well maybe not all of us will be surprised as we expected so very much of them! They pushed me to go on and continue doing. As this book goes to press, I just renewed my teaching certificate. Finally, I am continuing the non-profit work, filling our office with more volunteers and always finding more to do.

Joe Szwaja

One of the greatest joys I experience as a teacher is to interact with alumni, to reflect upon what they learned and how we worked together during their time at Nova. Reading the chapter that examines our school and my role in it during the WTO protests has provided me with a similar experience, albeit one that is different from the one-on-one reminiscence that normally characterize my interactions with former students. I find Celia's account of our school invaluable in that it weaves together different student perspectives on a particular class, including some valuable critiques and does so within a well articulated progressive pedagogy.

Reading Celia's account of our class brought back wonderful memories of the class and the protest. I always felt it was one of the boldest ones we've taught, as it ran the risk of intense criticism from parents and the district, as well as the possibility of students getting injured by the violence that took place. Clearly, we made mistakes; some students and parents felt that we hadn't prepared them adequately. Still, it was hard at the time to see quite how big it would be, and truly I think we did all we humanly could to inform students and parents of the risks that would ensue if their students took to the streets after our scheduled and supervised performance.

More than any class I have taught, this one was woven inextricably in with real and important historical events, ones that were changing right before our eyes. We have always said that we teach history in part to help students to inhabit and take an active role in it. Real struggles against real injustice are seldom tidy and this one was no exception. For all their flaws, this class and the protest seem to have helped inspire a number of our students to learn about and take an important part in one of the greatest struggles for social justice and democracy of our times. Three of our students were featured in a poignant photograph in *Five Days that Shook the World* by Alexander Cockburn and Jeffrey St. Clair (2001) and they deserved it, as they were a big part of the protest and stayed peaceful and positive in the face of significant government violence. Many of our students in this class passed a lot of difficult tests—some on paper and some on the pavement of Seattle.

We still teach about the WTO, but the particular struggles we involve ourselves in have changed: now, for example, we work on linking up with communities in Guatemala and East Timor who have born the ravages of our government's often rapacious foreign policy. Yet, the quest to use history and *all* our academic disciplines to help prepare and involve students in the messy, joyous struggle for a world of justice is alive and well at Nova. This is perhaps best shown by the words of one of our current students:

> My name is Tristan Quan; I've been attending Nova High School since September of 2006. I've attended several classes taught by Joe Szwaja throughout my years at Nova. Reading [the chapter about Joe's class] definitely correlated with a lot of what I've experienced since coming here. The tradition of community-focused education has continued at our school; my education has always held lessons that reach further than just the school doors. For example, I've been part of a class called "Science Geeks at Bailey Gazert" this past semester. The goal in this course was for every student to create and lead a science project for a class of fifth graders to take part in each week.
>
> The Sweat, No Sweat Fashion Show definitely remains as a strong example in many of Joe's classes. In a course focused around the 1860s, the revolutions that happened in that era, and how they affected more recent struggles, we referenced the globalization class and it strongly influenced what we learned about with respect to the WTO. We even had students who participated in the original fashion show come in and regale us with their first-hand experiences and how they had been involved with the WTO protest.
>
> I've also been heavily involved for the past three years with Nova's social justice trips to Guatemala. I first got involved when I took a class focused on one such trip during the second semester of 2009. Since then, I've spearheaded a lot of the organizing and fundraising connected to the two ensuing trips to Guatemala to link up with ex-refugee communities. Other actions I've taken include presenting a speech to the Seattle School Board pertaining to Language Arts Curriculum Alignment and being part of a successful effort by our American Government class to convince the district not to impose changes which we felt would harm our Language Arts Department.

Joe has really helped spur me into action in the school and the community. He has introduced me to countless different ideas and actions, which I never had learned about from a history teacher before. I am proud to walk in some of the same footsteps as my Nova predecessors and to be part on our proud, ongoing social justice tradition.

Lance Powell

The author of this book could not have picked a better week to follow me around if the goal was to see students engaged in social justice issues. Sadly, the efforts of the students, staff and community were somewhat in vain. At the end of that year, the entire administration of Thurgood Marshall Academic High School had either been terminated or had resigned, and the academic status and higher credit requirement of TMAHS was mandated to be reduced to that of the other public schools in the San Francisco Unified School District. While most teachers, including myself, hung on for one more year to help stabilize the school with the new administrators, at the end of that year, I, along with several other teachers, was ready to move on. The Thurgood Marshall I remember was one that was built on the idea that adults would hold all students to high standards and all students were capable of going on to higher education. To me, it felt a bit like a think tank with an abundance of talented and enthusiastic teachers. Although there is no doubt that Thurgood Marshall still has good teaching going on, it is most certainly a different school today. It is one that draws students only from the immediate neighborhood, and has a much lower college admissions rate than when it was an "academic" high school requiring more credits and attracting students from across the city.

I look back on my TM experience with fond memories—it's where I learned how to teach. At the time I was observed by Celia Oyler, I was a younger and less experienced educator than today … one who today would most certainly run a somewhat different classroom than as described in this book. However, I still feel that making lessons relevant is critical to engaging students. I don't consider myself to be a radical or an activist, but if I can make a social justice issue a vehicle to meeting a learning objective, I believe that not only does the learning become more relevant, it teaches students to actively participate in their community and that there is value in that.

From Thurgood Marshall I hopped on another social justice train when I was the last of six teachers hired to start June Jordan School for Equity, a new small school in the same area as Thurgood Marshall, the southeast side of San Francisco. This school was born from the idea that there had to be an alternative school model that could be developed that would systematically prevent students from falling through the cracks, which they can often do, in comprehensive high schools in lower socioeconomic neighborhoods. Before I was hired, a small grassroots group of educators rallied students and parents and gained community support that mounted to the point that the superintendent of the district had to bow down to their demands. Ironically, this alternative school materialized just as Thurgood Marshall was forced to into a more conventional mode.

Starting a brand new school was a phenomenal experience. June Jordan School for Equity was based on the small school model made popular by Deborah Meier in New York. Alternative assessments, teachers teaching dual "cored" subjects like math/science and English/social studies (or humanities) in small classrooms, community service, project based learning and advisory systems, were all at the heart of how this teacher led school was to be different from conventional high schools. At this school, social justice issues, both local and global, were woven into the curricula across the school. Students would debate the different sides of propositions being voted on it California, research global conflicts in their humanities classes and learn about environmental justice in their science classes, with me. The exceptionally talented staff at this school was extremely reflective of their teaching practices and prided itself on being progressive with regards to social justice issues. However, despite the idealistic approach and what quickly became an incredibly tight community of students, teachers, and parents, as is commonly the case with small schools, especially young ones still stabilizing, teacher sustainability increasingly became an issue for me. After what seemed like a lifetime of investing so much of myself at June Jordan, when my former assistant principal from Thurgood Marshall contacted me with a position down the Peninsula at Menlo-Atherton High School, I made the tremendously difficult choice to accept it.

Menlo-Atherton High School has proven to be an extremely interesting place to work. Many falsely assume that because this school is located in the wealthy community of Atherton, California, it only serves affluent students. This couldn't be further from the truth. MAHS has a diverse group of students from over twenty feeder middle schools coming from both extremely poor and extremely wealthy neighborhoods. This comprehensive high school falls on the polar opposite end of the spectrum as the exceptionally progressive June Jordan School for Equity. Perhaps because this large school has around 150 certified staff, incorporating social justice issues into the curricula so that every student is exposed to these issues seems exponentially more difficult ... or perhaps it's because social justice isn't as valued by the staff as a whole.

I have, however, found my calling. During the first four years at this school, I coordinated the California Partnership Academy, which is a career technical education program that targets students at risk of not graduating from high school. As I work with a team of teachers that share a group of common students, it feels to me almost like teaching in a small school. Because of this, I was able to bring many of the best practices I learned at June Jordan, and we have been able to morph them into workable practices at our site. I am very proud of the progress my team has made in developing this program that was in shambles when we took it over. When we started, a mere 3% of our 150 students made the honor roll first quarter. After the first quarter of this year, 48% made it.

I am also proud of a course I developed that I believe also is in and of itself a tool of activism in that it is creating social change. The name of the course is Environmental Analysis through Chemistry, or Environmental Chemistry. Traditional chemistry is a lab science course that qualifies as an accredited course by the University of California, Berkeley. It is commonly the second lab science course that students take. However, chemistry can be an incredibly abstract and seemingly meaningless subject for students. Sadly, this course acts as a gatekeeper, largely determining which students qualify to go straight into four-year colleges. This is because the second year of lab science is a University of California/California State University requirement, but for most high schools, it is not a graduation requirement. Consequently, this sets up a path of least resistance scenario and contributes directly to the achievement gap. Although I believe chemistry can be confusing for students from all socioeconomic groups, the ethnic groups underrepresented in the sciences and higher education are predominantly Hispanic, African American, and Pacific Islanders.

As a science teacher, I have long seen the environment as a very effective way to make science relevant. By using the environment as a lens to study chemistry, I believe it gives chemistry more meaning. Because the course meets all the chemistry standards, UC Berkeley accredited the course as a "lab science" course. The main difference between this course and a traditional chemistry course is that this course anchors chemistry concepts into the environment every step of the way. So many issues showing up in the newspaper facing the United States can be incorporated into chemistry lessons—issues ranging from dwindling fuel supplies, solid waste management and fresh water availability, distribution and pollution. This course also sets the stage for lots of field trips and community service opportunities as well as job possibilities. My students are literally getting dirty all over the watershed. I believe there is value in this because they are becoming environmental stewards and are getting involved in their communities. I have conducted research around the students and am confident that students are not only learning chemistry, they understand why what they are learning is important and they are meeting the lab science requirement for four-year colleges in California.

I am pleased to report that three other teachers in my district are teaching Environmental Chemistry in addition to me. My mission though is to get this course to really get wheels and expand across the state as a way to hook kids into science, have them become environmental stewards and become educated on issues of environmental justice and to become college ready. This school year has been an exciting one because much of my work has been recognized. I am proud to have been named by the California League of High Schools as their Educator of the Year for the Bay Area of California.

Derrlyn Tom

When I first started teaching, California was in the throes of Proposition 187, one of the most anti-immigrant and anti-child propositions ever placed on its ballot. As a new teacher, I knew my position against anything anti-child would need to be in the forefront. I swore I would never turn in any student of mine—nor his or her family—to Immigration simply because they could not show me, a public school teacher, any document of their immigration status. To this day, as a public school teacher and educator, I want all children and their families to have equal access to the one thing they can always have throughout their lives: an education. Proposition 187 here in California helped to shape my political views of why good, quality, public education is so vital for all. It has also taught me that fighting for social justice takes many generations. And the struggle has profoundly taught me to be better, both as a teacher and as a community member.

Being active in politics and policy-making at all levels is fundamental when we think about the future of public education in this country. Many of my students here at Mission High School come from Mexico and Central America, immigrants and refugees fleeing from political and economic turmoil in their home countries. Many of my students were brought here as young children, minors with very little say. And now that they are facing the challenge of being ready for the next step—a college education—they are once again barred and stigmatized because of their immigration status. For this reason, it is imperative that the DREAM Act pass and as educators we support all our students in pursuit of their dreams.

As an educator, I've always tried to instill in my students that taking control of their future means taking action now. As Malcolm X said, "Education is an important element in the struggle for human rights. It is the means to help our children and people rediscover their identity and thereby increase self-respect. Education is our passport to the future, for tomorrow belongs to the people who prepare for it today." In January 2003, I was sentenced to six months in Federal prison for a Class B misdemeanor. I was arrested in November 2002 for trespassing onto Ft. Benning, Georgia's School of the Americas (SOA), currently known as the Western Hemisphere Institute of Security Cooperation (WHINSEC). My civil disobedience was an act against the training of Latin American paramilitaries who return to their countries to oppress their poor. Because our tax dollars pay for this "terrorist camp," I had to speak out against the oppression and brutal takeovers of many Central and South American governments. I believe, as an educator that I cannot shy away from injustices, especially injustices that impact my students. While in prison, I heard many stories from so many women about their experiences and their "failure" in school. I realized then that it is the system that truly failed them. I shared with them many stories of my students and what so many of them have tolerated or risked to even attend school and obtain an education. As in the prison system, nothing will change within the education system if the "parts" or the people do not take risks. My students, and the women I met in prison risk so much every day of their lives … living in a toxic environment, crossing a hostile border, and being subjected to daily abuse by the people from whom they should feel love and protection. Being a teacher has taught me to take risks to create a better system; one that all my students deserve.

Brian Schultz

In the waning weeks of the students' fifth-grade year, the Chicago Board of Education decided to shut down the Byrd Community Academy. Perhaps not so ironically, the school board cited the reason for closure as low enrollment, rather than the shamefully inadequate facilities the students had identified and chronicled throughout the school year. Although not regretting their yearlong efforts, the students were understandably frustrated, saddened, and angered by this decision, since they had worked long and hard to help their community through their social action curriculum project. Many people, including me, pondered whether the students might take away a lesson that their voices did not count, or that the actions of a group of fifth graders were simply to be marginalized and disregarded. Their resolve to this day both shows and teaches me otherwise.

Following the school closure, most of the children were transferred to a relatively new building in the neighborhood—one of their originally identified alternative solutions to getting a whole new Byrd school. The students found themselves in a better facility despite quickly affirming what they had already come to know dearly: a school is not merely a structure, but instead is a space of community where ideas and authority can and ought to be shared. Adjusting to different classroom structures coupled with navigating a rival neighborhood school, were both symbolic and literal reminders of the emergent and complicated nature of real life curricula. New challenges the students faced in the classroom mirrored the changes the city's gentrification and displacement effort had done to notions of community we had come to share.

The Byrd school was no longer used for teaching and learning even though the district used the building for administrative purposes on and off over the past half-dozen years. As high-priced condominiums and townhomes were put up in the footprint of the high-rise tenements buildings that came down, the school property was rumored to have been on the auction block for tens of millions of dollars, but the school board apparently held out for more. During the summer of 2010 city building permits were issued for significant renovations and alterations to the structure—some 8 million dollars worth—not for the children of Cabrini Green, but in an apparent complex property swop with the Chicago Archdiocese for a building adjacent to one of Chicago Public Schools' flagship, selective-enrollment high schools. The former Archdiocese building has become the elite school's annex.

Almost seven years have passed since Celia visited Room 405 to witness the young activist students' efforts to push the Chicago Board of Education to make good on their erstwhile promise of a new school for the Cabrini Green community. During this time, many of the students from that classroom and I have stayed in touch as they matriculated through late elementary and high school. While a couple of students already have graduated high school, the rest (as I understand it) remain in school finishing their senior years. This is quite a feat since Chicago, as with most large urban school districts, has abysmal graduation rates with only about half the students starting ninth grade finishing twelfth grade.

A handful of the former Room 405 Byrd students and I have remained close. Over the years, we have presented together at conferences and co-written book chapters and journal articles. With prompting from me, the students and I are interested in sharing our perspectives about how young people can teach teachers through their insights regarding what motivates and engages city kids in school. Particularly noteworthy are the students' thoughts stemming from our experiences teaching and learning together where they used their voices in purposeful, powerful ways to solve a problem important to them. In a recently co-authored book chapter, six students collaborated with me to offer thoughts on "kids as teacher educators" (Schultz et al., 2009). In a natural continuation of the lines of inquiry we started together many years ago, the piece encourages educators to listen to and learn from students. By offering choices and flexibility in their learning, we argue, young people may be more readily engaged and excited about what schooling can offer them. We purport the importance of getting parents involved in classrooms, and relay how critical it is for schools to be involved in their communities while making certain that communities have access and opportunities within schools. Perhaps most profoundly, the students discuss the significance of letting children ask the questions most relevant to their lives in classroom spaces and beyond.

In thinking about writing this reflective epilogue about my endeavors with and alongside the Room 405 students, I thought it would be appropriate to gain insight from them directly. Certainly I share my thoughts readily about how our journey together was transformative, especially for me, but I am also keenly interested in learning from my former students. Quite honestly this reflection would be incomplete without input from them. One student, Malik, and I recently visited the site of the old Byrd school. As we peered into what is now a construction area, Malik shared some provocative sentiments about not only that year when he and his classmates fought for a better place to learn, but also about how the students and the community deserved something better. As he gazed at a partially reconstructed building that was once Byrd Community Academy, Malik said, "I think it's nice but, why couldn't they keep Byrd right here?" We continued talking as we walked into a gated hard-hat zone. Observing the changes to the school building, Malik continued,

There are new windows. And they built another section to the school. I wish they had done this when we were fighting for our school. That's crazy. They could have done this for us when we were here. I think they were trying to get us—they had a plan. They knew they were going to close the buildings down just to wipe us out of the way.... They are going to keep this for those kids—different race kids but not African American kids ... and keep us on the other side. Interesting. When we wanted a new school, why couldn't they build us a new school? Why couldn't they do this for us? I just hope they let the kids that want to make it from Cabrini come here to this school. They can be a part of this school, too.

Malik's commentary should give us pause. With all the nonstop rhetoric swirling in a national debate about our educational system's dire need for reform through higher standards, more accountability, and letting market forces control public schooling, we should stop and listen to someone that has the most at stake. As state legislators make grave policy decisions in hopes of competing for federal education dollars, we need to hear the message that emerged from a curricular campaign of fifth graders who wanted something better for themselves and their community. Malik's thoughts and questions ought to prompt us all to reflect, ask more questions, and take action.

Eric Rofes

by Celia Oyler

After spending a week with Eric Rofes in Arcata, California, we stayed in fairly regular contact. When we saw each other, we talked a lot about our respective research, and I peppered him with questions that perplexed me.

I greatly admired how Eric merged his activism seamlessly with his teaching; this was seen in many ways, but particularly in the North Coast Educational Summit, which he originated. The summit was a gathering at Humboldt University of educators, writers, and activists from the region. Eric used the summit as a way to both organize about educational justice (and justice through education), as well as teach people how to organize a conference. Eric was deeply committed to movement building and the summit was his local instantiation of that vision.

Eric is sorely missed. Please visit www.ericrofes.com to read more about Eric and view some of his writings.

Barbara Regenspan

It is a humbling experience to read Celia's chapter about my work in the "Social Action as Curriculum" course. I am reminded how heavily our socially constructed selves are constructed by the socio-political realities of the historical eras in which we live. Already when Celia collected data for her chapter about my work, the "Social Action as Curriculum" course that she observed was less overtly political than two years earlier, when an initiative of some of our EdD program students to create and enact "Teachers for Peace" spilled over into our elementary education program. During the months leading up to the war against Iraq, when my "Social Action as Curriculum" course met in one of the University's downtown leased facilities, approximately half of the students walked with me up the street during our 5:00 break to join Binghamton's weekly anti-war demonstration sponsored by Broome County Peace Action.

At that time, at least three students in "Social Action as Curriculum" taught English to local Iraqi men who organized with the anti-sanctions organization Voices in the Wilderness. For two years students in our elementary education program supported these men, most of them young fathers with children in the local schools, to address very well-attended sessions at the local YMCA's Anti-Racism Day where mainstream Binghamton families engaged in dialogue with them about Islam, life in Iraq, the impact of the sanctions, and other questions related to war, peace, U.S. policies, and the Middle East. Other elementary education students were finally able to interest the wives of the Iraqi men in English language lessons as well, which led to shared meals and expansive conversation in the anteroom of the local mosque for myself and my students. Another "Social Action as Curriculum" student supported Teachers for Peace by hosting a regional meeting on anti-war children's literature.

By the time Celia came to research my class, Voices in the Wilderness had been declared an illegal terrorist organization, and Teachers for Peace had lost momentum. We did host one meeting for regional teachers on "How to Critically Teach the War in/against Iraq," but "Social Action as Curriculum" definitely shifted from its clear social action focus to the approach more in line with service learning that Celia observed. My relative comfort with that shift was sincere, in that I did not want to become either dogmatic or beleaguered in response to the increasingly muffled student and teacher anti-war spirit, which I interpreted as a response to general increasing political repression of both subtle and unsubtle varieties.

Still, when during the term following Celia's visits, my department chair asked me to remove the Teachers for Peace bumper stickers and collection cans from the education office and from tables in our hallway in the Academic B building, charging the inappropriateness of political partisanship in our work, I became discouraged even though I was not actually vulnerable as a tenured and generally valued faculty member. But her challenge exacerbated the uncertainty I was feeling in relation to future direction for my work at a time when my students were experiencing fewer opportunities to question the validity of the war in their classrooms. When Colgate University offered me a position leading their secondary English and History certification and MAT programs, I reasoned that perhaps I could put energy into long-term advocacy for a high school history and literature curriculum that questioned war as a part of its foundation.

Now at Colgate University, I do not have a "Social Action as Curriculum" course, and I do miss the elementary education focus that put me regularly in touch with the energy of young children and those adults and young adults who were drawn to them. Still, my activist spirit is channeled in mostly gratifying ways into two related areas: 1) addressing the challenges of more generally pursuing socially critical (and anti-war) education during a reactionary political era in an environment of significant economic privilege, and 2) supporting the socially critical work of new education faculty and graduate students in New York State through my leadership of the historic NY State Foundations of Education Association. (Celia Oyler was a recent keynoter who inspired new faculty with the example of her own activist work.)

In my small department at Colgate, I enjoy the powerful commitment of my colleagues to use a variety of genres of literature and experience to support critical social inquiry. We also contribute to the university's mandated (for all students) CORE curriculum. (In "The Challenges of Modernity," where the teaching of *The Communist Manifesto* is required along with other canonical works of "late modernity," even our most conservative economics students are often surprised by the accuracy of its critique of capitalism.) I teach philosophy of education, curriculum theory, and politics in education to larger numbers of students who will not necessarily pursue teacher education, but whom I address as compassionate, social-justice-pursuant-allies of teachers, to varying effects. I also teach a much smaller number of students who will earn teacher certification at Colgate. In both types of work, I often feel the same quality of joy I experienced in "Social Action as Curriculum." I do enjoy the challenge of developing socially critical curriculum with my prospective high school teachers, especially as our cooperating teachers often value the influence of feminists like Nel Noddings and historians like the late Howard Zinn on the history and literature curricula our students generate.

Increasingly, the Lave and Wenger (1991) paradigm of "legitimate peripheral participation" provides me with a model for work in the education of teachers and their allies that I have sought to export through my leadership of the New York State Foundations of Education Association. Lave and Wenger posit "communities of practice" into which we invite our students. That is, we conceive of ourselves as relative "masters" of communities of practice in different and appropriate areas, and we create opportunities for students to participate first peripherally, and gradually more centrally, in the experiences into which our own (necessarily partial) "mastery" in those communities has invited us. One such "community of practice" for me has been that of critical literacy including critical media literacy.

Project Looksharp at Ithaca College has been a powerful teacher in critical media literacy practices for myself and my students; Looksharp directly feeds anti-imperialist, anti-racist teacher education with its excellent and free K–12 curriculum materials, most of it available on the Internet; further, its week-long summer institute has provided socially critical teaching methods for the visual thinking strategies we have introduced to our students. Then our own IT staff at Colgate has been willing to train our students to use image and video-editing software to produce their own films. I see increasing mastery of digital story-telling produced over the past few years in all of my courses; digital storytelling, by its nature demands re-evaluation of personal experience; when situated in a critical social foundations course, that re-evaluation gains both social relevance and depth. Many students have now responded to variations on the following assignment: "Create a 280–350 word voiceover and its illustrative film that uses critique from our course to re-evaluate an educational memory of your choice."

This assignment has produced some marvelous results including, during my first two years at Colgate, the posting by Educator's Roundtable on their website of two collectively produced films in my "American School" courses that critique high stakes testing. As well, students have presented films at the annual New York State Foundations of Education Association Conference, educating educators with their increasing "mastery." One student teacher who taught American History with particular effectiveness created and screened at NYSFEA a film linking a cousin's lack of engagement in school with his repeated re-enlistments for service in Iraq, despite the deterioration of his relationship with his wife and young children and his apparent indifference to the war's official rationale, process and effects. Recently, two other students screened films that narrated their own educational histories of accreted social ignorance, successfully interrupted by the teaching of Howard Zinn's (2010) *A People's History of the US* by one beloved high school teacher. A student from India re-evaluated how he was encouraged by token economy behavioral reinforcements to work uncritically in school to gratify others, without considering social aims. At the end of his film he asked, "Will I continue on the same path, now that I understand my implicatedness in the fragility of the social contract?" Twice groups of students have screened their films at local Chenango County Peace Alliance meetings.

I know that this is a time when socially critical educators, facing the domination of testing, accreditation, and standards-driven curricula in both the public schools and in teacher education, can feel quite desperate. Yet I appreciate the possibility for us to allow that desperation to give way to a spirit of life-loving experimentation, if we can agree to hold deep compassion for ourselves and our colleagues. For me, such compassion grows only to the extent that I nurture myself spiritually through meditation and other contemplative practices. In these uncertain times I hope to become bolder at integrating both arts and contemplative practices into my work with my students, in the hope that they will reinvent a kind of "social action as curriculum" that works for them and their own students.

APPENDIX

Notes on Methodology and Methods

My work as a classroom-based curriculum researcher is marked by my commitment to make meaning *with* teachers, as well as *about* them (Heron, 1995). My work and my research orientation are best described as "advocacy research." I have a point of view which provoked and sustained my inquiry. In the case of this study, my point of view is that schools should be sites for engaging children and youth in community- and globally-centered learning. That is, one reason to go to school is to learn about our local and global world so that we can each be fully engaged with it. Such engagement is truly limitless: it involves studying genres that people have already invented (poetry, non-fiction, science experiments, drama, painting, mathematics proofs, cartography, debate, a cappella singing, etc.), then recreating these genres with new content. It also can involve the creation of new genres, or new modes of expression, or new media to share those genres and modes; someone, after all invented YouTube.

When schools invite learners to engage with the world, each act of engagement is a new creation. It is my assumption that most people walking this planet want these engagements to be healing, and productive, and passionate. And it is also my experience that most children and youth seek connection and meaning as they organize their daily encounters with the world. Plainly put, most people want to connect with others in positive ways. When given the chance in a classroom to bring something into being (a relationship, a product that demonstrates their knowledge, or even a question), they are eager to engage. They are capable of sustaining attention and commitment when given the necessary supports from peers and teachers.

Teachers are no different. Most teachers I have known seek to create unique engagements each day that are designed at the intersection of the knowledge humans have codified, the learning zone of the students, and the requirements of the school, society and state. Each lesson, then, in any classroom is a unique lesson. Even if the lesson comes from a book of scripts, each time the script is enacted in a classroom, the outcomes will differ based on the learners and the teacher and what they bring to the engagement and what they take away. Each lesson, then, is an encounter among people and the knowledge systems of our world.

Given this reality, and knowing that my research endeavors are also engagements with the world, I seek to advocate for schooling practices that create space and possibilities for teachers to move towards intentional social action curriculum. How better to do this than to find teachers engaged in such practices, look carefully at what they are doing in a few of their unique engagements (lessons), and then carefully analyze these engagements? Thus, even though I approach this research advocating for social action curriculum, it is extremely important to consider all the evidence related to the issues under study.

Uncritical portraits cannot uncover the dangers and challenges of integrating social action projects into the curriculum. Therefore, in this research, I did not act as an uncritical cheerleader bent on producing a rosy portrait for practices I think are good. Rather, I took the stance of critical friend: to ask hard and intrusive questions, to write about aspects of the work that are complicated and require nuance, and to show the warts and "the bumps" (see Oyler, 1996).

That is not to say, however, that this book represents everything I saw, heard, thought about, or concluded. In a study with transcripts and field notes and literature review that are couple of feet tall, I had to make many decisions about what to highlight and what to leave on the cutting room floor. If I were writing a book focused exclusively on pedagogical effectiveness, I probably would not offer teachers the opportunity to use their real names as there are conclusions I drew that position some teachers in a more negative light. However, in this book, my focus was on issues of power and authority related to social action projects, so I leave many other very interesting aspects of the data unexplored.

Data Collection

By the second case, I had evolved my method: start with an initial interview with the teacher, make a schedule to observe and interview other people, audiotape and take field notes during teaching episodes, close with an exit interview with the teacher. Throughout my time at the site, I collected a wide range of artifacts (see section on Data Management for details).

Teacher Interviews

At each site, I began with an interview with the teacher asking about project details, constraints, and responses. I also posed questions about motivation to teach with social action projects, their own education, and their pedagogical aims. Finally, I asked about specific classroom practices, including student assessment. At the first teacher interview, I also designed a schedule for the week. The teacher suggested people to interview, class periods to observe, told me about field trips planned, suggested other leads I could follow.

Other Interviews

Interviews were conducted with whoever would talk to me at each site: colleagues of the teacher, school leadership, parents, and secretaries. In all K–12 schools, I spoke with administrators; I spoke with parents at two sites; and I spoke with school secretaries (always a rich source of information!). By the third case, I began doing an initial and an exit interview with each teacher: the initial interview was to build rapport, create a schedule, and hear how the project had gotten started; the exit interview was to ask detailed questions about curriculum and instruction and to probe for matters of teacher authority, power, politics, and imposition. The student interviews were conducted outside of regular classroom time as I did not want to interfere with students' instructional schedules.

Interviews were conducted in all sorts of conditions. For instance, in one school, my transcripts and field notes are punctuated by mice sightings—students hardly blink an eye while I am distracted by little brown mice darting in and out of closets.

Semi-Structured Interview Protocols

At each site I wrote teacher, student, administrator and community member questions ahead of time. Some teachers wanted to see the questions ahead of time, others did not want them. In all interviews, I used a semi-structured format: arriving with my questions, stating the purpose of the interview, asking if the person had any questions to ask me—both at the beginning of the interview as well as at the end. In most all interviews, I did not stick to the interview protocol, particularly if the person was talking a lot. Even if the conversation seemed "off the topic" to me, I sought primarily to build rapport and wanted the person to talk and not feel that I was overly directing the conversation. In that way, by the end of many interviews, many of my previously formed questions had been answered. If not, I told the person I wanted to consult my list of questions and see if there was anything more I needed to ask. In most all cases, the interviewee also had a copy of the pre-formulated questions so could consult the list as well.

In looking back on my five years of collecting data for this project in which I did eighty-three interviews, I notice in re-reading the transcripts that I am a good interviewer: there is little evidence of interruption; the utterances by the interviewees are long and most of my utterances are fairly short. At various points in most interviews, there came a time in the conversation, however, when I elaborated more extensively on the underlying central questions of my study: What sorts of negotiations occurred in the classroom around the teacher's politics? In what ways did the teacher's politics frame, shape, motivate, sway, influence the knowledge and skills being taught and learned?

Group Interviews with Students

Whenever possible, I held group interviews with students. I felt that this venue would help the students feel less "on the spot" and that a conversation could be facilitated that would allow students to position themselves differently and to sometimes take on different points of view. I wanted to probe for the "underbelly" of the story, not wanting to paint a romantic, Hollywood version of teaching for social action. But knowing that I wanted to hear stories that involved critical analysis or criticism, I also did not want the students to feel awkward about saying potentially "negative" things about their teacher to a total stranger. Thus, I thought that a group conversation could alleviate some anxiety.

Classroom Observations

For all classroom teaching periods I observed, I audio-recorded with cassette size tapes. My recording equipment included a Sony PZM microphone which did an excellent job of capturing much classroom talk, even from far corners of the room. If the participation structure involved whole group instruction, I put the microphone near the teacher as my focus in the study was on the teacher and the curricular and pedagogical decisions of the teacher. When the instructional method involved the students dividing into small groups, I selected one group (sometimes with the teacher's recommendation) and asked permission of the group members to leave the equipment at their table. Sometimes such permission was denied, in which case I thanked the group members for being frank with me and went on to another group.

While observing and audio-recording, I also hand wrote field notes of the details the audio tape would not capture: bulletin boards, students' physical gestures, teachers' use of physical space and facial expressions. Additionally, I made note of what appeared to be significant oral exchanges.

Field Notes and Analytic Memos

At the end of each day in the field, I entered my field notes into a Word document and wrote analytic memos regarding the questions and observations I had. In preparation for the final, exit interview with the teacher, I used all my questions posed throughout the week to generate the interview protocol. In the final teacher interview, I also included open-ended time for her/him to tell me anything they thought I should be sure to know and understand.

Back Home after Data Collection

Verbatim Transcriptions

When I returned home from the field, I transcribed the audio tapes of classroom teaching episodes. I then merged the transcriptions with my observational field notes, making a chronological record of my data collection. I kept my observer comments in my field notes, but I maintained a separate file for analytic memos.

I paid Michelle Mondo to do most transcriptions of individual interviews with teachers and some students as well. In all cases, after receiving the transcriptions, I listened to the tape again and filled in question marks and made corrections as necessary.

Data Management

I put all artifacts from each case into a folder, along with all transcripts, field notes, and analytic memos.

When all data collection was finished for all cases, I made one table that inventoried all the audiotapes by name of the person/s interviewed. Also on that table was a list of all other sources of data, including classroom observations periods, and all artifacts. Artifacts included: online links to data such as the *Democracy Now!* radio interview; rubrics teachers used; leaflets; posters; digital photographs of classrooms, including bulletin boards in the hallways; copies of student work, course syllabi; newspaper articles used in class or referred to by interviewees; background information on the social issue of the case, including media referred to by interviewees, such as videos and books or brochures from community-based organizations.

Data Analysis

Data analysis was iterative and began with each moment in a classroom when I listened to one speaker rather than another. That is, even when collecting data, the researcher is making a decision about what not to listen to, or what not to record. Researchers must continually ask ourselves, what matters here?

Data analysis continued when I divided my field notes page with three columns—time, activity/utterance, observer comments. The ongoing observer comments on every day of data collection can be understood as my second iteration of analysis. This analytic process continued each night when I opened my field notes, typed them into my computer, and then wrote an analytic memo.

Data analysis continued back home when I transcribed the classroom teaching tapes, group interview tapes, or filled in the missing words from the transcriber's interview tapes. While editing transcripts, I often highlighted speakers' comments, made jottings in the margins, or wrote myself new analytic memos.

When my entire data set was complete, I went back to my initial literature review, read more related scholarship, and generated three questions to guide my next round of data analysis in which I read through all the data from start to finish.

1. What advocacy and activism activities did the students engage in and how were they structured for learning? (Wade, 2000)
2. What role does the "public good" play in classroom instruction and in the teachers' motivations? (Barber, 2003; Parker, 2003)
3. What opportunities existed for students to engage with multiple viewpoints? What opportunities existed for discussion where difference and pluralism were visible? (Arendt, 1958/1988)

While re-reading all the data, I highlighted portions that related to these three questions, and made many notes in the margins with questions I had or when I noticed particular patterns or themes. With notes on each case, I began writing narratives of each case. Using my notes on major themes, I outlined each case chapter and inserted the data related to that theme.

Transcriptions in Text

When people speak, we use a variety of filler words, such as "you know," or we make false starts and repeat a phrase. Likewise, some people say "um" or "uh" as they seek to answer questions, or tell a story. Qualitative researchers, as we seek to present our research participants' experiences, histories, and stories, have a choice to make in regard to how much we *clean* the oral transcripts. There are sometimes strong reasons to keep hesitations and backtracking in the final excerpt of a transcript, as it can deepen the reader's impression of the participant's possible feelings and potentially provide a more nuanced understanding. When interviewees paused while talking, I indicate this on the transcription with a dash. The more the dashes there are in the direct quote, the longer was the pause.

In this project (and indeed, in almost all my other research), I am not comfortable with my narration being the only cleaned up one. That is, because I am writing the story, I get to choose and re-choose my words, sometimes dozens of times a day. Yet, the people who generously volunteered for me to be part of a focus group, or be interviewed, or be observed while teaching, get locked into a verbatim transcript they uttered at one moment in time. They, because of my authorial control and power, are not free to go back years later and edit their words. Thus, throughout the final version of this book, I have edited many oral transcripts to render my participants as eloquent speakers. When any word was deleted, I indicated this by using ellipses. On many occasions throughout the book, I also shortened longer transcripts by taking out entire utterances. The deletion of what was transcribed as sentences is indicated by four ellipses rather than three.

Likewise, for ease of reading and understanding, I have sometimes taken out the speaker's original words and replaced a word to assist the reader in deriving the meaning I took from the speaker's utterance. This is, of course, a judgment call on my part. As much as possible I tried to stick very closely to the speaker's original words. Whenever I made a word or phrase substitution, I marked it with brackets: [word replaced].

Transcription Notation

- - - -   Dashes indicate pause when speaking. The number of dashes roughly corresponds to length of pause.
....   Ellipses indicate words or sounds deleted. Four ellipses indicate a sentence-like utterance was deleted.
[ ]   Brackets indicate a word or phrase was substituted to more closely convey my interpretation of the speaker's meaning.
/   A backslash indicates the speaker was interrupted.

Names, Pseudonyms, and Editing the Public Record

It is traditional in educational research to employ pseudonyms for students, teachers, and schools. In the case of the students, I gave all minors pseudonyms; sometimes first names, and sometimes both first and last when I deemed it relevant to convey ethnicity. For adult students, I used real names when the student asked me to do so in written permission. Otherwise, all adult students have pseudonyms.

In my past research, I have avoided providing pseudonyms for teachers as much as possible, wanting people to get credit for their work, particularly in this era of outrageous teacher bashing. Additionally, many of the cases in this book are fairly traceable via public record. The details of the cases would be difficult to change and still maintain the power of the original story. In other cases—such as Tar Creek—the people want the case to be named because they want as much publicity about the issue as they can get. In each case, I offered the teacher to use a pseudonym, have me obscure give-away details, and to be granted anonymity. No one chose that. In every case I sent back my final words to each of them for fact-checking. In the case of Eric Rofes, as he died before the book was written, I sent the chapter about him to his husband. He has approved the use of his real name.

Every teacher (and Eric's husband) had edits for me. There was one teacher who asked me to delete a particular passage that s/he did not want to have in print; in other cases, teachers corrected small details or chronology I had gotten wrong. In a few cases, teachers asked if I could make a small change in wording that seemed to change the nuance of the sentence. (To be honest, I did not always understand the difference between my original and their edits, but I did not belabor the point as I wanted to make sure that they could live with everything said about them.) Responding to a close-up look inside one's classroom is not uncomplicated, of course, as much time elapsed between when I collected the data and the teacher read my final version of the chapter. As one teacher said when speaking with me on the telephone, "I've learned a lot since you came to observe me and I don't think I'd make the same decisions today, but that is what you observed and heard, so I can live with it being in print."

NOTES

Chapter 4

1. Recently renamed the Western Hemisphere Institute for Security Cooperation, the U.S. Army School of the Americas provides combat training for Latin American soldiers at Fort Benning, Georgia. Known by many as an academy for teaching torture, it has been a site of ongoing protest for decades (see School of the Americas Watch—www.soaw.org—for information). The year after I visited her classroom, Ms. Tom was arrested at the protest and was subsequently sentenced to six months in federal prison, which she served.
2. Proposition 21, "The Gang Violence and Juvenile Crime Initiative," passed in 2000, was called by opponents "California's War on Youth Initiative."

Chapter 5

3. To keep the data set coherent, all student pseudonyms in this chapter are consistent with the ones Brian uses in his book.
4. During my final interview, Brian and I decided to write an article together so we had more conversations after formal data collection concluded (see Schultz & Oyler, 2006).

Chapter 6

5. Choices included: Grace Lee Boggs (1998), *Living for Change*; Peter Medoff & Holly Sklar (1999), *Streets of Hope: The Fall and Rise of an Urban Neighborhood*; Suzanne Pharr (1996), *In the Time of the Right: Reflections on Liberation*; and Fred Rose (2000), *Coalitions Across the Class Divide: Lessons from the Labor, Peace, and Environmental Movements*.

Chapter 7

6. Barbara's book—*Parallel Practices: Social Justice-focused Teacher Education and the Elementary School Classroom* (2002)—has an entire chapter devoted to the class and also an entire chapter

riffing on Maxine Green's (1988) notion of the dialectic of freedom particularly in relation to learning to teach.

7. The class was actually a combination of student teaching seminar and *Social Action as Curriculum* and the two classes were merged; the combined class is co-taught. Although I interviewed the co-instructor as part of my study, I do not take up the other half of the class content in my analysis here.

REFERENCES

Adams, F. (1975). *Unearthing seeds of fire: The idea of Highlander.* Winston-Salem, NC: John Blair.

Adams, M., Bell, L. A., & Griffin, P. (2007). *Teaching for diversity and social justice* (2nd ed.). New York: Routledge.

Arendt, H. (1958/1988). *The human condition* (2nd ed.). Chicago: University of Chicago Press.

Auerbach, S. (2007). From moral supporters to struggling advocates: Reconceptualizing parent roles in education through the experience of working-class families of color. *Urban Education, 42*(3), 250–283.

Barber, B. (2003). *Strong democracy: Participatory politics for a new age.* Berkeley: University of California Press.

Bell, B., Gaventa, J., & Peters, J. (Eds.). (1990). *We make the road by walking: Myles Horton and Paulo Freire.* Philadelphia: Temple University Press.

Bigelow, B. (1997). The human lives behind the labels: The global sweatshop, Nike, and the race to the bottom [Electronic version]. *Rethinking Schools, 11*(4), 1–16.

Bobo, K., Kendall, J., & Max, S. (2001). *Organizing for social change: A manual for activists* (3rd ed.). Santa Ana, CA: Seven Locks Press.

Boggs, G. L. (1998). *Living for change: An autobiography.* Minneapolis: University of Minnesota Press.

Bomer, R., & Bomer, K. (2001). *For a better world: Reading and writing for social action.* Portsmouth, NH: Heinemann.

Bomer, R., Dworin, J. E., May, L., & Semingson, P. (2008). Miseducating teachers about the poor: A critical analysis of Ruby Payne's claims about poverty. *Teachers College Record, 110*(12), 2497–2531.

Bondy, E., & Ross, D. D. (2008). The teacher as warm demander. *Educational Leadership, 66*(1), 54–58.

Bondy, E., Ross, D. D., Gallingane, C., & Hambacher, E. (2007). Creating environments of success and resilience: Culturally responsive classroom management and more. *Urban Education, 42*(4), 326–348.

Bourdieu, P. (1986). The forms of capital (R. Nice, Trans.). In J. G. Richardson (Ed.), *Handbook for theory and research for the sociology of education* (pp. 241–258). New York: Greenwood Press.

Brady, M. (2004, May 22). Priceless lesson: Teacher, students put learning into action, show what can be done. *Orlando Sentinel*, p. A19.

Brown, J. (Interviewer). (2010, October 27). *The PBS NewsHour: W.S. Merwin on becoming the new poet laureate* [Television broadcast]. Washington, D.C.: Public Broadcasting Service. Retrieved December 7, 2010, from http://www.pbs.org/newshour/bb/entertainment/july-dec10/merwin_10-27.html

Bryan, D. (1993). Teaching for global responsibility through student participation in community. In S. Berman, & P. La Farge (Eds.), *Promising practices in teaching social responsibility* (pp. 236–255). Albany: SUNY Press.

Carlson, T. (1997). *Making progress: Education and culture in new times.* New York: Teachers College Press.

Carlsson-Paige, N., & Lantieri, L. (2005) A changing vision of education. In N. Noddings (Ed.) *Educating citizens for global awareness* (pp. 107–121). New York: Teachers College Press.

Cockburn, A., & St. Clair, J. (2001). *Five days that shook the world: The battle for Seattle and beyond.* New York: Verso.

Delpit, L. (2006). *Other people's children.* New York: New Press.

Dewey, J (1902). *The child and the curriculum.* Chicago: University of Chicago Press.

Epstein, S., & Oyler, C. (2008) "An inescapable network of mutuality:" Building relationships of solidarity in a first grade classroom. *Equity and Excellence in Education, 41*(4), 406–416.

Foster, M. (2002, July). Using call-and-response to facilitate language mastery and literacy acquisition among African American students. ERIC Clearinghouse on Languages and Linguistics. (Digest number: EDO-FL-02-04).

Foucault, M. (1980). *Power/knowledge: Selected interviews and other writings, 1972–1977* (C. Gordon, Ed. & Trans.). New York: Pantheon.

Freire, P. (2005). *Education for critical consciousness.* New York: Continuum Press.

Freire, P. (1980). *Pedagogy of the oppressed.* New York: Continuum Press.

Gaye, M. (1971). What's going on. On *what's going on* [Album]. Detroit, MI: Motown Records.

Gee, J. (1999). Critical issues: Reading and the new literacy studies: Reframing the National Academy of Sciences report on reading. *Journal of Literacy Research, 3,* 355–374.

Gibson, J. L. (1993). Political freedom: A sociopsychological analysis. In G. Marcus & R. L. Hanson (Eds.), *Reconsidering the democratic public* (pp. 113–138). University Park: Pennsylvania State University Press.

Gledhill, L. (2002, March 18). Report links school success to health care. *San Francisco Chronicle,* p. A19.

Goodwin, A. L. (Ed.). (1997). *Assessment for equity and inclusion: Embracing all our children.* New York: Routledge.

Greene, M. (2010, Winter). Prologue to art, social imagination and action. *Journal of Educational Controversy, 5*(1). Retrieved January 12, 2011, from http://www.wce.wwu.edu/Resources/CEP/eJournal/v005n001/p001.shtml

Greene, M. (1988). *The dialectic of freedom.* New York: Teachers College Press.

Hampton, H. (Producer/director). (1987). *Eyes on the prize* [Motion picture]. United States: Blackside.

Heath, S. B. (1983) *Ways with words: Language, life, and work in communities and classrooms.* New York: Cambridge University Press.

Henry, A. (1995). Growing up Black, female, and working class: A teacher's narrative. *Anthropology and Education Quarterly, 26*(3), 279–305.

Heron, J. (1995). *Co-operative inquiry: Research into the human condition.* New York: Sage.

Hollibaugh, A. (2000). *My dangerous desires.* Durham, NC: Duke University Press.

Horton, M., with Kohl J., & Kohl, H. (1997). *The long haul: An autobiography.* New York: Teachers College Press.

Irvine, J. J., & Fraser, J. W. (1998, May 13). Warm demanders: Do national certification standards leave room for the culturally responsive pedagogy of African American teachers? *Education Week, 17* (35), 56–57.

Isaac, K. (1992). *Civics for democracy: A journey for teachers and students.* Washington, D.C.: Essential Books.

Jones, S. (2006). *Girls, social class, and literacy: What teachers can do to make a difference.* Portsmouth, NH: Heinemann.

Kahne, J., & Middaugh, E. (2006). Is patriotism good for democracy? A study of high school seniors' patriotic commitments. *Phi Delta Kappan, 87*(8), 600–607.

Kahne, J., & Westheimer, J. (2006, July). The limits of political efficacy: Educating citizens for a democratic society. *PS: Political Science and Politics, 39*(2), 289–296.

Kaye, C. B., & Cousteau, P. (2010). *Going blue: A teen guide to saving our oceans, lakes, and rivers.* Minneapolis, MN: Free Spirit Publishing.

Kesson, K., & Oyler, C. (1999). Integrated curriculum and service learning: Linking school-based knowledge and social action. *English Education, 31*(2), 133–146.

Kilpartick, W. H. (1918). The project method [Electronic version]. *Teachers College Record, 19*(4), 319–335.

King, M.L.K, Jr. (2011). *Why we can't wait* [Kindle edition]. New York: Beacon Press. Retrieved from Amazon.com.

Kirshner, B. (2008). Guided participation in three youth activism organizations: Facilitation, apprenticeship, and joint work. *The Journal of the Learning Sciences, 17,* 60–101.

Kounin, J. S. (1970). *Discipline and group management in classrooms.* New York: Holt, Rinehart & Winston.

Kovacs, P. (2010). *The Gates Foundation and the future of U.S. public schools.* New York: Routledge.

Kozol, J. (1992). *Savage inequalities: Children in America's schools.* New York: Harper.

Kreisberg, S. (1992). *Transforming power: Domination, empowerment, and education.* Albany: SUNY Press.

Kumashiro, K. (2000). Toward a theory of anti-oppressive education. *Review of Educational Research, 70*(1), 25–53.

Ladson-Billings, G. (1994). *Dreamkeepers: Successful teachers of African American children.* San Francisco: Jossey-Bass.

Ladson-Billings, G. (1995). But that's just good teaching: The case for culturally relevant pedagogy. *Theory into Practice, 34*(3), 159–165.

Ladson-Billings, G. (2005). Differing concepts of citizenship: Schools and communities as sites of civic development. In N. Noddings (Ed.), *Educating citizens for global awareness* (pp. 69–80). New York: Teachers College Press.

Lareau, A. (2003). *Unequal childhoods: Class, race, and family life.* Berkeley: University of California Press.

Lareau, A., & Horvat, E. M. (1999). Moments of social inclusion and exclusion: Race, class and cultural capital in family-school relationships. *Sociology of Education, 72,* 37–53.

Lave, J., & Wenger, E. (1991). *Situated learning: Legitimate peripheral participation.* Cambridge, England: University of Cambridge Press.

Levstik, L., & Barton, K. (2005). *Doing history: Investigating with children in elementary and middle schools* (3rd ed.). Mahwah, NJ: Erlbaum.

Lindquist, T. (1995*). Seeing the whole through social studies.* Portsmouth, NH: Heinemann.

Lipman, P. (2011). *The new political economy of urban education: Neoliberalism, race, and the right to the city.* New York: Routledge

Medoff, P., & Sklar, H. (1999). *Streets of hope: The fall and rise of an urban neighborhood.* Boston: South End Press.

Menzel, P., & Mann, C. C. (1995). *Material world: A global family portrait.* San Francisco: Sierra Club Books.

Obama, B. (1998). *Dreams from my father: A story of race and inheritance.* New York: Three Rivers Press.

Oyler, C. (1996). *Making rooms for students: Sharing teacher authority in Room 104.* New York: Teachers College Press.

Oyler, C. (2001, Spring). Democratic classrooms and accessible instruction. *Democracy and Education, 14*(1), 28–31.

Oyler, C., & Becker, J. (1997). Teaching beyond the progressive-traditional dichotomy: Sharing authority and sharing vulnerability. *Curriculum Inquiry, 27,* 453–467.

Oyler, C., & the Preservice Inclusion Study Group (2006). *Learning to teach inclusively: Student teachers' classroom inquiries.* Mahwah, NJ: Erlbaum.

Parker, W. C. (2003). *Teaching democracy: Unity and diversity in public life.* New York: Teachers College Press.

Payne, R. (2001). *A framework for understanding poverty.* Highlands, TX: aha! Process, Inc.

Pharr, S. (1996). *In the time of the right: Reflections on liberation.* Berkeley, CA: Chardon Press.

Pratt, C. (1948). *I learn from children: An adventure in progressive education.* New York: Simon & Schuster.

Ravitch, D. (2010). *The death and life of the great American school system.* New York: Basic Books.

Regenspan, B. (2002). *Parallel practices: Social justice-focused teacher education and the elementary school classroom.* New York: Peter Lang.

Reagon, B. J. (1983). Ella's song. On *Sweet Honey In the Rock, we all...everyone of us* [Album]. Chicago: Flying Fish Records.

Reagon, B. J. (2000). Coalition politics: Turning the century. In B. Smith (Ed.), *Home girls: A Black feminist anthology* (pp. 343–355). Rutgers, NJ: Rutgers University Press.

Ringold, F. (1996). *Tar beach.* Albuquerque, NM: Dragonfly Books.

Rocha, Z. (1999). Helder Camera Helder, o dom: Uma vida que marcou os rumos da Igreja no Brasil [Helder, the gift: A life that marked the direction of the Church in Brazil]. Petrópolis, Brazil: Editora Vozes.

Rofes, E. (Ed.). (1981) *The kids book of divorce: By, for, and about kids.* Lexington, MA: Lewis.

Rofes, E. (Ed.). (1984). *The kids book about parents.* Boston: Houghton Mifflin.

Rofes, E. (Ed.). (1985a) *The kids book on death and dying: By and for kids.* Boston: Little, Brown & Company.

Rofes, E. (1985b). *Socrates, Plato, and guys like me: Confessions of a gay schoolteacher.* New York: Alyson Books.

Rose, F. (2000). *Coalitions across the class divide: Lessons from the labor, peace, and environmental movements.* Ithaca, NY: Cornell University Press.

Ross, E. W., & Gibson, R. (2007). *Neoliberalism and education reform.* New York: Hampton Press.

Sax, L. J. (2004, Summer). Citizenship development and the American college student. *New Directions for Institutional Research, 122,* 65–80.

Schultz, B. (2008). *Spectacular things happen along the way: Lessons from an urban classroom.* New York: Teachers College Press.

Schultz, B. D., Banks, P., Brewer, L., Davis, S., Easter, T., Pruitt, K., & Thomas, R. (2009). Kids as teacher educators: Looking, listening, and learning from students. In J. Burdick, J. A. Sandlin, & T. Daspit, T. (Eds.), *Complicated conversations and confirmed commitments: Revitalizing education for democracy* (pp. 195–207). Troy, NY: Educator's International Press.

Schultz, B., & Oyler, C. (2006). We make this road as we walk together: Sharing teacher authority in a social action curriculum project. *Curriculum Inquiry, 36*(4), 423–451.

Scott, N. (1999). *Tar Creek anthology: A legacy.* Miami, OK: Miami High School Cherokee Volunteer Society. Unpublished manuscript.

Scott, M. P., & Jim, R. (2002). *Tar Creek anthology 2: Our toxic place.* Vinita, OK: LEAD (Local Environmental Action Demanded) Agency.

Shepard, B., & Hayduk, R. (Eds.). (2002). *From ACT UP to the WTO: Urban protest and community-building in the era of globalization.* New York: Verso.

Style, E. (1988). Curriculum as window and mirror. In M. Crocco (Ed.), *Listening for all voices: Gender balancing the school curriculum* (pp. 6–12). Summit, NJ: Oak Knoll School Monograph.

U.S. Environmental Protection Agency (1997). Record of decision: Residential areas operable unit 2, Tar Creek Superfund Site, Ottawa County, Oklahoma. Dallas Texas: U.S. Environmental Protection Agency. Retrieved March 14, 2011, from http://www.epa.gov/region6/6sf/oklahoma/tar_creek/ok_tar_creek_ou2_rod_res_199708.pdf

Varlotta, L. E. (1997). Confronting consensus: Investigating the philosophies that have informed service-learning's communities. *Educational Theory, 47,* 453–476.

Vasquez, J. (1988). Contexts of learning for minority students. *The Educational Forum, 52,* 243–253.

Wade, R. (2000). *Building bridges: Connecting classroom and community through service-learning in social studies.* Silver Spring, MD: National Council for the Social Studies.

Wade, R. (Ed.). (1997). *Community service-learning: A guide to including service in the public school curriculum*. Albany: SUNY Press.

Wade, R. C., & Saxe, D. W. (1996). Community service-learning in the social studies: Historical roots, empirical evidence, critical issues. *Theory and Research in Social Education, 24*, 331–359.

Walker, T. (2000). The service/politics split: Rethinking service to teach political engagement. *PS: Political Science and Politics, 33*(3), 646–649.

Zeichner, K. M., & Liston, D. P. (1990). Traditions of reform in U.S. teacher education. *Journal of Teacher Education, 41*(3), 3–20.

Zinn, H. (2002). *You can't be neutral on a moving train: A personal history of our times*. Boston: Beacon Press.

Zinn, H. (2010). *A people's history of the United States: 1492-present*. New York: Harper Perennial Modern Classics.

Zorn, E. (2004, March 23). Pupils welcome all to see their dreary reality. *The Chicago Tribune*, p. B1.

INDEX